The LABEL BOOK

— OF CLOTHING CULTURE

Published and distributed worldwide by
DAAB MEDIA GMBH
Scheidtweilerstrasse 69
50933 Cologne / Germany
Tel. + 49 221 690 48 210
Fax + 49 221 690 48 229
www.daab-media.com

Join our community
www.edaab.com and present your
work to a worldwide audience

Printed in Italy
www.graficheflaminia.com

ISBN 978-3-942597-25-8

EDITOR
Dr. Dr. Thomas Rusche

CONCEPT
Ralf Daab and Thomas Rusche

MANAGING EDITOR
Christiane Blass

COVER AND DESIGN CONCEPT
Meiré und Meiré

LAYOUT
Conny Koeppl, vice versa

COPY EDITORS
Christiane Blass, Claudia Grönemeyer

TEXTS
Claudia Cosmo, Michaela Kühn,
Sabine Elsa Müller, Camilla Péus

ENGLISH TRANSLATION
Susan Ghanouni in association with
First Edition Translations Ltd, Cambridge

COPY PROOFREADING
Bev Zimmern in association with
First Edition Translations Ltd, Cambridge,
Yvonne Paris

THOMAS RUSCHE

The
LABEL
BOOK

— OF CLOTHING CULTURE

TRADITION — QUALITY — STYLE

INTRODUCTION

Clothing culture is not cheap and attractive, not fashionable and transitory, but timeless, of everlasting value, the highest expression of harmony, of decency and human dignity, which is at once both one's highest obligation and sweetest joy. (Cf. Johann Gottfried Herder)

Assembling the best of clothing culture in a single book has been a challenging project for everyone involved and I would like to begin by expressing my warmest thanks to all concerned. First and foremost to my visionary publisher, Ralf Daab, who encouraged me to produce this work, to Camilla Péus, Claudia Cosmo, Michaela Kühn and Sabine-Elsa Müller for their articles, to Lars Beusker for his impressive photographic work, to Meiré and Meiré for their excellent graphic design and, not least, to Christiane Blass, my meticulous project coordinator, who successfully handled all the different strands of the project. These strands lead us to some of the best manufacturers in the world of international clothing culture; it is they who form the backbone of our publication – my special thanks go to all of them!

In the midst of an increasingly hectic pace of life, seductive advertising and strident pronouncements about what is in or out, we would do well to reflect on the key priorities in all aspects of life. For generations, the key elements in clothes culture have been distinctive continuity and international distribution, not to mention traditional expectations in terms of high-quality materials, components, styles and finishing methods.

Our culture, with its rituals, forms and symbols, is the treasure chest of mankind. Culture cannot be expected to materialize overnight – culture must be created, and it is "the whole way of life of a people, from birth to the grave, from morning to night and even in sleep" (Thomas Stearns Eliot). Culture raises the quality of human activity to maximum perfection. Culture enriches whatever we are doing at the time. In dress, this means we must look to the occasion. Clothing culture is therefore governed by the respective occasion and manifests itself in clothes appropriate to different aspects of life, whether for work or leisure, for sitting round a conference table, attending a ball at the opera or taking a walk in the woods.

Clothing culture calls for high standards of quality. My clothes, like a second skin, must not only be comfortable, functional and appropriate to the occasion but should also be sensual, sophisticated and subtle. Whenever I touch this second skin during the course of the day, catch sight of myself wearing it and note the harmonious perfection of style and quality, I am filled with a wonderful feeling which carries me through the day and helps me through life in general.

Clothing culture is an indication of style awareness. Style is the dress of thought. It reflects the quality of my thinking (Arthur Schopenhauer). Style is the body of the spirit – clothes often reflect my inner state of mind. In this respect, people's clothing style reflects the state of their soul and helps them to express or hide inner emotions. Clothes can be a form of communication: consciously or unconsciously, I talk to myself, and everyone else I encounter, through my clothing. My clothes send out a constant stream of signals which is why they must be consistent with who I am: an embodiment of quality and style!

But how and where to find such high-quality products in which I can dress elegantly and which will express my personality without making myself look like a "fashion victim"? Nowadays, price is no longer an accurate indicator of a product's quality or style. Nor does the name necessarily tell the

full story. This LABEL BOOK poses the following questions: which brands have upheld their commitment to the quality and elegance for which their name is famous? Which manufacturers, despite all the price competition, still insist on top-quality raw materials and perfect workmanship? Which companies have succeeded in combining tradition and future trends to create products with timeless appeal? In these times of highly professional marketing campaigns, global production sites and multiple distribution channels, it has become much more difficult for customers to separate the wheat from the chaff. It is hoped that this book will go some way towards helping in this respect. THE LABEL BOOK introduces a collection of 43 different brands from the world of clothing culture which are among the best in their particular sector. Thanks to a shared passion for outstanding quality, traditional craftsmanship and timeless elegance, these companies have succeeded in creating distinguished products which are a source of lasting pleasure to the wearer thanks to the fact that – over years of wear – they have come to feel like a second skin. They still exist, these seasoned classics of clothing culture. Indeed, some companies have been demonstrating their commitment to tradition, quality and style for the past 100 years with every new collection launched!

Thanks to our own association with these firms, which, in some cases, spans many decades – the Hamburg cravatier Laco was supplying my grandfather over 75 years ago – I can personally vouch for the fact that all the brands listed in this Label Book relate to top-quality products which will satisfy the highest expectations. The collection is, of course, entirely subjective, filtered from several generations of personal experience and a systematic analysis of constructive, critical feedback from over 100,000 loyal and discerning SØR customers. Our selection of best brands for this LABEL BOOK does not claim to be complete since, for various reasons, it was not always possible for all the companies approached to take part in this complex research project.

I would also like to beg your indulgence for the fact that, given our own company's particular traditions, the emphasis is mainly on men's clothing. A further reason for this is the fact that the world of women's fashion is governed to a greater degree by changing styles, and ladies consequently change their wardrobes more frequently. It follows, therefore, that men's fashion lasts longer and is less susceptible to new trends. But, here too, it is the exception that proves the rule. This is why we are delighted to present this selection of famous labels of international clothing culture, which will fulfil the highest expectations of both men and women.

Perhaps the House of SØR, with its traditional outlook and roots dating back to the 19th century, is not a bad starting-point from which to compile such a tribute to these masters in the arts of weaving, tailoring, knitting, shoemaking and fashion craftsmanship. I hope at any rate that this international publication will serve to champion the cause of a classically timeless clothes culture for which I predict a great future in our fast-paced 21st century.

I hope that you will now enjoy looking behind the scenes of both the great labels and the less familiar "hidden champions" of a fascinating industry which has now held my family in its sway for five generations.

Sincerely,
Thomas Rusche
Oelde /Berlin, September 2012

EINLEITUNG

Das Beste der Kleidungskultur in einem Buch zu versammeln, ist ein herausforderndes Projekt für alle Beteiligten, denen ich zu Beginn herzlich danken möchte. Allen voran dem visionären Verleger Ralf Daab, der mich zu dieser Publikation ermutigt hat, Camilla Péus, Claudia Cosmo, Michaela Kühn und Sabine Elsa Müller für ihre Textbeiträge, Lars Beusker für beeindruckende Fotoreportagen, Meiré und Meiré für die großartige grafische Gestaltung und nicht zuletzt der umsichtigen Projektkoordinatorin Christiane Blass, in deren Händen alle Fäden zusammenliefen. Diese Fäden führen uns zu den besten Herstellern der internationalen Kleidungskultur; sie bilden das Rückgrat unserer Publikation – ihnen allen gilt mein besonderer Dank!

In einer Zeit zunehmender Hektik, verführerischer Werbung und lärmender In und Out Diktate tut uns die Besinnung auf das Wesentliche in allen Lebensbereichen gut. Das Wesentliche der Kleidungskultur ist seit Generationen ihre unverwechselbare Kontinuität und internationale Verbreitung sowie ihr traditioneller Anspruch an höchste Qualität von Materialien, Zutaten, Schnitten und Verarbeitungsweisen.

Unsere Kultur ist mit ihren Riten, Formen und Symbolen die Schatztruhe der Menschheit. Kultur kann der Mensch nicht von heute auf morgen wollen – Kultur muss ich erschaffen: „Im täglichen Lebensvollzug beginnend von der Geburt bis zum Grabe, vom Morgen bis in die Nacht und selbst im Schlaf" (Thomas Stearns Eliot). Kultur steigert die Qualität der menschlichen Tätigkeit zur größtmöglichen Vollkommenheit. Kultur vollendet das Jeweilige – das Jeweilige der Kleidung ist der Anlass. Kleidungskultur ist deshalb anlassbezogen und konkretisiert sich in der anlassgerechten Kleidung für die Wechselfälle des Lebens im Beruf und in der Freizeit, am Konferenztisch, auf dem Opernball und beim Waldspaziergang.

Kleidungskultur beinhaltet einen hohen Qualitätsanspruch. Meine Kleidung sollte als zweite Haut nicht nur bequem, nützlich und anlassgerecht sein, sondern auch sinnlich, raffiniert und delikat. So oft ich am Tag meine zweite Haut berühre, mich darin sehe und die harmonische Vollkommenheit von Stil und Qualität erlebe, entsteht ein wunderbares Gefühl, das mich durch den Tag trägt und mir durch mein ganzes Leben hilft. Kleidungskultur ist Ausdruck von Stilempfinden. Der Stil ist das Kleid meiner Gedanken, the dress of thought. Stil drückt die Qualität meines Denkens aus (Arthur Schopenhauer). Stil ist der Leib des Geistes – die Kleidung oftmals das Abbild meines inneren Zustands. In diesem Sinn spiegelt der Kleidungsstil den Zustand der Seele und hilft dem Menschen, Inneres auszudrücken oder zu verbergen. Kleidung ist Kommunikation, bewusst oder unbewusst spreche ich mit meiner Kleidung zu mir selbst und zu allen anderen, denen ich begegne. Mit meiner Kleidung sende ich permanent Signale. Deshalb sollte sie mir entsprechen: voller Qualität und Stil!

Wie und wo aber finde ich diese qualitätvollen Produkte, die mich stilvoll kleiden und meiner Persönlichkeit Ausdruck verleihen, ohne mich als Fashion Victim zu verkleiden? Heute ist es nicht mehr allein der Preis, der mir sichere Auskunft darüber gibt, ob ein Produkt von hochwertiger Qualität und gutem Stil ist. Auch der Name verrät nicht immer alles. So stellen wir uns mit diesem LABEL BOOK die Frage: Welche Marke hält heute noch dieses stilvolle Qualitätsversprechen, für das der

Name stehen sollte? Welche Hersteller setzen ungeachtet aller Preiskämpfe nach wie vor auf beste Rohstoffe und handwerkliche Perfektion? Welchen Unternehmen ist es gelungen, Tradition und Zukunft überzeugend miteinander zu verbinden und Produkte von zeitloser Gültigkeit zu schaffen?

In unserer Zeit der hochprofessionellen Marketing-Kampagnen, globalen Produktionsstätten und multiplen Vertriebskanäle ist es für den Kunden bisweilen gar nicht so einfach, die Spreu vom Weizen zu trennen. Genau dazu möchte diese Publikation einen Beitrag leisten. THE LABEL BOOK stellt eine Auswahl von 43 Marken der Kleidungskultur vor, die zu den besten in ihrem jeweiligen Segment zählen. Diesen Unternehmen gelingt es, mit ihrer Leidenschaft für hochwertige Qualität, traditionelle Handwerkskunst und zeitloses Stilniveau Produkte mit Charakter zu schaffen, die nachhaltig Freude machen, weil sie – über Jahre getragen – zur zweiten Haut des Menschen werden: Es gibt sie eben noch, diese bewährten Markenklassiker der Kleidungskultur, die zum Teil schon über 100 Jahre lang mit jeder Kollektion Tradition, Qualität und Stil aufs Neue unter Beweis stellen!

Bei all diesen im Label Book versammelten Marken kann ich aufgrund der oftmals schon jahrzehntelangen Zusammenarbeit – so belieferte der Hamburger Cravatier Laco bereits vor über 75 Jahren meinen Großvater – persönlich versichern, dass es sich um qualitätsvolle Produkte handelt, die höchsten Ansprüchen gerecht werden. Selbstverständlich ist diese Auswahl subjektiv, gefiltert durch meine generationenübergreifende Erfahrung und die systematische Auswertung der wohlwollend kritischen Resonanz unserer über 100.000 loyalen und anspruchsvollen SØR-Kunden. Bei der Selektion der besten Marken für das LABEL BOOK erheben wir allerdings schon deshalb keinen Anspruch auf Vollständigkeit, weil es aus unterschiedlichen Gründen nicht allen angefragten Unternehmen möglich war, an diesem komplexen Research Project teilzunehmen.

Auch bitte ich um Verständnis, dass aufgrund der Tradition unseres Hauses der Schwerpunkt auf der Herrenbekleidung liegt. Das liegt allerdings darüber hinaus auch darin begründet, dass die Damenwelt mehr Wert auf den Wechsel der Mode legt und ihre Garderobe dementsprechend schneller austauscht. Herrenmode ist also naturgemäß langlebiger und weniger trendbestimmt. Ausnahmen bestätigen auch in diesem Fall die Regel. Deshalb freuen wir uns über die hier versammelten renommierten Label der internationalen Kleidungskultur, die den höchsten Erwartungen der Kundinnen und Kunden gerecht werden können.

Vielleicht ist der Blick aus dem traditionsreichen Hause SØR, dessen Wurzeln bis ins 19. Jahrhundert zurückreichen, nicht die schlechteste Perspektive, um eine solche Hommage an die Meister des Weber-, Schneider-, Stricker-, Schuhmacher- und Modistenhandwerks zu verfassen. Ich hoffe jedenfalls, mit dieser internationalen Veröffentlichung eine weitere Lanze für die zeitlos gültige Kleidungskultur zu brechen, der ich im schnelllebigen 21. Jahrhundert eine große Zukunft voraussage.

Nun wünsche ich Ihnen viel Vergnügen bei dem Blick hinter die Kulissen der großen Marken und weniger bekannten Hidden Champions einer faszinierenden Branche, die meine Familie seit nunmehr fünf Generationen in ihren Bann zieht.

Herzlichst,
Ihr Thomas Rusche
Oelde / Berlin, im September 2012

CONTENT / INHALT
— FROM 1734 UNTIL TODAY

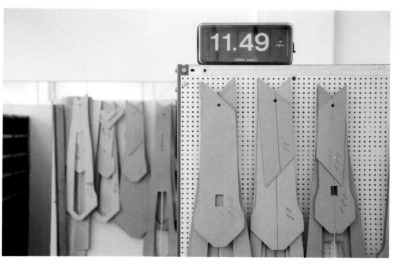

ALBINI

"The Albini Group
has been producing the
best shirt fabrics
in the world since 1876."
Silvio Albini

WEAVERS OF FINE FABRICS

The Albini Group is a traditional, family-run firm of Italian cloth manufacturers with an impressive history. The foundation stone was laid by Zaffiro Borgomanero, who established the firm under the name of Z. Borgomanero & C. in 1876 in Albino, situated in Bergamo province. After just one year of business, Borgomanero had acquired more than 40 mechanical weaving looms and 44 employees. In 1884, the company was awarded a bronze medal at the Turin industrial exhibition – the first major commendation for this producer of shirt fabrics, whose express aim was to produce top-quality fabrics. The firm continues to operate according to this ethos to this day and its success is self-evident.

In 1891, by which time the company had grown to over 100 looms and 90 workers, Borgomanero, who had no children of his own, left the company to his nephew, Giovanni Albini. As President of the Bergamo Chamber of Commerce, Albini was one of the most important figures of local industry. In 1907, he also played a leading role in the foundation of the Industrial Union of Bergamo, which consisted mainly of textile companies. In 1919, he handed ownership of the business to his sons: his son Riccardo took over Industrie Riunite Filati whilst the weaving mill, henceforth known as Società Dr Silvio Albini & C., went to his son Silvio.

In 1968, responsibility passed to the fourth generation, to the brothers Giancarlo, Marino, Piero and Gianni. Even now, the firm is still a family-run business and the fifth generation to run the company now comprises Silvio, Fabio, Andrea and Stefano Albini. Since 1984, the President of the Albini Group, Silvio Albini, has focused on expanding the business internationally.

TRADITION MEETS INNOVATION

One of the most important achievements in the firm's history was the acquisition in 1992 of two traditional British brands, Thomas Mason and David & John Anderson, which brought with it an historical archive comprising 700 books of fabric designs and a remarkable record of textile history. The archive represents a priceless asset which, according to Silvio Albini, forms a bridge between the traditional and modern. Not only does this in-house museum bear witness to the classic brands but it is also a source of inspiration for the designers of the Albini Group and its customers.

The company now comprises eight production sites worldwide, five of them in Italy, two in Egypt and one in the Czech Republic, and employs 1,300 workers for the five different labels – Albiate 1830, Cotonificio Albini, Thomas Mason, David & John Anderson, Albini Donna. It offers a range of over 20,000 fabrics to meet the requirements of its demanding, international clientele. The product palette ranges from sporting to elegant. Seventy per cent of the group's products are exported to around 80 different countries. The Albini Group is now regarded as a label of absolute excellence in the international market.

There are two words which perfectly sum up the Albini Group's philosophy: heritage and innovation. Whilst the oldest book in the archive dates from 1845, the fabrics are produced on state-of the-art looms. This combination of traditional and modern elements is also reflected in the architecture of the firm's headquarters. Silvio Albini's succinct and confident summing-up of the Albini Group's success is as follows: "the Albini Group has been producing the best shirt fabrics in the world since 1876". This success is based on tradition, passion, highest quality standards and innovation. Other important elements reflected in product quality now also include sustainability and environmental protection – in other words, the focus is on eco-friendly issues.

The Albini group, after years of constant effort and significant investment on the frontline of energy saving, has given life to Albini Energia (energy). This new Group company was born out of their experience gained over the years in energy optimisation and the exploitation of alternative sources. In recent years this has led to the installation of three CHP groups, a photo-voltaic plant along with numerous other energy saving measures to improve the efficiency of the production buildings and sites.

Andrea, Stefano, Silvio & Fabio Albini

COMPANY	UNTERNEHMEN
Albini Group	Albini Group
FOUNDED IN	GEGRÜNDET
1876	1876
FOUNDER	GRÜNDER
Zaffiro Borgomanero	Zaffiro Borgomanero
HEADQUARTERS	HAUPTFIRMENSITZ
Albino, Bergamo, Italy	Albino, Bergamo, Italien
CEO	GESCHÄFTSFÜHRUNG
Albini Family	Familie Albini (Silvio Albini
(Silvio Albini CEO	Geschäftsführer und
and President)	Vorstandsvorsitzender)
EMPLOYEES	MITARBEITER
More than 1,300	Über 1.300
PRODUCTS	PRODUKTE
Fabrics	Stoffe
TURNOVER 2011	UMSATZ 2011
121 million Euros	121 Millionen Euro
EXPORT COUNTRIES	EXPORTLÄNDER
Worldwide, 80 countries	Weltweit, 80 Länder

DIE EDLEN TUCHMACHER

Giza 87 cotton selection on one of Albini's cotton fields in Egypt
Auswahl der Giza 87 Baumwolle an einem Baumwollfeld von Albini in Ägypten

Die Albini Group ist ein traditionsbewusstes Familienunternehmen italienischer Tuchmacher mit beeindruckender Geschichte. Den Grundstein legte Zaffiro Borgomanero. Unter dem Namen Z. Borgomanero & C. gründete er den Betrieb im Jahre 1876 in Albino in der Provinz Bergamo. Nach nur einem Jahr verfügte Borgomanero bereits über 40 mechanische Webstühle und 44 Mitarbeiter. 1884 wurde die Marke auf der Gewerbeausstellung in Turin mit der Bronzemedaille ausgezeichnet. Die erste wichtige Anerkennung für den Hemdenstoffproduzenten, der den Fokus bewusst auf die Hochwertigkeit seiner Produkte gelegt hatte. Nach dieser Überzeugung produziert das Unternehmen noch heute, und der Erfolg gibt ihm recht.

Im Jahr 1891, in der Zwischenzeit besaß Borgomanero bereits über 100 Webstühle und 90 Mitarbeiter, vererbte der kinderlos gebliebene Geschäftsmann die Firma an seinen Neffen Giovanni Albini. Als Präsident der Handelskammer von Bergamo wurde Albini eine der wichtigsten Größen der lokalen Wirtschaft. So war er 1907 auch maßgeblich an der Gründung der Industriegewerkschaft von Bergamo beteiligt, die überwiegend aus Textilunternehmen bestand. 1919 übergab er seinen Besitz an seine Söhne: Die Industrie Riunite Filati erhielt sein Sohn Riccardo, die Weberei, die fortan Società Dr. Silvio Albini & C. hieß, ging an seinen Sohn Silvio.

1968 fiel die Verantwortung an die vierte Generation, die Brüder Giancarlo, Marino, Piero und Gianni. Bis heute ist das Unternehmen in Familienhand und wird in fünfter Generation von Silvio, Fabio, Andrea und Stefano Albini repräsentiert. Seit 1984 konzentriert sich Silvio Albini, Geschäftsführer der Albini Group, darauf, das Unternehmen international auszubauen.

TRADITION TRIFFT INNOVATION

Eine der wichtigsten Errungenschaften in der Firmengeschichte war der Erwerb der beiden britischen Traditionswebereien Thomas Mason und David & John Anderson im Jahre 1992. Seitdem lagern 700 Bücher mit historischen Stoffmustern in den Archiven und erzählen von textiler Vergangenheit. Ein Wert, der nicht in Zahlen zu fassen ist und der laut Silvio Albini eine Brücke zwischen Tradition und Moderne schlägt. Denn das Archiv ist nicht nur Zeugnis der traditionellen Marken und ein hausinternes Museum, sondern gleichzeitig Inspirationsquelle für die Designer der Albini Group sowie für deren Kunden.

Das Unternehmen umfasst heute acht Produktionsstätten weltweit, fünf davon in Italien, zwei in Ägypten und eine in der Tschechischen Republik. Über 1.300 Mitarbeiter arbeiten für fünf verschiedene Marken – Albiate 1830, Cotonificio Albini, Thomas Mason, David & John Anderson, Albini Donna – und halten ein Angebot von mehr als 20.000 Stoffen bereit, um den Wünschen der anspruchsvollen, internationalen Kunden zu genügen.

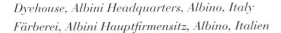

Dyehouse, Albini Headquarters, Albino, Italy
Färberei, Albini Hauptfirmensitz, Albino, Italien

The modern logistics centre in Gandino, Italy
Das moderne Logistikcenter in Gandino, Italien

Die Produktpalette reicht von sportlich bis elegant; 70 Prozent der Produkte werden in rund 80 Länder exportiert. Auf dem internationalen Markt ist die Albini Group heute eine der absoluten Premium-Marken.

Zwei Begriffe geben die Philosophie der Albini Group perfekt wieder: Erbe und Innovation. Während das älteste Buch im Archiv von 1845 datiert, wird in der Produktion mit den modernsten Webstühlen gearbeitet. Die Verbindung von Tradition und Moderne spiegelt sich auch in der Architektur des Firmensitzes wider. Silvio Albini fasst den Erfolg der Albini Group prägnant und selbstbewusst zusammen: „Die Albini Group produziert die besten Hemdenstoffe der Welt, seit 1876." Dieser Erfolg gründet auf Tradition, Leidenschaft, höchsten Qualitätsstandards und Innovation.

Heute gehört dazu auch Nachhaltigkeit, der Schutz der Umwelt bzw. der Fokus auf umweltfreundliche Maßnahmen, die sich auch in der Produktqualität widerspiegeln.

Nach Jahren stetigen Einsatzes und erheblicher Investitionen im Bereich des Energiesparens hat die Albini Group nun Albini Energia gegründet. Dieser neue Firmenbereich ist aus der jahrelangen Erfahrung in der Energieoptimierung sowie in der Förderung alternativer Ressourcen entstanden. In den letzten Jahren wurden – neben zahlreichen Energiesparmaßnahmen – drei Blockheizkraftwerke und eine Fotovoltaik-Anlage in Betrieb genommen, um die Effizienz der Produktion zu verbessern.

Book of samples from the Thomas Mason archive
Musterbuch aus dem Thomas Mason Archiv

ALLUDE
— SINCE 1993

"Cashmere will never go
out of fashion."
Andrea Karg

EXTRAVAGANCE IN CASHMERE

When Andrea Karg, founder of Allude, Munich's premier cashmere label, talks about one of her biggest successes, there is a definite look of pride in her eyes. In March 2012, the creative head of Allude pulled off a real coup: a show of her cashmere collection was staged for the very first time in Paris at the Grand Palais – and, what is more, the fixture was included in the official show calendar alongside labels such as Chanel, Chloé, Givenchy, Isabel Marant and Stella McCartney. "Having successfully been represented on the French market for around eight years, we have now been allowed to take our place alongside the world's great names – an international accolade!" enthuses Andrea Karg. "The entire collection featured berry tones, with a few sequin details adding a glamorous touch – and jazz music courtesy of Nina Simone."

Since she and her husband, Christian Karg, founded the company in 1993, Allude, with its staff of around 50 employees, has really taken off. Their aim was to find innovative new ways of using cashmere, to lose the typical prim image of cashmere twin sets, conservative V-necked pullovers and college-style cardigans. Andrea Karg is a law graduate who has also worked as a model. Her original aim was to try out all the different ways in which cashmere could be used instead of simply relying on the inherent desirability of the material itself. It was about time cashmere finally conquered the high-end fashion market.

Andrea Karg did in fact succeed in completely revamping the cashmere image, proceeding very gently at first, then with increasing determination. She was one of the first designers to dye the durable cashmere yarns, which she imports from China from the best farms in the world, in strong, vibrant colours. "Cashmere just absorbs colour brilliantly", comments the head of the company. She has also enjoyed experimenting with mixing materials. Hers was the first label to combine cashmere with silk and chiffon, inserting extremely elegant, semi-transparent back panels, trendy elbow patches and luxurious knitted jackets with appliquéd silk collars. She introduced cashmere garments which were skin-tight, loose and flowing or ribbed. She conceived unusual cashmere looks such as asymmetrical tops with short trains, knitted coats, soft, fluffy hoodies and floor-length tube dresses. Her collection even included shorts and culotte slip bloomers. "Our silhouettes have become more figure-hugging and subtly sexy for self-confident women", says Andrea Karg.

Andrea Karg has always been fascinated with the countless facets of the female image. The way women are depicted in contemporary art has often served as a source of inspiration. Her personal favourites include the expressive works by South African artist Marlene Dumas and the late French artist, Louise Bourgeois. A passionate collector herself, Andrea Karg has a collection of "her" women in the long corridor of her Munich apartment, which is hung with portraits of artists, including British-born Chris Ofili and a faceless portrait of Swiss painter, Albrecht Schnider.

"I'M ALWAYS READY TO TRY SOMETHING NEW."

Her main concern when designing new creations is the way that cashmere drapes around the female body. The company's name is, after all, borrowed from the English verb "to allude". A perfect fit is consequently rather less important in this respect. In addition to some of her more unusual designs, the firm's creative head has revamped timeless favourites such as pullovers embellished with trendy details and hand-crafted touches. Allude has progressed in just two decades from the narrow V-neck in 15 colours to a stylish cashmere fashion collection comprising coats, skirts, trousers, pullovers, waistcoats, tops and pants", lists Andrea Karg, who, despite her tall model's stature, still likes wearing high heels. Now the mother of two grown-up twins, she is adding a children's collection to supplement the firm's menswear line. In the USA and France, she is celebrating considerable success with her "Resort" collection aimed at exclusive department stores and boutiques. At home in Germany, she collaborates with the Falke company, which designs tights exclusively for Allude.

She is soon to grace the company's advertising campaign with herself as the label's "role model". "I am always ready to try something new and am quite happy to take risks", claims the founder of Allude, who actually sees no risks at all in the direction Allude is heading: "After all, cashmere will never go out of fashion."

Andrea Karg

COMPANY	UNTERNEHMEN
Allude GmbH	Allude GmbH
FOUNDED IN	**GEGRÜNDET**
1993	1993
FOUNDERS	**GRÜNDER**
Andrea & Christian Karg	Andrea & Christian Karg
HEADQUARTERS	**HAUPTFIRMENSITZ**
Munich, Germany	München, Deutschland
CEO	**GESCHÄFTSFÜHRUNG**
Andrea Karg	Andrea Karg
EMPLOYEES	**MITARBEITER**
Around 50 personnel,	Rund 50 Mitarbeiter,
15 of them in Munich	davon 15 in München
PRODUCTS	**PRODUKTE**
Cashmere fashion:	Kaschmirmode:
coats, skirts, pullovers,	Mäntel, Röcke, Pullover,
waistcoats, tops and	Westen, Oberteile und
pants	Hosen
EXPORT COUNTRIES	**EXPORTLÄNDER**
Approx. 200 German	Ca. 200 deutsche
premium outlets, approx.	Premium-Adressen, ca.
700 high-end retailers in	700 Premium-Händler in
Asia, Europe and USA	Asien, Europa und USA

ALLUDE

EXTRAVAGANZ IN KASCHMIR

Wenn Andrea Karg, die Gründerin des Münchner Kaschmir-Labels Allude, von einem ihrer größten Erfolge erzählt, ist ihr ein gewisser Stolz anzusehen. Im März 2012 gelang der Kreativchefin ein Coup: Erstmals wurde ihre Kaschmir-Kollektion im Pariser Grand Palais gezeigt – und der Termin im offiziellen Show-Kalender neben Labels wie Chanel, Chloé, Givenchy, Isabel Marant und Stella McCartney eingetragen. „Da wir schon seit rund acht Jahren erfolgreich auf dem französischen Markt vertreten sind, durften wir uns bei den großen Namen der Welt einreihen – ein internationaler Ritterschlag!", begeistert sich Andrea Karg. „Die gesamte Kollektion war in Beerentöne getaucht, dazu ein paar glamouröse Paillettendetails – und Jazzklänge von Nina Simone."

Seit sie und ihr Mann Christian Karg Allude 1993 gründeten, gewinnt die Firma mit rund 50 Mitarbeitern stetig an Bedeutung. Ihre Motivation war es, Kaschmir neu und anders zu verwenden, sich abzuheben von den typisch-braven Kaschmir-Twinsets, den biederen V-neck-Pullovern und Cardigans im College-Stil. Alle Möglichkeiten des Kaschmirgarns austesten, statt sich nur auf die Überzeugungskraft des Materials zu verlassen, war damals das Ziel der studierten Juristin, die auch als Model jobbte. Kaschmir sollte endlich auf dem High-Fashion-Markt ankommen.

Andrea Karg gelang es tatsächlich, das Kaschmir-Image gründlich umzukrempeln, erst zaghaft, dann immer konsequenter. Als eine der Ersten ließ sie die langlebigen Kaschmirgarne, die sie von den weltweit besten Farmen aus China bezieht, in kraftvoll leuchtenden Tönen einfärben. „Kaschmir nimmt Farbe einfach super an", erklärt die Firmenchefin. Experimentierfreudig war sie auch mit Material-Mixturen. Als erstes Label kombinierte sie Kaschmir mit Seide und Chiffon, setzte hochelegante, halbtransparente Rückenteile ein, trendige Ellbogen-Patches oder wertete Strickjacken mit applizierten Seidenkragen auf. Bei ihr tauchte Kaschmir hauteng, fließend und gerippt auf. Sie erdachte außergewöhnliche Kaschmir-Looks wie asymmetrische Tops mit kurzer Schleppe, Strickmäntel, kuschelige Hoodies und bodenlange Tubedresses. Selbst Shorts und Culottes, die bauchnabelhohen Slips, fehlten nicht im Programm. „Unsere

Allude is famous for its luxury knitwear, including opulent thick-knits.
Feinster Strick bis hin zu opulenten, mehrfädigen Aufmachungen – diese Qualitäten machen Allude aus.

Silhouetten wurden firgurbetonter und subtil sexy für selbstbewusste Frauen",
so Andrea Karg.

Das Frauenbild mit seinen unzähligen Facetten fasziniert Andrea Karg schon
lange. Die Darstellung von Frauen in der zeitgenössischen Kunst dient ihr immer wieder als Inspirationsquelle. Persönlich begeistern sie die expressiven Arbeiten der südafrikanischen Künstlerin Marlene Dumas und der verstorbenen
Französin Louise Bourgeois. Im langen Flur ihrer Münchner Wohnung hat die
passionierte Sammlerin „ihre" Frauen versammmelt. Dort hängen unter anderem Porträts von Künstlern wie dem Briten Chris Ofili oder die gesichtlosen
Kopfumrisse des Schweizer Malers Albrecht Schnider.

„ICH PROBIERE IMMER MAL WIEDER ETWAS NEUES AUS."

Beim Entwerfen neuer Kreationen kommt es ihr darauf an, wie die Kaschmirgarne
den Frauenkörper umspielen. Schließlich bedeutet der Firmenname Allude „sich
anschmiegen" – abgeleitet vom englischen „to allude". Der perfekte Schnitt ist
dabei erstmal zweitrangig. Neben ausgefalleneren Entwürfen wertet die Kreativchefin auch zeitlose Favoriten wie Pullover mit trendigen Details und handwerklichem Touch auf. „Allude ist in nur zwei Dekaden vom schmalen V-Neck in 15
Farben zur stylishen Fashion-Kollektion aus Kaschmir mit Mänteln, Röcken,
Hosen, Pullovern, Westen, Oberteilen und Pants avanciert", bilanziert Andrea
Karg, die trotz ihrer Modelgröße gerne High Heels trägt. Neben einer Herrenlinie entwirft die Mutter von inzwischen erwachsenen Zwillingen auch eine Kin-
der-Kollektion. In den USA und Frankreich feiert sie mit einer Resort-Kollektion
für exklusive Kaufhäuser und Boutiquen Erfolge. Hierzulande kooperierte sie
mit der Firma Falke, die exklusiv für Allude Strumpfhosen entwarf.

Bald wird sie selbst, als „role model" der Marke, die Anzeigenkampagne zieren.
„Ich probiere immer mal wieder etwas Neues aus und bin gern bereit, Risiken
einzugehen", sagt die Allude-Gründerin, die in der grundsätzlichen Ausrichtung von Allude überhaupt kein Risiko sieht: „Schließlich wird Kaschmir nie aus
der Mode kommen."

Allude on the catwalk of the
Prêt-à-Porter show at the historic
Grand Palais in Paris
Allude auf dem Catwalk der Prêt-
à-Porter-Schauen im ehrwürdigen
Grand Palais in Paris

ANDREA FENZI
— SINCE 1962

"To succeed in this
league, we listened
to our intuition
and worked hard."
Mario Ferrari

TWO SEWING-MACHINES PLUS A LOT OF COURAGE AND PASSION

The first thing you notice is its lightness, its almost weightless quality. A typical cashmere pullover by Andrea Fenzi barely weighs any more than a shirt; it is finely woven but nevertheless robust. Similarly, the stretchy, soft merino wool pullovers produced by this small, but elegant manufacturer in the Italian town of Visano, about 30 kilometres southwest of Lake Garda, incorporate a feel-good factor. The popularity of this soft, downy knitwear manages to survive the changing seasons and changing fashion trends and the elegant knitwear collections by Andrea Fenzi symbolise the firm's excellence in knitwear and knitted goods.

Ester and Mario Ferrari founded their textile company at the beginning of the 1960s, equipped with just two manual sewing-machines, a good deal of courage and imagination and, above all, a passion for knitwear. The German market became interested in their soft, downy cashmere pullovers and merino wool knitwear even before Italian retailers. Consequently, it was in Munich that Mario Ferrari presented his first collection in 1966. He swore that he would not return home again until he had assembled a list of potential clients. A year went by – then the first orders began to roll in. One purchase order read: 93,000 pullovers, to be ready in three months. "At that time, we only had the capacity to make 3,000 pullovers a month", recalls the firm's boss. Consequently, the Ferrari family hired all the seamstresses it could find in the area around the factory. They borrowed money from banks and personally collected the raw materials from the factories themselves in a little red Fiat "Bianchina". Their venture into this clothing sector proved successful and they have been producing top-quality cashmere goods in Visano ever since. This luxury knitwear is now exported all over the world.

It was not long before Commendatore Mario Ferrari, his wife Ester Tononi and son Dottore Cesare Ferrari were supplying the international market, e. g. USA, Russia, China, Korea, Hong Kong and Japan. "To succeed in this league, we followed our intuition and worked hard", comments Mario Ferrari. Nowadays, Andrea Fenzi, the Ferrari family's manufacturing company, is part of the Doratex group, one of the most modern enterprises in Europe with over 300 employees and a creative team which is always on the look-out for the latest trends. Thanks to strong demand from Europe, America, the Middle East and Asia, 50 per cent of the Andrea Fenzi Collection now includes polo shirts, T-shirts and sweat-shirts, in addition to its high-quality cashmere and merino wool products. New designs featuring trendy colours and modern details are combined in a classic style.

Every pullover represents over 50 steps which are carried out by hand. Such attention to detail, the efforts to improve quality and fit and the tireless search for new styles are unique. The Ferrari family has been producing clothes according to these criteria for three generations and its Andrea Fenzi label is governed by clearly defined guidelines. Only wool from the world's best cashmere producers are used in their products. These are meticulously checked for quality, transferred to specially equipped bobbins before being turned into top-quality knitwear on computer-operated knitting machines. The cutting, finishing and checking of each individual piece is done by hand, regardless of whether the garment is a classic man's pullover, which might be worn to complement a business outfit, or an item of men's leisurewear.

RICE STITCH LUXURY IN KNITWEAR

Andrea Fenzi is famous for other products besides its cashmere knitwear. It also has an international clientele for various articles produced using a rice stitch, so-called because it produces a raised pattern resembling grains of rice, also known as purl stitch or "grana di riso". This special knitting stitch pattern, which is created using old Stoll machines from the 1920s, produces an unusual elasticity. Rice stitch pullovers and sleeveless pullovers are usually made from Australian merino wool and likewise are a symbol of Andrea Fenzi's exclusivity. Few people can resist this Italian-style elegance. The Pope, along with numerous actors and artists, is one of the most famous wearers of this uniquely timeless, luxury knitwear.

Cesare & Mario Ferrari, Ester Tononi

COMPANY	UNTERNEHMEN
Andrea Fenzi – Doratex S.p.A.	Andrea Fenzi – Doratex S.p.A.
FOUNDED IN 1962	GEGRÜNDET 1962
FOUNDERS Mario Ferrari, Ester Tononi	GRÜNDER Mario Ferrari, Ester Tononi
HEADQUARTERS Visano (Brescia), Italy	HAUPTFIRMENSITZ Visano (Brescia), Italien
CEO Cesare Ferrari, Gianluigi Bresciani, Mario Riccieri, Massimo Gorini, Diego Ronchi, Mariateresa Scalmana	GESCHÄFTSFÜHRUNG Cesare Ferrari, Gianluigi Bresciani, Mario Riccieri, Massimo Gorini, Diego Ronchi, Mariateresa Scalmana
EMPLOYEES 60	MITARBEITER 60
PRODUCTS Premium and luxury knit-wear: jumpers, pullovers, blazers, t-shirts, scarves, bonnets	PRODUKTE Premium- und Luxus-Strickwaren, Pullover, Blazer, T-Shirts, Schals, Mützen
ANNUAL PRODUCTION 250,000–300,000 items	JAHRESPRODUKTION 250.000–300.000 Artikel
EXPORT COUNTRIES Ex USSR Countries, Europe, Hong Kong, Japan, Korea	EXPORTLÄNDER Europa, Hongkong, Japan, Korea, Länder der ehemaligen UdSSR

Wearing machine in the factory
Webmaschine in der Produktion

MIT ZWEI NÄHMASCHINEN, MUT UND LEIDENSCHAFT

Als Erstes fällt auf, wie leicht er ist, beinahe schwerelos. Ein typischer Kaschmirpullover von Andrea Fenzi wiegt kaum mehr als ein Hemd, ist kleinmaschig gewebt, aber dennoch robust. Auch die elastischen, weichen Merinopullover der kleinen, aber feinen Manufaktur im italienischen Städtchen Visano, etwa 30 Kilometer südwestlich des Gardasees, sind zum Wohlfühlen gemacht. Der Trend zu kuscheligem Strick überdauert Jahreszeiten und Moden, und die feinen Strick-Kollektionen von Andrea Fenzi stehen für die hohe Kompetenz der Firma in Strick- und Wirkwaren.

Ester Tononi und Mario Ferrari gründeten das Textilunternehmen zu Beginn der 1960er-Jahre, ausgestattet mit zwei handbetriebenen Nähmaschinen, einer Menge Mut, viel Fantasie und vor allem der Passion für Strick. Noch vor den italienischen Händlern haben sich die deutschen für die flauschigen Kaschmirpullover und Merinostrickwaren interessiert. 1966 präsentierte Mario Ferrari deshalb seine erste Kollektion in München. Er schwor sich, nicht eher wieder nach Hause zu fahren, bevor er nicht eine Liste potenzieller Kunden zusammengetragen hätte. Ein Jahr verging – dann trudelten die ersten Bestellungen ein. Auf einem der Orderscheine stand: 93.000 Pullover, fertigzustellen in drei Monaten. „Wir hatten damals allerdings nur Kapazitäten für 3.000 Pullover pro Monat", erinnert sich der Firmenchef. Also stellte die Familie Ferrari kurzfristig alle Näherinnen an, die sie im Umkreis der Manufaktur finden konnte. Sie lieh sich Geld von Banken und holte die Rohmaterialien mit ihrer kleinen roten „Bianchina" von Fiat persönlich in den Fabriken ab. Der Einstieg in die Branche gelang. Seither werden in Visano Kaschmirprodukte allererster Güte produziert und weltweit am Luxusstrickmarkt vertrieben.

Bald schon fertigten Commendatore Mario Ferrari, seine Frau Ester Tononi und ihr Sohn Dottore Cesare Ferrari für den internationalen Markt mit den Ländern USA, Russland, China, Korea, Hongkong und Japan.

„Um in dieser Liga anzukommen, haben wir auf unsere Intuition gehört und hart gearbeitet", sagt Mario Ferrari. Heute gehört Andrea Fenzi, die Manufaktur der Familie Ferrari, zur Firmengruppe Doratex, eines der modernsten Unternehmen Europas mit über 300 Beschäftigten und einem Kreativteam, das stets auf der Suche nach den neuesten Trends ist.

Neben den High-Quality-Erzeugnissen aus Kaschmir und Merino bestehen mittlerweile 50 Prozent der Andrea-Fenzi-Kollektion aufgrund der großen Nachfrage aus Europa, Amerika, dem Mittleren Osten und Asien aus Poloshirts, T-Shirts und Sweatshirts. Im klassischen Stil verbinden sie neue Schnitte mit modischen Farben und modernen Details.

In jedem Pullover stecken über 50 Handarbeitsschritte. Die Liebe zum Detail, das Streben nach Verbesserung von Qualität und Passform sowie die unermüdliche Suche nach neuen Stilen sind einzigartig. Die Familie Ferrari fertigt schon in dritter Generation nach diesen Kriterien und unterzieht ihre Marke Andrea Fenzi klar definierten Richtlinien: Nur Garne weltbester Kaschmirerzeuger kommen zum Einsatz. Sie werden akribisch genau auf Qualität geprüft, auf eigene, speziell ausgerichtete Garnspulen übertragen und dann auf neuesten computergesteuerten Strickmaschinen zu feinsten Strickwaren verarbeitet. Der Zuschnitt, die Konfektionierung und die Kontrolle jedes einzelnen Teils erfolgt von Hand, ganz gleich ob es sich um den klassischen Herren-Pullover handelt, der oft als Ergänzung zum Businessoutfit getragen wird, oder um die Herren-Freizeitbekleidung.

REISKORN-LUXUS IN STRICK

Die Marke Andrea Fenzi ist aber nicht nur bekannt für ihre Kaschmirprodukte. Weltweit gibt es eine Fangemeinde für die verschiedenen „Reiskorn"-Artikel, auch Perlfangmuster oder „grana di riso" genannt. Das besondere Maschenbild, das auf alten Stoll-Maschinen aus den 1920er-Jahren entsteht, liefert eine einzigartige Elastizität. Die Reiskorn-Pullover und -Pullunder sind meistens aus australischer Merinowolle hergestellt und stehen ebenfalls für Exklusivität à la Andrea Fenzi. Dieser italienischen Eleganz können sich nur wenige entziehen. Der Papst gehört neben vielen Schauspielern und Künstlern zu den berühmtesten Trägern dieses einzigartig zeitlosen Luxus in Strick.

Successful showroom collaboration with Cesare Ferrari
Effektive Zusammenarbeit mit Cesare Ferrari im Showroom

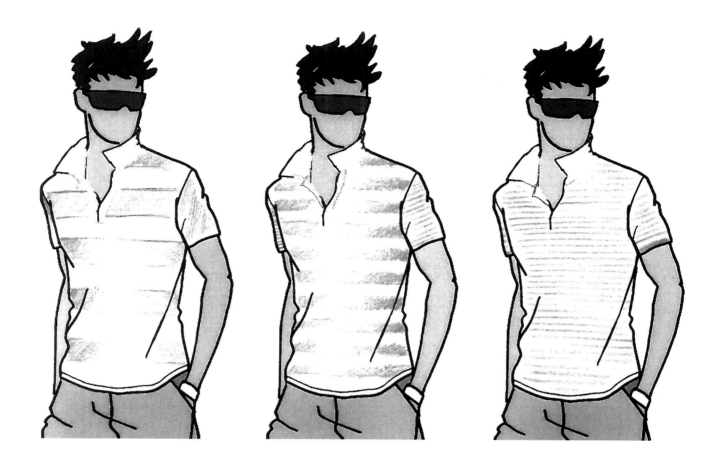

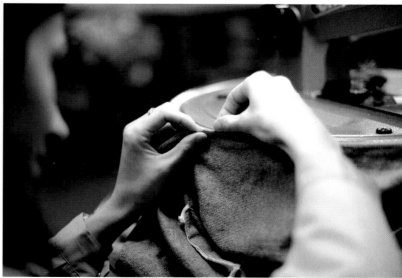

ASCOT
— SINCE 1908

"A suit and shirt without a tie is like shoes without laces!"
Jan Moese

HANDMADE IN KREFELD

For more than 100 years, Ascot, a family-run firm, has been producing hand-sewn ties from high-quality materials. Karl Moese established the business in 1908 in Krefeld, a town famous for velvet and silk, where he gained an international reputation as a tie manufacturer. To this day, every Ascot product bears a label stating "Made by Hand in Germany". "This is not likely to change in the future", remarks the current managing director, Jan Moese. As far as he is concerned, there is no question of moving production abroad: "During the past decades, we have accumulated so much know-how that we would not dream of outsourcing production to Asia or Eastern Europe – particularly not now when ties are experiencing a fashion revival", predicts the head of the firm, adding that the four generations who have so far contributed to the firm's successful history had something very important in common: "It is the vision of a perfectly crafted, high-quality product which was and still is the motivation which drives us and our employees." No fewer than 80 per cent of all ties produced in Germany in this Lower Rhineland town are exported to clients throughout Europe, North America, Australia and Asia.

One of the main guiding principles at Ascot is that exclusive ties should never be sewn by machine. Only hand-sewing guarantees optimum volume, a high degree of elasticity and durability. For this reason, when choosing a tie, never be afraid to feel, scrunch or roll up the material – a genuine Ascot will survive this kind of quality control treatment unharmed. "The idea for the label's name was conceived by Erwin Moese towards the end of the 1940s during a visit to England, which took him to the small town of Ascot in the county of Berkshire", explains Jan Moese. On his return to Germany, Erwin Moese, who was head of the firm at that time, immediately registered the name throughout Europe with the Patent Office in Munich. With that, "Ascot" became the firm's premium brand name and remains so to this day. In British English, a classic Ascot is the term for a very wide silk tie which is normally worn with a morning coat, grey-striped trousers and a silver-grey top hat or worn by British high society at the annual horse racing events at Ascot. The forerunner of the Ascot tie dates from the late 18th century. A famous English dandy of the period, by the name of Beau Brummell, introduced the fashion of wearing an elaborately knotted cravat, a looser version of the Ascot knot as worn by the sophisticated middle classes with formal morning dress. The modern-day Ascot tie lives up to its historic role models.

Jan & Wolfgang Moese, Barbara Pauen

PASSIONATE ABOUT STYLE AND QUALITY

Between 450 and 500 styles of tie are produced in the large Krefeld production rooms each season – in each case, two samples from each square metre of fabric. The raw silk for the fabric is produced in China before being processed and dyed in Italy. "Chinese silk is too shiny and lacks the right feel and scrunch factor", explains Jan Moese. It is this, in particular, that is an essential characteristic of high-quality ties. A passion for style and quality is what sets the Ascot label apart. Materials such as cashmere, wool and silk are selected in collaboration with the world's best weaving firms.

It takes a total of 20 individual steps to fashion a top-quality Ascot tie from the luxury fabric. Once the pattern is cut out, the top layer is placed over the interlining and pinned in place. The two sections are then stitched together, leaving a hollow cavity, using a single length of thread, 1.60 m long. Hand-stitching guarantees that the upper section and interfacing fit together perfectly. The interlining itself consists of a slightly roughened wool mixture which gives the finished tie a soft, supple quality, which makes it easier to knot and helps it recover its original shape quickly after wear. The lining is made from pure silk, even in the case of lighter fabrics such as crêpe de chine. A true connoisseur can identify an Ascot tie from the cut of the fabric: all three sections of the tie, as well as the interfacing and lining, are cut out at a 45-degree angle. This gives the tie a certain amount of elasticity, ensures that it hangs well and does not twist. A true fan is not concerned with any of this and simply enjoys the pleasure of wearing an Ascot tie. "Ideally", comments Jan Moese, "he will look in the mirror and think that he and his tie look great, if not irresistible!"

COMPANY	UNTERNEHMEN
Ascot Karl Moese GmbH	Ascot Karl Moese GmbH
FOUNDED IN	GEGRÜNDET
1908	1908
FOUNDERS	GRÜNDER
Karl and Gertrud Moese	Karl und Gertrud Moese
HEADQUARTERS	HAUPTFIRMENSITZ
Krefeld, Germany	Krefeld, Deutschland
CEO	GESCHÄFTSFÜHRUNG
Jan Moese (managing partner), Wolfgang Moese, Barbara Pauen (partner)	Jan Moese (Geschäftsführender Gesellschafter) Wolfgang Moese, Barbara Pauen (Gesellschafter)
EMPLOYEES	MITARBEITER
Approx. 40	Ca. 40
PRODUCTS	PRODUKTE
Ties, knitted ties, scarves, bow ties, pocket handkerchiefs	Krawatten, Strickkrawatten, Schals, Schleifen, Ziertücher
ANNUAL PRODUCTION	JAHRESPRODUKTION
Approx. 100,000 items	Ca. 100.000 Artikel
EXPORT COUNTRIES	EXPORTLÄNDER
Asia, Australia, Europe, North America	Asien, Australien, Europa, Nordamerika

Perfect combination of tweed and checks
Tweed und Karos perfekt kombiniert

HANDMADE IN KREFELD

Seit über 100 Jahren produziert das Familienunternehmen mit dem Namen Ascot handgenähte Krawatten aus hochwertigen Materialien. 1908 hatte Karl Moese die Manufaktur in der Samt- und Seidenstadt Krefeld gegründet, die mit ihrer Krawattenproduktion Weltruhm erlangte. Bis heute ziert jedes Ascot-Produkt ein Etikett mit den Worten „Made by Hand in Germany". „Daran soll sich auch in Zukunft nichts ändern", erklärt der heutige Geschäftsführer Jan Moese. Die Produktion der Krawatten ins Ausland zu verlegen, kommt für ihn nicht in Frage: „Wir haben in den letzten Jahrzehnten so viel Know-how aufgebaut, dass wir nicht daran denken, die Produktion nach Asien oder Osteuropa auszulagern – schon gar nicht jetzt, da die Krawatte ein Mode-Revival erlebt", prognostiziert der Geschäftsführer und erläutert, dass die vier Generationen, die an der erfolgreichen Geschichte bisher mitwirkten, etwas Entscheidendes verbindet: „Es ist die Vision vom perfekt gemachten, qualitativ hochwertigen Produkt, die uns und unsere Mitarbeiter angetrieben hat und noch immer antreibt." Nicht weniger als 80 Prozent aller in Deutschland gefertigten Krawatten erreichen heute aus der Stadt am Niederrhein Kunden in ganz Europa, Nordamerika, Australien und Asien.

Eine der wichtigsten Überzeugungen im Hause Ascot lautet: Exzellente Krawatten kommen nie unter die Nähmaschine. Denn nur Handnähte garantieren maximales Volumen, hohe Elastizität und Haltbarkeit. Daher gilt auch beim Aussuchen einer Krawatte: keine Scheu beim Anfassen, Knautschen und Rollen des Materials – eine echte Ascot besteht den Qualitätstest unbeschadet. „Die Idee zu dem Markennamen kam Erwin Moese Ende der 1940er-Jahre auf einer Reise durch England, bei der er auch in dem Städtchen Ascot, im britischen Landstrich Berkshire vorbeikam", erzählt Jan Moese. Zurück in Deutschland ließ sich der damalige Firmenchef den Namen sogleich beim Patentamt in München europaweit sichern. Seither ist Ascot die Premium-Marke der Firma Karl Moese. Im britischen Englisch bezeichnet man als klassische „Ascot" eine sehr breite, zum Plastron gefaltete Seidenkrawatte, die normalerweise zum Cut mit grau gestreifter Hose und silbergrauem Zylinder getragen wird, so von der britischen High Society beim alljährlichen Pferderennen in Ascot. Der Vorgänger der Ascot-Krawatte stammt bereits aus dem späten 18. Jahrhundert. Damals führte ein Dandy namens Beau Brummell die Mode einer gekonnt gewickelten Krawatte in England ein, eine lose gebundene Version des Ascot-Knotens, die in der gehobenen Mittelschicht zur formellen Morgenkleidung getragen wurde. Die Ascot-Krawatte von heute steht zu ihren historischen Vorbildern.

MIT LEIDENSCHAFT FÜR STIL UND QUALITÄT

In der großen Krefelder Produktionshalle entstehen pro Saison 450 bis 500 Krawatten-Modelle – jeweils zwei Stück aus einem Quadratmeter Stoff. Die Rohseide für das Textil wird zwar in China produziert, veredelt und gefärbt wird der Stoff aber in Italien. „Die chinesische Seide ist zu glänzend, ihr fehlen der Griff und der Knirsch", so Jan Moese. Genau das ist jedoch ein wesentliches Merkmal hochwertiger Krawatten. Die Leidenschaft für Stil und Qualität ist bezeichnend für Ascot. Materialien wie Kaschmir, Wolle und Seide werden in Zusammenarbeit mit den weltweit besten Webern ausgewählt.

Insgesamt 20 Arbeitsschritte entfernen den edlen Stoff von der hochwertigen Ascot-Krawatte. Nach dem Zuschnitt wird der Oberstoff um die Einlage gelegt, mit Nadeln vorgesteckt und beide Materialien durch einen einzigen, rund 1,60 Meter langen Faden hohl genäht. Die Handnaht ermöglicht den perfekten Sitz zwischen Oberstoff und Einlage. Die Einlage selbst besteht aus einer leicht angerauten Wollmischung, die der Krawatte einen weichen, fließenden Griff verleiht. So lässt sie sich leicht binden und kehrt nach dem Tragen schnell in ihre ursprüngliche Form zurück. Das Futter besteht aus reiner Seide, selbst bei leichten Qualitäten wie Crêpe de Chine. Der wahre Kenner identifiziert eine Ascot-Krawatte am Zuschnitt des Stoffes: Alle drei Teile der Krawatte sowie Einlage und Futter werden im Winkel von 45 Grad zugeschnitten. Dadurch bekommt die Krawatte Elastizität, einen glatten Fall und dreht sich nicht. Der wahre Liebhaber macht sich darüber keine Gedanken und empfindet es einfach nur als sehr angenehm, eine Ascot zu tragen. „Idealerweise", meint Jan Moese „schaut er in den Spiegel und findet sich und seine Krawatte super, ja unwiderstehlich!"

Tie patterns waiting to be used.

Krawattenschablonen warten auf ihren Einsatz.

The central inside seam is sewn by hand.
Die Krawattenhohlnaht wird per Hand genäht.

Cutting out ties from a template
Krawattenzuschnitt per Schablone

BARBOUR

"All of our collections remain true to our heritage. We draw on over 100 years of experience to create fit for purpose, quality clothing that is relevant to today's customer."
Dame Margaret Barbour

TOP QUALITY AND FUNCTIONAL

"Bill Tennant was out fishing in his open boat off the coast of Northern Ireland when his outboard motor suddenly cut out and he found himself drifting further and further out to sea, into a storm with winds reaching gale force 8. The coastguard estimated his chances of survival as being extremely small. If the sea did not get him, hypothermia would almost certainly finish him off. More than thirty hours later, as the storm began to abate, Bill Tennant was found. Apart from suffering from exhaustion, he was still in good health and his clothes underneath his Barbour jacket were dry." Among the letters which accompany the thousands of jackets returned to Barbour each year for repairs are many which relate similar adventures to the one experienced by Bill Tennant. His jacket was also sent in for repair and is probably still serving him faithfully to this day.

John Barbour, the company's founder, made it his mission to protect people from the extreme vagaries of the weather. He was the second son of a family whose roots date back to the 14th century and grew up on a farm in Galloway in southwest Scotland. His daily experience of shepherding sheep in a harsh, barren landscape gave John Barbour the idea of developing clothing which would offer the wearer protection against extreme weather conditions. In 1870, aged 20 years, he put his ideas into practice and left the family farm. In 1894, encouraged by his wife Margaret to make the most of his abilities and experience, he founded the company J Barbour & Sons, manufacturers of oilskins and rainwear, in the up-and-coming port of South Shields.

John Barbour soon became the leading manufacturer of oilskins on the British north coast and did not only supply seamen but anyone who earned their living working outdoors, such as farmers, labourers, guides and shepherds. In 1908 the company published its first catalogue to cope with the large demand from Britain's colonies. Only four years later, in 1912, Barbour already delivered to distant countries such as Argentina, Australia, Brazil, Canada, East Africa, Chile, Jamaica, Newfoundland, Rhodesia, New Zealand and the Chinese metropolis Hong Kong.

Barbour produced weatherproof clothing for the British armed forces during both World Wars. It was this period which resulted in the company's credo that all products from the house of Barbour must not only be of the highest quality but be functional as well. This maxim was also extended to motorsports. From 1936 to 1977, Barbour supplied British as well as international motor racing teams with clothing made of robust, waxed cotton. The iconic "Barbour International", a biker-style jacket, remains part of the Barbour collection to this day.

SUPPLIER TO THE BRITISH ROYAL FAMILY

There is no superfluous frippery to be found on Barbour products. Every detail serves a purpose: little tabs on the breast pockets for fishing hooks, spacious pockets for holding tools designed for both country and town dwellers. The uncompromising quality and authenticity which is the hallmark of the Barbour family company have always been appreciated by the British Royal Family. Barbour has been carrying the title "supplier to the British Royal Family" for many decades as a symbol of recognition for the Barbour family's services to Great Britain.

Maintaining a sense of tradition whilst remaining open to progress is the motto of Dame Margaret, who has been chair of the company since 1972. Today's collections comprise far more than just weatherproof clothing: in addition to its range of jackets, this British lifestyle label also offers trousers, knitwear, polo shirts, blazers, shirts, blouses, accessories and shoes.

Barbour employs 750 people worldwide and maintains a presence in 40 countries. The classic wax jackets are still produced in Barbour's own factory in South Shields. Ideas for each new collection come from the Barbour archives which date back to 1908. Barbour's authenticity and heritage are two of the reasons why an increasing number of young people are attracted to the label. Some musicians at the famous Glastonbury festival in 2007 sparked a revival of the Barbour jacket, whilst in 2006, the film "The Queen" sent crowds of people rushing into the Barbour store on Madison Avenue in New York, all of them coveting a jacket like the one worn by Helen Mirren in the film. Sales of "Beaufort" jackets doubled overnight.

The wax jackets are still made by hand in Barbour's factory in South Shields, where the company was founded. Time here seems to have stood still. The

John Barbour

COMPANY	UNTERNEHMEN
J Barbour & Sons Ltd	J Barbour & Sons Ltd
FOUNDED IN	**GEGRÜNDET**
1894	1894
FOUNDER	**GRÜNDER**
John Barbour	John Barbour
HEADQUARTERS	**HAUPTFIRMENSITZ**
South Shields, UK	South Shields, UK
CEO	**GESCHÄFTSFÜHRUNG**
Dame Margaret Barbour (Chair), Steve Buck (Managing Director)	Dame Margaret Barbour (Vorstandsvorsitzende), Steve Buck (Geschäftsführer)
EMPLOYEES	**MITARBEITER**
750	750
PRODUCTS	**PRODUKTE**
Jackets, knitwear, shirts, polo shirts, trousers, shoes, accessories	Jacken, Strick, Blusen, Hemden, Poloshirts, Hosen, Schuhe, Accessoires
ANNUAL TURNOVER	**JAHRESUMSATZ**
2010: 89.8 million British Pounds	2010: 89,8 Millionen Britische Pfund
EXPORT COUNTRIES	**EXPORTLÄNDER**
Worldwide, 40 countries	Weltweit, 40 Länder

Barbour

sewing machines clatter away just as they did 100 years ago, using 15,000 stitches to construct a jacket which is impermeable to water. The fabric is treated with an old, secret impregnation formula and finished with big metal zips and heavy-duty metal buttons, producing the end result of a functional and top-quality Barbour "Beaufort" or "Bedale" style wax jacket. Old jackets can be returned to the customer service for servicing, in other words, for re-waxing or repair. Sometimes, these jackets carry tales of adventure, like that of Bill Tennant, who, thanks to his Barbour jacket, survived 30 hours on a storm-tossed sea and remained safe and dry.

FUNKTIONAL UND VON HÖCHSTER QUALITÄT

„Bill Tennant war mit seinem offenen Boot zum Fischen vor der Küste Nord-irlands unterwegs, als plötzlich der Außenbordmotor ausfiel und er auf die offene See hinausgetrieben wurde, hinein in einen Sturm der Windstärke 8. Die Küstenwache gab ihm eine äußerst geringe Überlebenschance. Wenn er nicht dem Meer zum Opfer fallen würde, dann sicherlich dem Kältetod. Nach über 30 Stunden, als der Sturm allmählich nachließ, fand man Bill Tennant. Er war zwar erschöpft, aber gesund und die Kleidung unter seiner Barbour-Jacke trocken." Zwischen den Tausenden von Jacken, die jährlich zu Barbour in die Reparatur geschickt werden, befinden sich viele Begleitschreiben mit ähnlich abenteuerlichen Geschichten wie der von Bill Tennant. Auch seine Jacke wurde wieder instand gesetzt und leistet ihm wahrscheinlich noch heute treue Dienste.

Den Menschen vor den extremen Widrigkeiten des Wetters zu schützen, dazu fühlte sich Firmengründer John Barbour verpflichtet. Als zweiter Sohn einer Familie, deren Wurzeln bis ins 14. Jahrhundert zurückreichen, wuchs er auf einer Farm in Galloway im Südwesten von Schottland auf. Das tägliche Schafe-hüten in der kargen und rauen Landschaft brachte John Barbour auf die Idee, Kleidung zu entwickeln, die Schutz gegen die extremen Wetterbedingungen bieten sollte. 1870, im Alter von 20 Jahren, ließ er Taten folgen und verließ die elterliche Farm. Ermutigt von seiner Frau Margaret, seine Fähigkeiten und Er-fahrungen zu nutzen, gründete er 1894 in der aufstrebenden nordenglischen Hafenstadt South Shields die Firma J Barbour & Sons, Hersteller von Ölhäuten und Regenbekleidung.

John Barbour entwickelte sich schon bald zum führenden Lieferanten von Ölhäuten an der britischen Nordseeküste und belieferte nicht nur Seeleute, sondern all jene, die ihren Lebensunterhalt im Freien verdienten, wie Bauern, Arbeiter, Fuhrmänner und Schäfer. 1908 brachte die Firma ihren ersten Katalog heraus, um auch der großen Nachfrage aus den britischen Kolonien gerecht zu werden. Nur vier Jahre später, im Jahre 1912, lieferte Barbour bereits in ferne Länder wie Argentinien, Australien, Brasilien, Kanada, Ostafrika, Chile, Jamaika, Neufundland, Rhodesien, Neuseeland und in die chinesische Metro-pole Hongkong.

Während der beiden Weltkriege produzierte Barbour wetterfeste Kleidung für das britische Militär. Schon aus dieser Zeit stammt das Credo des Unterneh-mens, dass alle Produkte aus dem Hause Barbour von höchster Qualität und

The popular classic: the "Beaufort" waxed jacket
Der populäre Klassiker: die Wachsjacke „Beaufort"

kompromisslos funktional sein müssen. Das gilt auch für den Motorsport. Von 1936 bis 1977 stattete Barbour britische sowie internationale Motorradteams mit Bekleidung aus der robusten gewachsten Baumwolle aus. Die Biker-Jacke „Barbour International" ist noch heute Bestandteil der Kollektion.

HOFLIEFERANT DES BRITISCHEN KÖNIGSHAUSES

Überflüssigen Schnickschnack sucht man vergeblich bei den Barbour-Produkten. Jedes Detail erfüllt eine Funktion; kleine Schlaufen an den Brusttaschen für Angelhaken, geräumige Taschen für allerlei Utensilien sowohl für die Countryside als auch für die urbanen Träger. Die kompromisslose Qualität und die Authentizität, für die das Familienunternehmen Barbour steht, wird seit jeher auch von den britischen Royals geschätzt. Der Titel „Hoflieferant des britischen Königshauses" schmückt Barbour schon seit Jahrzehnten und zeichnet damit auch die Verdienste der Familie Barbour für Großbritannien aus.
Die Tradition im Blick behalten und sich trotzdem dem Fortschritt nicht verschließen, so lautet das Motto von Dame Margaret Barbour, die das Unternehmen seit 1972 führt. Die Kollektionen beinhalten heute weitaus mehr als

Barbour's two-way zip fastening
Barbours Zwei-Wege-Reißverschluss

wetterfeste Kleidung; Hosen, Strickwaren, Poloshirts, Blazer, Hemden, Blusen, Accessoires und Schuhe ergänzen neben den Jacken die Kollektion der britischen Lifestyle-Marke.

Barbour beschäftigt weltweit 750 Mitarbeiter und vertreibt seine Produkte in über 40 Ländern. Die klassischen Wachsjacken werden noch heute in der eigenen Produktionsstätte in South Shields gefertigt. Ideen für die aktuellen Kollektionen liefert das Barbour-Archiv, welches bis 1908 zurückreicht. Barbours Authentizität und das historische Erbe sind zwei der Gründe, warum auch immer mehr junge Menschen sich zu der Marke hingezogen fühlen. Beim Auftritt auf dem berühmten Glastonbury Festival 2007 sorgten einige Musiker für eine kleine Renaisssance der Barbour-Jacken. Und schon 2006 löste der Kinofilm „The Queen" einen Ansturm auf den Barbour-Store in der Madison Avenue in New York aus. Alle wollten die Jacke haben, die Helen Mirren in dem Film trägt. Über Nacht verdoppelte sich die Anzahl der verkauften „Beaufort"-Jacken.

Approximately 120 seamstresses are now employed in the South Shields factory.
In der Produktionsstätte in South Shields sind heute rund 120 Näherinnen beschäftigt.

In Barbours Produktionsstätte am Gründungsstandort in South Shields werden noch heute Wachsjacken von Hand gefertigt. Hier scheint die Zeit stehen geblieben zu sein. Wie vor 100 Jahren rattern die Nähmaschinen vor sich hin, um mit 15.000 Stichen eine Jacke zu fertigen, durch die kein Tropfen Wasser dringen kann. Die Stoffe sind mit einem speziellen Wachs imprägniert, dessen Rezeptur Barbour bis heute geheim hält. Aus dieser gewachsten Baumwolle, grobzähnigen Reißverschlüssen und soliden Metallknöpfen entstehen Barbours funktionale und hochwertige Wachsjacken wie die Modelle „Beaufort" und „Bedale". Ein Kundenservice steht eigens für die Instandsetzung getragener Jacken zur Verfügung, dort erhalten sie eine neue Wachsschicht oder sie werden repariert. Und manchmal erzählen diese Jacken Geschichten, wie die von Bill Tennant, der dank seiner Barbour-Jacke 30 Stunden auf stürmischer See wohlbehalten und trocken überstanden hat.

Pages/Seiten 44–45
Items found in the pockets of jackets sent to the Customer Service department
Fundstücke aus den Taschen der Jacken, die an den Kundenservice gesandt wurden

View of the production hall in the 1950s
Blick in die Produktion in den 1950er-Jahren

The first Barbour store, South Shields
Erster Barbour-Store, South Shields

BOGNER
— SINCE 1932

"A winter without Bogner is like a desert without sand."
Sven Hannawald

SPORTINESS,
QUALITY AND COMFORT

Willy Bogner describes supplying clothes to celebrities such as golf ace Bernhard Langer or Claudia Schiffer as kitting them out with a "B". The little silver "B" in question dangles from zips and jacket pockets, discreetly signalling the garment's origins. Meanwhile, his designs are no longer only worn by sports enthusiasts on the slopes of St. Moritz, Courchevel and Kitzbühel but also by trendsetters on the boulevards of New York, Moscow and Munich. Willy Bogner's home town of Munich in Bavaria is also home to this internationally successful label's design and cutting studios where the visitor is immediately struck by the informal atmosphere. Around 450 employees work in Munich for Willy Bogner and his wife Sônia, both of whom make a point of always being available to their team. Willy Bogner sets great store on "remaining firmly grounded".

"REMAINING GROUNDED"

This same attitude was also shared by Willi Bogner Senior, the founder of the firm. In 1932, working from a Munich backyard, he began importing skis, skiing equipment and knitted goods from Norway. With the advantage of a sportsman's expert eye – he won 11 German championship titles in cross-country skiing and ski-jumping in the Nordic combination – his new company became a success. Bogner has long been regarded as the inventor of sports fashion and in the 1950s it was described as the "Dior of ski fashion". Maria Bogner created a real fashion sensation when she invented stretch trousers with stirrup straps which were even worn by Marilyn Monroe to great advantage. Willy Bogner Junior, the couple's youngest son, followed in his father's footsteps as a prominent sports-man, winning altogether 70 trophies in 300 races. As if this were not enough, he became a leading ski cameraman, filming action shots for James Bond movies and celebrating international success with his own sports film "Fire and Ice". During a fashion shoot, he fell in love with Brazilian model Sônia Ribeiro. Together, they built his parents' firm into a major fashion business which has expanded dramatically, particularly in recent years. Since 1980, the company has acquired a further eleven Bogner licences to produce further lines such as Bogner Leather, Jeans, Shoes, Gloves, Man Shirts, Eyes, Perfumes and Bogner Ski clothing.

Since 1936, Bogner has been the official outfitter of the Germany winter Olym-pics team and in summer 2012 kitted out the summer Olympic team for the first time. However, regardless of whether the garment in question is a high-tech ski suit, an outdoor jacket, knitted products or classic jeans, the collections offered by this Munich firm combine exclusivity with quality. The styles are extremely comfortable to wear, both in the city and on the slopes. Elegant, high-quality materials, first-class styles and bold colours are the hallmark of this label as are a whole host of innovative details. The list is long: decorative seams, leather zip garages and embroidery details, elbow patches, detachable fur collars and striking lining fabrics. A jacket should look good on the inside as well as outside. Willy Bogner describes the persuasive brand concept, which has made the Bogner label internationally famous, as a combination of "sportiness, quality, comfort and an awareness of the spirit of the times". It is this lifestyle, which resonates high fashion, functionality and luxury in equal measure, that sets the Bogner, Sônia Bogner and Bogner Fire + Ice labels apart from the crowd. At its heart is a passion for sport and fashion, which Bogner, with every new season, combines with an authentic lifestyle.

Willy & Sônia Bogner

COMPANY	UNTERNEHMEN
Willy Bogner GmbH & Co. KGaA	Willy Bogner GmbH & Co. KGaA
FOUNDED IN	**GEGRÜNDET**
1932	1932
FOUNDER	**GRÜNDER**
Willy Bogner Sr.	Willy Bogner sen.
HEADQUARTERS	**HAUPTFIRMENSITZ**
Munich, Germany	München, Deutschland
CEO	**GESCHÄFTSFÜHRUNG**
Willy Bogner Jr. and his wife Sônia Bogner	Willy Bogner jun. und seine Frau Sônia Bogner
EMPLOYEES	**MITARBEITER**
767 worldwide, 689 in Germany	767 weltweit, 689 davon in Deutschland
PRODUCTS	**PRODUKTE**
Sônia Bogner, Bogner (Man, Woman and Sport), Bogner Fire + Ice, Bogner Kids and 11 licences	Sônia Bogner, Bogner (Man, Woman und Sport), Bogner Fire + Ice, Bogner Kids und 11 Lizenzen
ANNUAL PRODUCTION	**JAHRESPRODUKTION**
Winter 2011 to summer 2012: 77,896 items (with licences); 65,624 items (without licences)	Winter 2011 bis Sommer 2012: 77.896 Artikel (mit Lizenzen); 65.624 Artikel (ohne Lizenzen)
EXPORT COUNTRIES	**EXPORTLÄNDER**
Worldwide, 35 countries	Weltweit, 35 Länder

BOGNER

Willy Bogner Sr. & Maria Bogner
Willy Bogner sen. & Maria Bogner

SPORTLICHKEIT, QUALITÄT UND KOMFORT

Mit einem „B" ausstatten – so nennt es Willy Bogner, wenn er Prominente wie Golf-Ass Bernhard Langer oder Claudia Schiffer einkleidet. Das silberne „B" baumelt dann an Reißverschlüssen und Jackentaschen und verrät dezent die Herkunft der Mode. Mittlerweile tragen jedoch nicht nur Sportbegeisterte Bogners Entwürfe auf den Pisten von St. Moritz, Courchevel und Kitzbühel, sondern auch Trendsetter auf den Boulevards von New York, Moskau und München.

In der bayerischen Heimatstadt Willy Bogners liegen auch die Design- und Schnittateliers des international erfolgreichen Labels. Was hier sofort auffällt, ist die familiäre Atmosphäre. Rund 450 Mitarbeiter arbeiten in München für Willy Bogner und seine Frau Sônia. Beide sind jederzeit für ihr Team ansprechbar. Willy Bogner liegt viel daran, „die Bodenhaftung zu behalten".

„DIE BODENHAFTUNG BEHALTEN"

Mit dieser Devise gründete auch Willy Bogner senior die Firma. 1932 begann er in einem Münchner Hinterhof, Ski, Zubehör und Strickwaren aus Norwegen zu importieren. Ausgestattet mit dem Kennerblick eines Spitzensportlers – er gewann als Langläufer und Skispringer elf Deutsche Meistertitel in der Nordischen Kombination – führte er das Unternehmen zum Erfolg. Bogner gilt schon früh als der Erfinder der Sportmode und in den 1950er-Jahren wird die Marke als „Dior der Skimode" bezeichnet. Eine echte Modesensation gelang Maria Bogner: Sie erfand die Stretch-Keilhose mit Fußsteg, die selbst Marilyn Monroes Kurven schmeichelte. Auch Willy Bogner jun., jüngster Sohn des Paares, ist ein sportliches Talent und gewinnt insgesamt 70 Pokale in 300 Rennen. Doch damit nicht genug. Er wird zu einem der besten Ski-Kameramänner, dreht Actionszenen für James-Bond-Streifen und feiert mit seinem eigenen Sportfilm „Fire and Ice" weltweit Erfolge. Bei einem Mode-Fotoshooting verliebt er sich in das brasilianische Model Sônia Ribeiro. Zusammen bauen sie das Unternehmen seiner Eltern zu einem Modekonzern aus, der gerade in den letzten Jahren stark expandiert. Seit 1980 sind zudem insgesamt 11 Bogner-Lizenzen hinzugekommen: z. B. Bogner Leather, Jeans, Shoes, Gloves, Man Shirts, Eyes, Parfums, Ski. Seit 1936 ist Bogner offizieller Ausstatter der deutschen Winter-Olympiamannschaft und im Sommer 2012 erstmals auch der Sommer-Olympiamannschaft. Aber ganz gleich ob Hightech-Skianzug, Outdoorjacke, Strick-Styles oder klassische Jeans – die Kollektionen des Münchner Unternehmens verbinden Exklusivität und Qualität. Die Mode trägt sich superbequem, in der City und auf der Piste. Edle und hochwertige Materialien, erstklassige Schnitte sowie Mut zur Farbe gehören ebenso zu den Leitlinien des Labels wie jede Menge innovativer Details. Die Liste ist lang: Ziernähte, lederne Reißverschlussgaragen und Stickereien, Ellbogen-Patches, abknöpfbare Pelzkragen und auffällige Futterstoffe. Ein Jacket soll innen wie außen einfach gut aussehen.

Das überzeugende Markenkonzept, das den sogenannten Bogner-Stil international bekannt gemacht hat, beschreibt Willy Bogner als eine Kombination aus „Sportlichkeit, Qualität, Komfort und sensiblem Zeitgefühl". Es ist dieser gleichermaßen modische, funktionale und luxuriöse Lifestyle, der die Marken Bogner, Sônia Bogner und Bogner Fire + Ice unverwechselbar macht – seine Seele ist die Leidenschaft für Sport und Mode, die Bogner Saison für Saison aufs Neue mit einem authentischen Lebensgefühl verbindet.

BOGNER

GRAZIA

Buono Magico N. 12:
Giacche a vento
Sconto 30°/₀

N. 563
Milano - A. XXIV
8 Dicembre 1951
L. 70

MODA PER LA MONTAGNA

BORSALINO

— SINCE 1857

"In the past we created generations of style, today we create the style of the new generations."
Roberto Gallo

FROM HAT TO CULT OBJECT

What happens when Alain Delon dons a Borsalino is demonstrated in Jacques Deray's film of the same title: Delon's film partner, the beautiful Catherine Rouvel, was not the only one who completely lost her composure. Countless numbers of female viewers were affected the same way. When "Borsalino" appeared on the cinema screens in 1970, it led to a worldwide revival of the fortunes of this Italian hat company. It constituted the rare occurrence of the cinema paying tribute to an item of clothing which, more than any other, has gone down in cinema history. The Borsalino is as much a part of the glamour surrounding the male hero figures of the 1930s, 40s and 50s and the films they starred in as beautiful women and black limousines. Al Capone and Humphrey Bogart, James Cagney and Orson Welles – where would these legends be without their elegant, distinctive hats?

Giuseppe Borsalino was one of the leading entrepreneurs during Italy's early industrial days. He is said to have had the "most talented hands of any hat maker". The fact is that before he struck out on his own, he took care to learn his trade from scratch. He left home at the age of twelve and worked as an apprentice for several hat makers in Italy and France. Upon his return in 1857, he set up his own business in his home town of Alessandria in Piedmont and soon became very successful. In addition to his creative talent, Giuseppe Borsalino also possessed a keen business acumen. He imported a modern machine, which had already revolutionised hat-making in Manchester and pioneered the introduction of special pension schemes, health and accident insurance for his workers as well as a factory school for the children. The former Borsalino factory, which in its heyday employed around 1,000 workers, now houses a very interesting hat museum documenting the firm's 150-year-old history and including examples of all the hat models ever produced on site – from the Fedora, the most classic of all Borsalino classics, to hats which have adorned crowned heads and the clergy. The museum also provides information about the laborious production process.

Giuseppe Borsalino

SEVEN WEEKS OF WATERING, FULLING, COLOURING AND BRUSHING

What distinguishes a genuine Borsalino from its many imitations is not only its elegant shape but also the product quality, which is impossible to achieve without top-quality raw materials and exceptionally well trained staff. It takes seven weeks to make an impeccable Borsalino from a mixture of different animal fibres. Complicated steaming procedures turn the loosely woven material into a firm, smooth felt by shrinking it to a fraction of its original size. It owes its special water-resistant properties to the fine, under-fur of hares, rabbits or coypu. The final product, which is made from 100 per cent natural materials, will only achieve the desired qualities of being absolutely crease-resistant and extremely light if the water treatment, fulling, colouring, and brushing procedures are carried out with the utmost care. The hat is then shaped, steamed, pressed, fitted with a sweat band and lining before being decorated with accessories, such as a hat band and bow, transforming the unformed raw material into an elegant hat. It is then pressed a second time, steamed and the last few, remaining hairs are removed until the unmistakeable Borsalino finally leaves the factory and is sent on its way. Approximately three-fifths of the hats produced are exported. Little has changed over the centuries with regard to the proportion of hats sold in Italy and abroad even though the overall quantity has dwindled compared to the firm's former glory days.

Fortunately, however, the hat business has begun to pick up. The golden days of the hat culture, which reached a climax in the 1950s, is currently enjoying a renaissance. Hats have become popular again thanks to stars such as Johnny Depp, Kate Moss and Naomi Campbell setting an example. The sexy addition of a man's hat emphasises a person's individual style in both men and women. "Borsalino S.p.A." has responded to this trend by introducing a young line which encourages people to experiment with their individual look. There are virtually no limits to people's imagination in this respect. Saucy shapes and striking details, not to mention painted-on comic figures, provide a fresh interpretation of the concept of a cosmopolitan appearance.

COMPANY
Borsalino S.p.A.

UNTERNEHMEN
Borsalino S.p.A

FOUNDED IN
1857

GEGRÜNDET
1857

FOUNDER
Giuseppe Borsalino

GRÜNDER
Giuseppe Borsalino

HEADQUARTERS
Spinetta Marengo
(Alessandria), Italy

HAUPTFIRMENSITZ
Spinetta Marengo
(Alessandria), Italien

CEO
Roberto Gallo

GESCHÄFTSFÜHRUNG
Roberto Gallo

EMPLOYEES
200

MITARBEITER
200

PRODUCTS
Men's and ladies' hats

PRODUKTE
Herren- und Damenhüte

EXPORT COUNTRIES
Worldwide

EXPORTLÄNDER
Weltweit

VOM HUT ZUM KULTOBJEKT

Was passiert, wenn Alain Delon einen Borsalino trägt, konnte man in Jacques Derays gleichnamigem Film erleben: Nicht nur Delons Filmpartnerin, die bildschöne Catherine Rouvel, verlor vollkommen die Contenance. Ähnlich erging es wohl zahllosen Zuschauerinnen. Als der Film „Borsalino" 1970 in die Kinos kam, verhalf er dem italienischen Unternehmen zu einem weltweiten Revival. Es ist der seltene Fall einer cineastischen Hommage an ein Kleidungsstück, das wie kaum ein anderes Kinogeschichte schrieb. Der Borsalino gehört zum Glamour des heroischen Männerbildes der 1930er-, 40er- und 50er-Jahre und der sich darum rankenden Filme wie die schönen Frauen und die schwarzen Limousinen. Al Capone und Humphrey Bogart, James Cagney und Orson Welles – was wären diese Legenden ohne ihre elegante und markante Kopfbedeckung?

Giuseppe Borsalino war eine der großen Unternehmerfiguren der industriellen Gründerzeit Italiens. Er soll über die „talentiertesten Hände, die man je bei einem Hutmacher finden konnte" verfügt haben. Tatsache ist, dass er sich gründlich in der Branche umsah, bevor er sich selbstständig machte. Mit zwölf Jahren verließ er sein Elternhaus und arbeitete als Lehrling bei verschiedenen Hutmachern in Italien und Frankreich. Nach seiner Rückkehr startete er 1857 im heimatlichen Alessandria im Piemont sein eigenes Unternehmen, das er schnell an die Spitze führte. Er importierte die erste englische Dampfmaschine und sorgte mit einer eigenen Pensions-, Kranken- und Unfallkasse sowie einer Werkschule für die Kinder vorbildlich für seine Arbeiter. Die alte Borsalino-Fabrik, die zu ihrer besten Zeit rund 1.000 Arbeiter beschäftigte, beherbergt inzwischen ein sehenswertes Hutmuseum. Dort kann man sich nicht nur über die 150-jährige Firmengeschichte informieren und sämtliche je vor Ort produzierten Hutmodelle bewundern – vom „Fedora", dem klassischsten aller Borsalino-Klassiker, bis zu den Kopfbedeckungen gekrönter Häupter und des Klerus. Man erfährt auch einiges über den langwierigen Fertigungsprozess.

SIEBEN WOCHEN WÄSSERN, WALKEN, FÄRBEN, BIMSEN

Was einen echten Borsalino von seinen zahlreichen Imitationen unterscheidet, ist neben der stilvollen Silhouette die Qualität. Und die ist ohne hochwertige Rohstoffe und hervorragend ausgebildete Mitarbeiter nicht zu haben. Es dauert sieben Wochen, bis aus den unterschiedlichen Tierhaar-Mischungen ein makelloser Borsalino wird. Komplizierte Dampfverfahren machen aus dem lockeren Verbund einen festen, geschmeidigen Filz, indem sie ihn zu einem Bruchteil seiner ursprünglichen Größe zusammenschrumpfen lassen. Seine besonderen wasserabweisenden Eigenschaften verdankt der Borsalino der feinen Unterwolle von Hasen, Kaninchen oder Nutria (Biberratte). Nur wenn das Wässern, Walken, Färben, Bimsen usw. äußerst schonend vonstattengeht, erreicht das 100-prozentige Naturprodukt die erwünschte, absolut knitterfreie und federleichte Qualität. Durch Formen, Dämpfen, Pressen, eingenähtes Schweißband und Futter sowie schmückende Accessoires wie Hutband und Schleife verwandelt sich der unförmige Rohling in einen ausgefeinten Hut. Dann wird ein weiteres Mal gebügelt und gedämpft, letzte überflüssige Härchen werden beseitigt, bis der unverwechselbare Borsalino endlich aus der Fabrikation entlassen und auf Reisen geschickt wird. Ungefähr drei Fünftel der Produktion gehen in den Export. Am Verhältnis zwischen der Anzahl der in und außerhalb Italiens verkauften Hüte hat sich über die Jahrhunderte wenig geändert, wenn auch die Gesamtzahl gegenüber den Glanzzeiten zurückgegangen ist.

Aber glücklicherweise ist Bewegung in das Hutgeschäft gekommen. Die Kunst, einen Hut zu tragen, ist eine der schönsten, fast verloren gegangenen und heute wieder zu entdeckenden Kulturleistungen. Stars wie Johnny Depp, Kate Moss oder Naomi Campbell machen es vor. Der sexy Touch eines Herrenhuts unterstreicht den persönlichen Stil bei Männern ebenso wie bei Frauen. Die Firma Borsalino S.p.A. antwortet auf den Trend mit einer jungen Linie, die zum Spiel mit den individuellen Looks auffordert. Der Fantasie sind dabei fast keine Grenzen gesetzt. Freche Formen und ausgefallene Details bis hin zu aufgemalten Comicfiguren interpretieren die Vorstellung von einem kosmopolitischen Erscheinungsbild neu.

The company has been despatching felt hats, meticulously packed, all over the world since the 1950s.
Bereits in den 1950er-Jahren werden die Filzhüte sorgfältig verpackt und weltweit versandt.

A Borsalino undergoes a series of around 80 steps before it achieves its final distinctive shape.
Above: The finest animal hair is sprayed with steam on a revolving bronze cylinder and condensed into a felt hat body.
In circa 80 Arbeitsschritten erhält der Borsalino seine unverwechselbare Form.
Oben: Feinstes Tierhaar wird mit Wasserdampf auf einen sich drehenden Bronzezylinder gesprüht und zu Stumpen verdichtet.

Page/Seite 57:
The 19th-century wooden felting machine is still in operation to this day.
Noch heute ist die aus Holz bestehende Maschine aus dem 19. Jahrhundert zur Filzbearbeitung in Betrieb.

BRIONI
— SINCE 1945

"We continue to create exclusive masterpieces to meet the demands for one of a kind wardrobes."
Francesco Pesci

FASHION FOR THE PERFECT GENTLEMAN

When Nazareno Fonticoli, a gentleman's tailor, and businessman Gaetano Savini opened a shop together in 1945, right after the end of the war, in the Via Barberini in Rome, they had a clear vision of their goal: to produce Italian tailoring at its most perfect! In order to capture the attention of the clientele they were hoping to attract, the newly founded firm was named Brioni, a title which immediately evoked an air of exclusivity reminiscent of what was once the most legendary resort on the Adriatic. And one other thing was clear right from the start: the new venture was not about individual garments but about style. Brioni's caters for the perfect gentleman's overall appearance from head to toe. With clothing ranging from sophisticated evening wear to sports clothes, from neckties to socks, the firm provides everything necessary for the style-conscious, jet-setting gentleman, who sometimes, when circumstances dictate, has to "live in his clothes". Like James Bond, the firm's most famous advertisement, whom Brioni clothed in five consecutive films, the firm's style is regarded as the epitome of unshakeable, meticulously coordinated, subtle elegance.

What is the firm's philosophy behind this impressive perfection? The magic words are – quite simply – tailoring excellence. The clothes are produced entirely in Italy in the Abruzzi town of Penne, a region with a long history of tailoring. To keep these roots alive and remain up-to-date with the latest developments, the company set up its own school of tailoring here in 1985, naming it after Nazareno Fonticoli. It was established to train a new generation of tailors. Production is carried out exclusively by hand – each model comprises five to seven thousand stitches, sewn by hand. Brioni practices the doctrine of the "220 individual steps" which an article of clothing must undergo during the tailoring process. Eighty of these alone are devoted to the elaborate pressing procedure. It is possibly this pressing routine which most clearly demonstrates the degree of perfectionism involved: the fabric is pressed every time a stitching stage is completed. This, in turn, necessitates a certain period of rest, depending on the type of fabric and how long the living fibres "work". Additional treatment is sometimes required to equip the fabric for the climate of the country in which it is to be worn.

Nazareno Fonticoli & Gaetano Savini

TIMELESS, UNIQUE, EXCELLENT

It goes without saying that only top-quality fabrics are used, mainly luxury products from Biella, northeast of Milan, known as the Italian "noble fibres valley"; silk has been obtained from Como since time immemorial. Only about 10 per cent of materials are imported and these are mainly fabrics produced exclusively for Brioni so that the colours and patterns will not be repeated anywhere else. Even these top-quality goods are meticulously checked for the tiniest defect, which might only just be visible to the naked eye. Brioni knows how important it is, when it comes to the cutting stage, to have a precise knowledge of the specific qualities of different fabrics and that in the case of fabrics with low elasticity (silk, linen, wool, gabardine, etc.), for example, any alterations need to be carried out on the model to ensure that the client has adequate freedom of movement and the garment is a perfect fit. Furthermore, every fabric requires a different type of lining.

All this offers us no more than the tiniest glimpse into a unique world of clothing culture. In the USA, Brioni stands for "power suits for managers", a promotional image which profits from its recognition value and is regarded as a passport to the upper eschelons of the business world. The number of Brioni retail stores has risen sharply in the past few years; Russia, the Middle East and the large cities of Asia, in particular, have witnessed a substantial increase. The traditional Brioni client is a bit like a member of a popular club which boasts the unique distinction that its members know about style and quality and insist on the highest standards in all areas. The exceptional excellence of its tailoring also bestows certain responsibilities on this family-run firm which it fulfils through its academic partnership with the Royal College of Art in London and the politecnico School of Design in Milan. Master tailors from the House of Brioni pass on their knowledge and skills to a new generation of art and design students from all over the world.

COMPANY Brioni S.p.A.	UNTERNEHMEN Brioni S.p.A.
FOUNDED IN 1945	GEGRÜNDET 1945
FOUNDERS Nazareno Fonticoli, Gaetano Savini	GRÜNDER Nazareno Fonticoli, Gaetano Savini
HEADQUARTERS Rome, Italy	HAUPTFIRMENSITZ Rom, Italien
CEO Francesco Pesci	GESCHÄFTSFÜHRUNG Francesco Pesci
EMPLOYEES 1,800	MITARBEITER 1.800
PRODUCTS Menswear	PRODUKTE Herrenbekleidung
EXPORT COUNTRIES Worldwide	EXPORTLÄNDER Weltweit

Every single suit bearing the Brioni
name is made by hand.
Jeder Anzug, der den Namen Brioni
trägt, ist handgefertigt.

MODE FÜR DEN
PERFEKTEN GENTLEMAN

Als der Herrenschneider Nazareno Fonticoli und der Unternehmer Gaeta-no Savini 1945, direkt nach Kriegsende, gemeinsam einen Laden in der Via Barberini in Rom eröffnen, haben sie eine klare Vision vor Augen: italienische Schneiderkunst in ihrer höchsten Perfektion! Um sich der anvisierten Klientel deutlich zu erkennen zu geben, adaptiert die Neugründung mit dem Namen „Brioni" auch gleich den Duft der Exklusivität eines der ehemals legendärsten Badeorte der Adria. Und noch etwas steht von Anfang an fest: Es geht nicht um das eine oder andere Ausstattungsstück, es geht um einen Stil. Brioni kümmert sich um den Auftritt des perfekten Gentleman von Kopf bis Fuß. Von der feins-ten Abendgarderobe bis zum Sportdress, von der Krawatte bis zur Socke hält das Unternehmen alles bereit für stilbewusste Männer des Jetset, die teils unter extremer Beanspruchung „in ihren Kleidern leben". Wie James Bond, seine be-rühmteste Verkörperung, für dessen Ausstattung Brioni in fünf Filmen hinterei-nander verantwortlich zeichnete, gilt der Brioni-Stil als Inbegriff für unerschüt-terliche, bis ins allerkleinste Detail abgestimmte, unaufdringliche Eleganz. Welche Firmenphilosophie steckt hinter dieser beeindruckenden Perfektion? Die Zauberformel heißt schneiderhandwerkliche Exzellenz ohne jedes Wenn und Aber. Produziert wird ausschließlich in Italien, im Abruzzen-Städtchen Penne, einer Gegend mit einer langen Tradition im Schneiderhandwerk. Um diese Wurzeln lebendig zu halten und sie mit den neuesten Entwicklungen zu verbinden, wurde dort 1985 die hauseigene Schneiderschule namens Naza-reno Fonticoli gegründet, um den Schneidernachwuchs zu qualifizieren. Die Produktion ist reine Handarbeit, das heißt im Klartext, in jedem Modell stecken fünf- bis siebentausend handgenähte Stiche. Brioni leistet sich die Doktrin der „220 Arbeitsschritte", die ein Bekleidungsstück im Schnitt zu durchlaufen hat. Davon werden 80 allein für die aufwendige Bügelprozedur beansprucht. Das Bügeln ist vielleicht eines der markantesten Elemente dieses Perfektionismus: Auf jede Nähphase folgt ein Bügelvorgang, der wiederum eine gewisse Zeit der Ruhe notwendig macht, je nach Art des Stoffes und je nachdem, wie lange die lebendige Faser „arbeitet", die übrigens mit entsprechenden Behandlungen eigens für das Klima des Bestimmungsortes gerüstet wird.

ZEITLOS, EINZIGARTIG, EXZELLENT

Als Stoffe kommen natürlich nur edelste Erzeugnisse in Betracht, im Wesentli-chen Luxusware aus Biella, dem italienischen „Tal der feinen Tuche" nordöstlich von Mailand; die Seide bezieht man seit jeher aus Como. Nur etwa 10 Prozent der Ware wird importiert, aber auch dann handelt es sich meist um exklusiv für Brioni hergestellte Stoffe, sodass sich bei keinem anderen Stück Farben und Muster wiederholen. Selbst diese Topqualitäten werden genauen Kontrollen auf winzigste Defekte unterzogen, die mit bloßem Auge gerade noch erkennbar sind. Wer weiß heute noch, wie wichtig die genaue Kenntnis der spezifischen Eigen-schaften der Stoffe für das Zuschneiden ist? Oder dass bei Stoffen mit geringer Elastizität (Seide, Leinen, Gabardine etc.) Änderungen am Modell vorgenommen werden müssen, um dem Kunden Bewegungsfreiheit und eine perfekte Passform zu garantieren? Jeder Stoff macht zudem ein bestimmtes Futter erforderlich.

RCA student and a young Master Tailor of Nazareno Fonticoli Tailoring School
RCA-Studentin und ein junger Schneidermeister der Schneiderschule Nazareno Fonticoli

All diese Beschreibungen geben nur einen kleinen Einblick in das Universum einer Kleiderkultur, die ihresgleichen sucht. In den USA steht Brioni für „power suits for manager", ein Aushängeschild, das von seinem Wiedererkennungswert profitiert und als Eintrittskarte in die obersten Etagen der Geschäftswelt gilt. Die Zahl der firmeneigenen Verkaufsboutiquen stieg in den letzten Jahren sprunghaft an; vor allem in Russland, dem Nahen Osten und in den Megastädten Asiens herrscht großer Zuwachs. Der klassische Brioni-Kunde ist so etwas wie ein Anhänger eines angesagten Clubs mit Alleinstellungsmerkmal, dessen Mitglieder etwas von Stil und Qualität verstehen und auf allen Gebieten höchste Ansprüche stellen. Mit diesem außerordentlichen Standard in der Schneiderkunst übernimmt das Familienunternehmen auch Verantwortung, der es in einer akademischen Partnerschaft mit dem Royal College of Art in London und der Scuola del Design des Politecnico di Milano Rechnung trägt. Dort geben die Schneidermeister aus dem Hause Brioni ihr Wissen und ihr Können an Kunst- und Design-Studenten aus der ganzen Welt weiter.

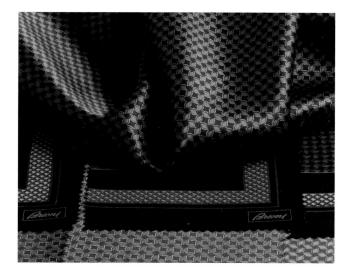

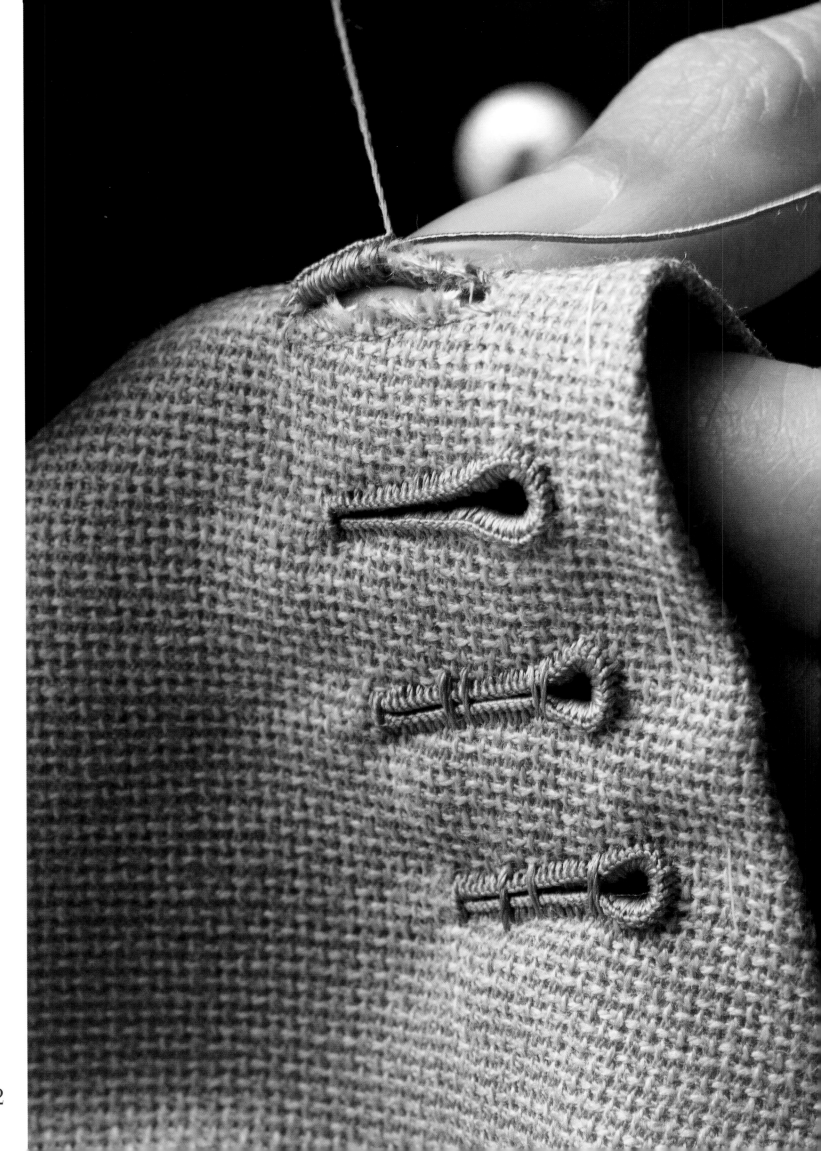

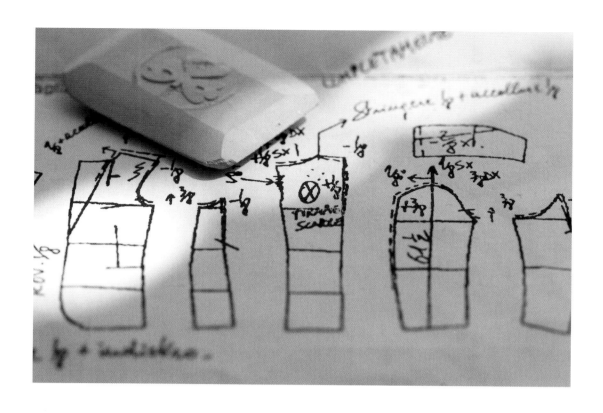

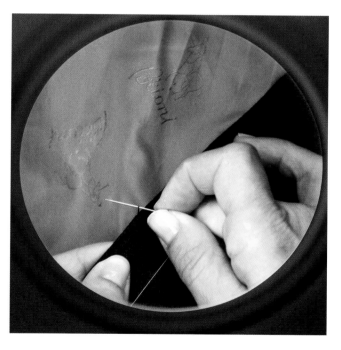

Brioni's impeccable attention to detail is shown in every single step, which is indispensable to creating a new masterpiece.
Brionis Sorgfalt im Detail zeigt sich in jedem einzelnen Schritt, der notwendig ist, um ein Meisterstück zu kreieren.

Sketches from the Brioni archive which has been declared
in 2009 "Italian cultural heritage" by the Italian Ministry
for Heritage and Culture
Skizzen aus dem Brioni-Archiv, das 2009 vom italienischen
Kultusministerium zum „italienischen Kulturerbe" erklärt
wurde

Pierce Brosnan, alias James Bond, wearing a Brioni three-piece suit in "GoldenEye", 1995.
Pierce Brosnan alias James Bond trägt einen Brioni-Dreiteiler in dem Film „GoldenEye", 1995.

CARUSO
— SINCE 1958

"All products
are 100 per cent
made in Italy."
Umberto Angeloni

CLASSIC AND YOUNG –
THE LOOK FOR GLOBAL PLAYERS

The star of the greatest tenor of all time, Enrico Caruso (1873–1921), never seems to set. The ongoing fascination for this artist has remained undiminished throughout decades, not to mention centuries. It arises from the combination of talent and charisma, so often associated with the glamorous world of opera and the Italian lifestyle in general, with its sensuality and instinctive flair for achieving the perfect look. What could be more natural, therefore, than to choose this world-famous style icon as the symbol and image of a fashion label, which not only stands for Italian tailoring excellence but also remains proud of its Neapolitan roots? Although the tenor and the firm's founder, Raffaele Caruso, are not related in any way, they nevertheless have many things in common: both men are prime examples of an internationally renowned product which is 100 per cent Made in Italy, they were both born in Naples and were

Umberto Angeloni

both fond of men's clothing. The label's signature garment, the "Caruso jacket", which is regarded as a tribute to Enrico, still stars in all the seasonal collections. During the late 1950s, the young tailor, Raffaele Caruso, like many others, moved to the more prosperous northern Italy to seek his fortune. He settled in the small town of Soragna in the Emilia-Romagna region, where, together with his wife and sister-in-law, he set up a workshop producing custom-made suits. This soon established itself and grew during the 1970s and 80s into a thriving concern. In 1990, their two sons joined the firm: Alberto assumed responsibility for production and technical innovation whilst Nicola was in charge of distribution and marketing. Meanwhile, the company now known as Caruso S.p.A., which went public in 2006, is run by Umberto Angeloni who bought it from the two brothers in 2009.

A STRONG IDENTITY WITH ITALIAN CULTURE

To this day, all elements of the collection are still produced in Soragna. This historic site in "Bassa Padana", the flat landscape of the Po river plain, remains an enclave of traditionally produced, top-quality garments. The latest designs are displayed to the international trade and press with Italian panache in the sophisticated atmosphere of the "Terrazza Caruso" in the Via Montenapoleone 5. Even though the arrival of Angeloni, Brioni's former chief executive, opened up contacts with international top brands and 60 per cent of production is now exported, the Caruso label is still defined, first and foremost, by its strong identity with Italian culture.

The label's styles and designs are not, however, bound by tradition. The Caruso look boasts a broad spectrum of products and a young style, which tend to appeal to customers in their 30s. The dynamic, quality-conscious global player can choose from six different styles, represented by six mannequins, which come from all over the world but share the same passion for the inimitable Caruso tailoring: Fefè from Naples, Tao from Shanghai, Pedro from Buenos Aires, Jean-Baptiste from Paris, Ricky from Los Angeles and Ji-Huan from Seoul. They are all dressed in elegant suits, sportswear, knitwear, trousers, shirts and ties.

In addition, Caruso's "Virtuoso Menswear" line also offers a range of special designs. Yet this is not the only area where the client's wishes are paramount. Fifteen of the 600 employees are devoted exclusively to customer service and advising clients. To maintain its reputation for outstanding quality and perfect fit, garments are still mainly sewn by hand. But what Caruso is famous for is the unbeatable value of its products, the perfect balance between quality and price. The company's compelling marketing image, from its Internet presence, to sales and distribution and the modern, functional architecture of the firm's headquarters, is based on a keen interest in the latest developments in technology and marketing. This label is an example of efficiency and authenticity working in successful symbiosis.

COMPANY	UNTERNEHMEN
Raffaele Caruso S.p.A.	Raffaele Caruso S.p.A.
FOUNDED IN	GEGRÜNDET
1958	1958
FOUNDER	GRÜNDER
Raffaele Caruso	Raffaele Caruso
HEADQUARTERS	HAUPTFIRMENSITZ
Soragna (Parma), Italy	Soragna (Parma), Italien
CEO	GESCHÄFTSFÜHRUNG
Umberto Angeloni	Umberto Angeloni
EMPLOYEES	MITARBEITER
600	600
PRODUCTS	PRODUKTE
Suits, jackets, tuxedoes, overcoats, pants, shirts, ties, knitwear	Anzüge, Jacken, Smokings, Mäntel, Hosen, Hemden, Krawatten, Strickwaren
ANNUAL PRODUCTION	JAHRESPRODUKTION
100,000 units of clothing	100.000 Kleidungsstücke
EXPORT COUNTRIES	EXPORTLÄNDER
Worldwide	Weltweit

CARUSO

Caruso Jacket

KLASSISCH UND JUNG –
DER LOOK FÜR GLOBAL PLAYERS

Der Stern des größten Tenors aller Zeiten, Enrico Caruso (1873–1921), scheint niemals unterzugehen. Der anhaltenden Faszination für diesen Künstler können die Jahrzehnte, ja Jahrhunderte, nichts anhaben. Sie erklärt sich aus der Verbindung von Talent und charismatischer Ausstrahlung, die mit der glamourösen Welt der Oper so eng verknüpft sind wie mit der italienischen Lebensart, der Sinnenfreude und dem Gespür für einen perfekten Auftritt. Was liegt also näher, als diese weltberühmte Stilikone zum Maßstab und Werbeträger für ein Mode-Label zu machen, welches sich als Botschafter italienischer Schneiderkunst nach wie vor auf seine neapolitanischen Wurzeln beruft? Zwar gibt es keine verwandtschaftlichen Verbindungen zwischen dem Tenor und dem Firmengründer Raffaele Caruso, es gibt aber zweifellos viele Gemeinsamkeiten. Sie sind weltweit ein wunderbares Beispiel für ein 100-prozentiges Produkt „Made in Italy": Beide erblickten in Neapel das Licht der Welt und beide zeichnen sich durch ein Faible für Herrenmode aus. So ist das Aushängeschild der Marke, das „Caruso Jackett", zu verstehen als Hommage an den legendären Tenor. Es bildet nicht umsonst die Speerspitze der saisonalen Kollektionen. Wie viele andere auch zog der junge Schneider Raffaele Caruso Ende der 1950er-Jahre in den prosperierenden Norden Italiens, um dort sein Glück zu versuchen. In dem kleinen Städtchen Soragna in der Emilia-Romagna gründete er mit Frau und Schwägerin eine Werkstatt für maßgeschneiderte Anzüge, die sich unter dem Namen Ma.Co. (Manufacture e Confezioni) schnell etablierte

The "Terrazza Caruso" in the
Via Montenapoleone 5 in Soragna
Die „Terrazza Caruso" in der
Via Montenapoleone 5 in Soragna

und sich in den 1970er- und 80er-Jahren zu einem florierenden Unternehmen entwickeln sollte. 1990 traten die beiden Söhne in die Firma ein: Alberto übernahm die Verantwortung für Produktion und technische Innovation, während Nicola sich um den Vertrieb und das Marketing kümmerte. Inzwischen wird das Unternehmen, das 2006 an die italienische Börse ging, unter dem Namen Raffaele Caruso S.p.A. von Umberto Angeloni geführt, der es den beiden Brüdern im Jahr 2009 abgekauft hatte.

VERBUNDEN MIT DER ITALIENISCHEN KULTUR

Bis heute werden alle Teile der Kollektion in Soragna gefertigt. Dieser historische Ort in der „Bassa Padana", dem flachen Land in der Po-Ebene, ist eine Enklave traditionell hergestellter, hochwertiger Produkte. Im gepflegten Ambiente der „Terrazza Caruso" in der Via Montenapoleone 5 werden der Presse und dem internationalen Markt die neuesten Modelle präsentiert. Auch wenn das Unternehmen mit dem Einstieg von Umberto Angeloni, dem ehemaligen Chef von Brioni, den Anschluss an die internationalen Top-Marken schaffte und inzwischen 60 Prozent der Produktion in den Export wandert, definiert sich Caruso zuallererst über seine Verbundenheit mit der italienischen Kultur. Diese Verpflichtung zur Tradition bezieht sich allerdings nicht auf die Schnitte und Designs. Der Caruso-Look zeichnet sich vielmehr durch eine große Bandbreite und einen jungen Stil aus. Das Unternehmen hat ermittelt, dass die Kunden im Durchschnitt zwischen 30 und 40 Jahre alt sind.

Dem dynamischen, qualitätsbewussten Global Player stehen sechs unterschiedliche Styles zur Verfügung. Repräsentiert werden sie von sechs Schaufensterpuppen aus der ganzen Welt, die die Leidenschaft für die unnachahmliche Caruso-Konfektion teilen: Fefè aus Neapel, Tao aus Schanghai, Pedro aus Buenos Aires, Jean-Baptiste aus Paris, Ricky aus Los Angeles und Ji-Huan aus Seoul. Sie alle tragen elegante Anzüge, Sportbekleidung, Strickwaren, Hosen, Hemden und Krawatten.

Darüber hinaus bietet Caruso mit seiner Linie „Virtuoso Menswear" auch Sonderanfertigungen an. Und nicht nur hier sind die Wünsche der Kunden oberstes Gebot. 15 der insgesamt 600 Mitarbeiter stehen allein für den Kundenservice und die Beratung zur Verfügung. Um die ausgezeichnete Qualität und eine optimale Passform zu gewährleisten, wird bei Caruso nach wie vor sehr viel in Handarbeit gefertigt. Wofür das Label aber vor allem steht, ist die unübertroffene Wertigkeit seiner Produkte bei einer perfekten Balance zwischen Qualität und Preis. Das Interesse an den neuesten Entwicklungen in Technik und Marketing bildet dabei die Basis für ein stringentes Profil, vom Internetauftritt über den Vertrieb bis hin zur modernen und zweckmäßigen Architektur der Firmenzentrale. Effizienz und Authentizität gehen bei dieser Marke eine überzeugende Symbiose ein.

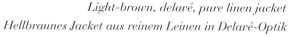

Light-brown, delavé, pure linen jacket
Hellbraunes Jacket aus reinem Leinen in Delavé-Optik

Page/Seite 75:
Sartorial tree
Schneiderbaum

CERRUTI
— SINCE 1881

"Only an excellent fabric can originate an excellent fashion. When designing our products, great care is paid to every single processing phase, combining tradition with technology and style."
Nino Cerruti

AN ITALIAN FASHION ICON

Since time immemorial, the name of Cerruti has stood for timeless elegance. The family tradition dates back to 1881 when Nino Cerruti's grandfather, Antonio, and his brothers Quintino and Stefano founded what is now the internationally famous weaving mill in Biella in Piedmont, Italy. It was run by Nino Cerruti's father until the latter's death, after which it was taken over in 1950 by Nino, who then abandoned his studies of political sciences and his plans to become a journalist. From that time on, the 19-year-old Nino Cerruti dedicated himself to fashion and, even today, aged over 80, he is still passionately involved in the family firm, which he runs jointly with his son Julian. He examines the fabrics with an expert eye, running his hands lovingly over the different textures. His sharp eyes call to mind a time when fashion was synonymous with excellence, a standard which Nino Cerruti still upholds to this day. His instinct for the aesthetic, coupled with his organisational talent, have turned him into an icon and yet he could not be more down to earth.

It was not enough for Beau Nino merely to follow in the footsteps of his fabric-manufacturing family. He wanted to break into the world of fashion, luxury and beautiful women and, in doing so, he made fashion history. In 1957, his first company Hitman presented a luxury, ready-to-wear menswear collection called Flying Cross. In 1967, he founded Cerruti 1881 Maison de Couture and opened his first menswear boutique of the same name in the Place de la Madeleine in Paris. This was followed a year later by his women's collection. A fashion show, which presented women's and men's fashions together, created a stir. He was the only designer to produce his own fabrics. From then on his label was known as Cerruti 1881. Giorgio Armani worked as a designer for Cerruti 1881 until 1970, before establishing his own label in 1974.

FASHION FOR THE BIG SCREEN AND FOR LIFE

The cornerstone of his international success was laid with the opening of the Cerruti 1881 boutique in Paris, a product of the passion and enthusiasm of Nino Cerruti, whose hard work and level-headedness had made his company internationally famous. Cerruti, whose trademark was to become a yellow pullover, thrown casually around the shoulders, created a brand, which was coveted by Hollywood stars and business people alike. The Cerruti 1881 label became synonymous with success and good taste.

Nino Cerruti has designed costumes for over 200 films, lending a magical presence to film stars both on and off screen. Marcello Mastroianni, Jean-Paul Belmondo, Robert Redford and Kathleen Turner, to name but a few, were all clothed and admired by this Italian maestro. Some of his most unforgettable outfits include those worn by Julia Roberts and Richard Gere in "Pretty Woman", by Sharon Stone and Michael Douglas in "Basic Instinct" and the suits worn in "Miami Vice". The 1980s would be practically unimaginable without the Cerruti 1881 label.

In 2001, Nino Cerruti sold 51 per cent of his company to an Italian financial holding company, which shortly afterwards forced him out of the firm. The 2002 spring/summer collection was the last one designed by Nino Cerruti. He commented in an interview: "A major reason for my withdrawal was the fashion industry itself. Where else would you find so much superficiality, egocentricity, so much fuss about nothing? Or such ignorance?"

However, anyone who thinks Nino Cerruti has retired is mistaken. In 2005, he acquired the Baleri furniture firm and four years later introduced the new brand of Cerruti Baleri furniture to Milan's furniture fair. Nino Cerruti has retained his passion for elegant clothes to this day, passing on his knowledge to his son Julian, who shares his aesthetic vision. The firm Lanificio F.lli Cerruti dal 1881 produces a total of eight top-class collections, ranging from "high end" to "casual chic". Every fabric bears testimony to Nino Cerruti's many years of experience and his striving for beauty and elegance as well as to the progressive approach of his son. Perfect craftsmanship and elegance, coupled with an instinct for the spirit of the time, Lanificio F.lli Cerruti dal 1881 unites tradition and modern technology. Nino and Julian Cerruti both count on eco-friendly production standards. The family firm is one of the best addresses for the finest Italian textiles and supplies its fabrics to international fashion houses like Chanel.

Julian & Nino Cerruti

COMPANY	UNTERNEHMEN
Lanificio F.lli Cerruti dal 1881	Lanificio F.lli Cerruti dal 1881
FOUNDED IN	GEGRÜNDET
1881	1881
FOUNDERS	GRÜNDER
Stefano, Antonio and Quintino Cerruti	Stefano, Antonio und Quintino Cerruti
HEADQUARTERS	HAUPTFIRMENSITZ
Biella, Italy	Biella, Italien
CEO	GESCHÄFTSFÜHRUNG
Daniele Sanzeni	Daniele Sanzeni
EMPLOYEES	MITARBEITER
420	420
PRODUCTS	PRODUKTE
Twice a year 3 fabric collections for men, women and urban-sports people	Zweimal jährlich 3 Stoffkollektionen für Herren, Damen und den sportlich urbanen Menschen
ANNUAL PRODUCTION	JAHRESPRODUKTION
3 million metres of fabric	3 Millionen Meter Stoff
EXPORT COUNTRIES	EXPORTLÄNDER
Worldwide	Weltweit

**LANIFICIO
F.LLI CERRUTI
DAL 1881**

75

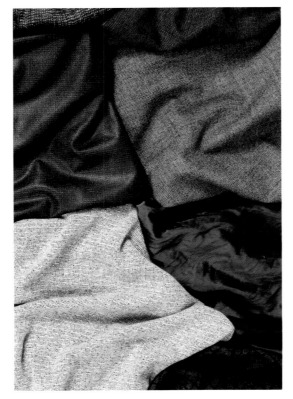

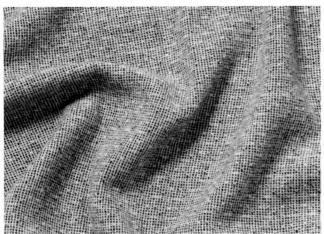

Above: Cashmere fabrics of the women's collection, Winter 2013
Below: Canvas of the Parcour Collection, Summer 2013
Oben: Kaschmirstoff für die Damen-kollektion, Winter 2013
Unten: Leinengewebe der Parcour-Kollektion, Sommer 2013

EINE ITALIENISCHE MODE-IKONE

Der Name Cerruti steht seit jeher für zeitlose Eleganz. Die Familientradition reicht zurück bis ins Jahr 1881, als Nino Cerrutis Großvater Antonio mit seinen Brüdern Quintino und Stefano die heute weltbekannte Weberei in Biella im italienischen Piemont gründete. Sie wurde von Nino Cerrutis Vater bis zu dessen Tod geleitet und 1950 von Nino übernommen, der sein Studium der Politikwissenschaften und seine Pläne, Journalist zu werden, damit aufgab. Fortan widmete sich der damals 19-Jährige der Mode und noch heute, mit über 80 Jahren, ist er mit Leidenschaft im Familienbetrieb tätig, den er gemeinsam mit seinem Sohn Julian führt. Mit Kennerblick streichen seine Hände liebevoll über die unterschiedlichsten Texturen. Die wachen Augen erzählen von einer Zeit, in der Mode noch höchsten Idealen entsprach und die Nino Cerruti bis heute beibehalten hat. Sein Gespür für Ästhetik, gepaart mit organisatorischem Talent ließen ihn zur Ikone werden. Dennoch liegt ihm nichts ferner als Starallüren.

Beau Nino war es nicht genug, bloß in die Fußstapfen der Stofffabrikanten-familie zu treten, er wollte in die Welt der Mode, des Luxus und der schönen Frauen eintauchen und sollte damit Modegeschichte schreiben. 1957 präsentierte er mit seinem ersten Unternehmen Hitman die luxuriöse Prêt-à-porter Herrenkollektion „Flying Cross". 1967 gründete er Cerruti 1881 Maison de Couture und eröffnete an der Place de la Madeleine in Paris seine erste gleichnamige Boutique für Herren. Ein Jahr später folgte die Damenkollektion. Eine Modenschau, bei der er Damen- und Herrenmode gleichzeitig präsentierte, sorgte für Aufsehen. Ebenso war er der einzige Designer, der seine eigenen Stoffe produzierte. Die Marke nannte er fortan Cerruti 1881. Bis zum Jahr 1970 arbeitete Giorgio Armani als Designer für Cerruti 1881, bevor er 1974 sein eigenes Label gründete.

MODE FÜR LEINWAND UND LEBEN

Der Grundstein für den internationalen Erfolg wurde mit der Pariser Cerruti-Boutique 1881 gelegt. Er gründete auf der Leidenschaft und Begeisterungs-fähigkeit Nino Cerrutis, der sein Unternehmen durch Fleiß und Besonnenheit zu Weltruhm geführt hat. Der Mann, dessen Markenzeichen ein lässig um die Schultern geworfener gelber Pullover werden sollte, etablierte eine Marke, die von Hollywood-Stars und Geschäftsleuten gleichermaßen geschätzt wurde. Cerruti 1881 wurde zum Synonym für Erfolg und guten Geschmack.

Nino Cerruti designte die Kostüme für über 200 Filme und verlieh den Schauspielern auf der Leinwand sowie im Privatleben eine magische Präsenz. Jean-Paul Belmondo, Marcello Mastroianni, Robert Redford und Kathleen Turner, um nur einige zu nennen, wurden vom italienischen Meister eingekleidet und verehrt. Unvergessen sind die Outfits von Julia Roberts und Richard Gere in „Pretty

Colour control book at the "White" fair, Milan 2012
Musterbuch zur Farbkontrolle auf der Messe „White", Mailand 2012

Woman", Sharon Stone und Michael Douglas in „Basic Instinct" oder die Anzüge der Hauptdarsteller in der Fernsehserie „Miami Vice". Die 1980er-Jahre sind ohne die Marke Cerruti 1881 nahezu unvorstellbar.

2001 verkaufte Nino Cerruti 51 Prozent seines Unternehmens an eine italienische Finanzholding, die ihn wenig später aus dem Unternehmen drängte. Die Kollektion Frühjahr/Sommer 2002 war die letzte, die von Nino Cerruti entworfen wurde. In einem Interview sagte er: „Ein wesentlicher Grund für meinen Rückzug war die Mode an sich. Wo finden Sie sonst so viel Oberflächlichkeit, Egozentrik, so viel Lärm um nichts? Eine derartige Ignoranz?"

Doch wer denkt, Nino Cerruti hätte sich damit zur Ruhe gesetzt, der irrt. 2005 erwarb er die Möbelfirma Baleri und präsentierte vier Jahre später die neue Marke Cerruti Baleri auf der Mailänder Möbelmesse.

Seine Liebe für elegante Kleidung hat Nino Cerruti sich bis heute bewahrt und gibt sein Wissen an Sohn Julian weiter, mit dem er seine ästhetische Vision teilt. So produziert das Unternehmen Lanificio F.lli Cerruti dal 1881 insgesamt acht hochwertige Kollektionen von High-End bis Casual Chic. Jeder einzelne Stoff ist durchwirkt von Nino Cerrutis jahrelanger Erfahrung und dem Streben nach Schönheit und Eleganz sowie den progressiven Ansätzen seines Sohnes. Handwerkliche Perfektion und Eleganz gepaart mit Zeitgeist. Lanificio F.lli Cerruti dal 1881 vereint Tradition und moderne Technologien. Besonderen Wert legen Nino und Julian Cerruti auf umweltfreundliche Produktionsstandards. Das Familienunternehmen ist eine der besten Adressen für feinste italienische Tuche und beliefert internationale Modehäuser wie Chanel mit seinen Stoffen.

Traditional fabric book, Winter 1904
Traditionelles Musterbuch, Winter 1904

Nino Cerruti at the "White" fair, Milan 2012
Nino Cerruti auf der Messe „White", Mailand 2012

Page/Seite 81:
Couture for the runway shows in Paris
Couture für die Laufstege in Paris

Soft
Reflat
Neck

Crepe
Legar

Split
Sleeves

Cashmere
Coat

Fold down
Boots.

Wardrobe
Waistcoat.
Shirt

Cashmere coat

Wool/silk knit
jacket

Cavalry twill
pants/silk voile
crepe

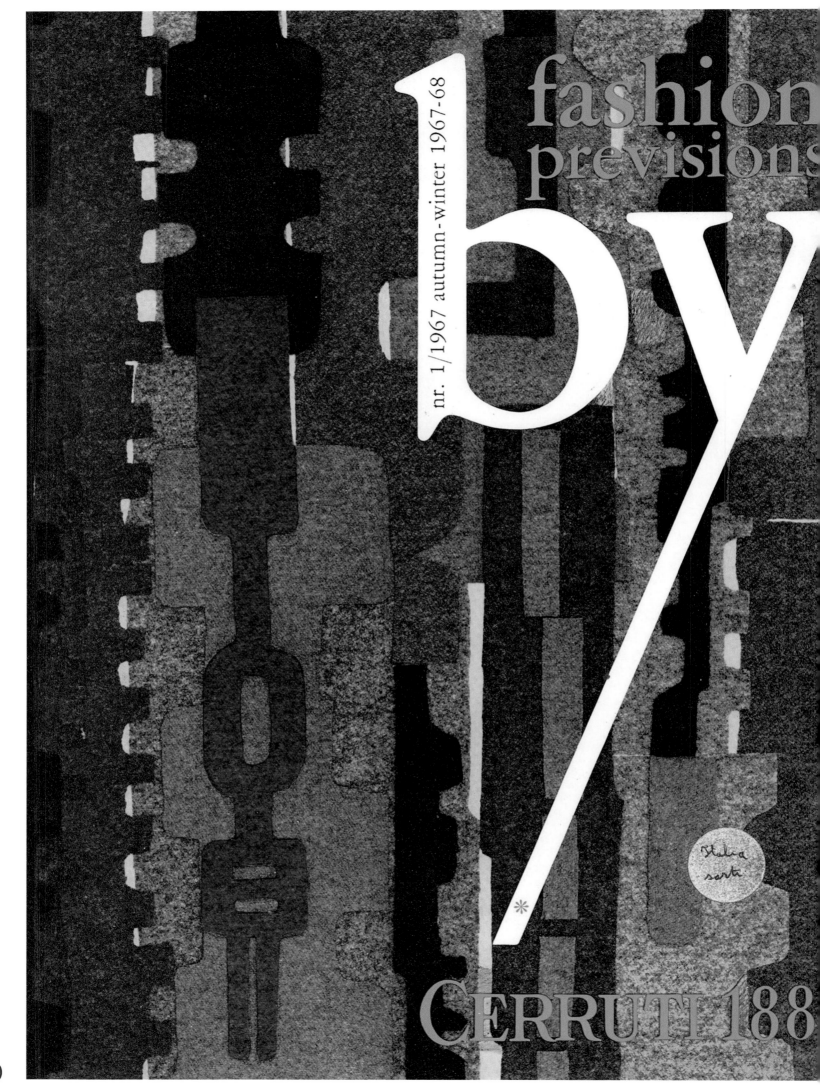

fashion
previsions

nr. 1/1967 autumn-winter 1967-68

by

CERRUTI 188

Italia
sarti

*Nino Cerruti at the weaving
department
Nino Cerruti in der Weberei*

*From above: Raw materials, warping, spinning
Von oben: Rohmaterialien, Schären, Spinnen*

DINKELACKER

"Once you have worn a Dinkelacker shoe, you will never wear any other brand."
Norbert Lehmann

COMFORT ELEVATED TO AN ART FORM

The lyre-shaped design on the wing cap is as exclusive as the figure on the bonnet of a luxury car. The ornamental pattern of holes is one of the distinctive features of a classic pair of Budapest shoes. For almost 150 years, Heinrich Dinkelacker, a traditional shoe-manufacturing company, has been producing handcrafted, welt-stitched men's shoes in the classic Budapest style, which are famous for their outstanding quality, reliable fit, elegant style and high degree of comfort. Welt-stitching is the ultimate skill in the art of shoemaking whereby the shoe upper is sewn to the sole with the seams elegantly disappearing into the invisible inner part of the shoe around the heel area. The special twine used for this purpose is coated with pitch to increase durability.

The Dinkelacker company was established in 1879 in the Baden-Württemberg town of Sindelfingen and, since the 1960s, has been producing both custom-made shoes as well as ready-to-wear styles in a small factory in the Budapest suburb of Budafok. The customer can choose from a range of 15 different lasts for shoe styles named "Buda" or "Oxford", for example. The all-time classic is "Rio" with its triple sole although the narrow "Lucerne" model has meanwhile also become a bestseller.

"MADE BY A MASTER CRAFTSMAN, WORN BY A CONNOISSEUR"

This is the motto of this family-run company which, since 2005, has displayed its comprehensive range of different styles in an elegant showroom at the firm's new headquarters in Bietigheim-Bissingen. After Burkhardt Dinkelacker, the grandson of the company's founder, decided to sell the business for reasons of age, the company was taken over by former Porsche boss, Wendelin Wiedeking, and his press spokesman, Anton Hunger, together with former IBM manager, Norbert Lehmann.

Remaining true to the philosophy of traditional craftsmanship, they expanded the product range by introducing a few style variations which make increased use of rubber profile soles and feature new shapes and styles. A pair of Budapest shoes from the house of Dinkelacker combines traditional reliability with modern ethos and provides the wearer with soft, but solid contact with the ground. This is guaranteed by the complex construction of the layered sole in every single shoe. The insole, middle sole and outer sole with its Dinkelacker logo are hand-sewn together, whereby the inner sole forms the basis of the shoe. It is cut out around the shape of the last and consists of 4-mm thick, pit-tanned leather. Welt-stitched Dinkelacker shoes are also renowned for the extremely fine leather used in their manufacture. The choice of material for the uppers ranges from French aniline calf, to Italian buffalo calfskin and ochre-yellow calfskin to cordovan, made from horse hide, made by the famous Horween Leather Company of Chicago.

There is a further element in the manufacture of Dinkelacker shoes which turns them into works of art: time. Over the course of 12 to 15 days, the master shoemaker will complete a process involving approximately 300 individual steps. While this time-consuming process is being carried out, almost entirely by hand, the shoe remains clamped to the last the whole time, long enough for it to mature into its ultimate shape.

One of the most physically strenuous steps is attaching the shoe to the last. Once the respective shank has been pulled over the last, the upper is clamped to the last using so-called "lasting tacks" where it remains for several days. The shoemaker then makes any necessary adjustments needed to tweak the shoe into the perfect shape.

Other procedures, such as hollowing out the inner sole to make the insole lip or the delicate task of hammering 60 brass pins into the sole by hand, represent a deliberate shift from and marked contrast to the usual fast pace of modern life. The finishing touches in the manufacture of a Dinkelacker shoe include the "abrading" whereby the edge of the sole is trimmed using a special knife. Before this, the master craftsman applies the edge dressing to the rim of the shoe, imprinting one notch at a time into the material. The signature of the master craftsman, located inside the shoe, is a guarantee of excellence, which anyone wearing Dinkelacker shoes experiences at every step.

Wendelin Wiedeking & Norbert Lehmann

COMPANY	UNTERNEHMEN
Heinrich Dinkelacker GmbH	Heinrich Dinkelacker GmbH
FOUNDED IN	GEGRÜNDET
1879	1879
FOUNDER	GRÜNDER
Heinrich Dinkelacker	Heinrich Dinkelacker
HEADQUARTERS	HAUPTFIRMENSITZ
Bietigheim-Bissingen, Germany	Bietigheim-Bissingen, Deutschland
CEO	GESCHÄFTSFÜHRUNG
Norbert Lehmann, Wendelin Wiedeking, Anton Hunger (partners); Norbert Lehmann, Christoph Renner, Marion Beißwanger (Managing Directors)	Norbert Lehmann, Wendelin Wiedeking, Anton Hunger (Gesellschafter); Norbert Lehmann, Christoph Renner, Marion Beißwanger (Geschäftsführer)
EMPLOYEES	MITARBEITER
46	46
PRODUCTS	PRODUKTE
Hand-stitched men's shoes	Rahmengenähte Herrenschuhe
ANNUAL PRODUCTION	JAHRESPRODUKTION
Approx. 10,000 pairs	Ca. 10.000 Paar
EXPORT COUNTRIES	EXPORTLÄNDER
Austria, Japan, Russia, Switzerland	Japan, Österreich, Russland, Schweiz

HEINRICH DINKELACKER

FEINSTE BUDAPESTER HANDARBEIT SEIT 1879

KOMFORTABLES KUNSTWERK

Burkhardt Dinkelacker

Die Lyra auf der Flügelkappe ist genauso exklusiv wie eine Figur auf der Kühlerhaube eines Luxusautos. Das ornamentartig angeordnete Lochmuster gehört zu den typischen Merkmalen eines klassischen Budapester Schuhs. Und das Traditionsunternehmen Heinrich Dinkelacker steht seit fast 150 Jahren für rahmengenähte Herrenschuhe in Budapester Handwerkstradition, die sich durch höchste Qualität, Passformbeständigkeit, Eleganz und Tragekomfort auszeichnen. Die Rahmennähung ist die Königsdisziplin der Schuhmacherhandwerkskunst. Bei dieser Fertigungsart wird das Schuhoberteil mit der Sohle vernäht, wobei die Nähte eleganterweise vor dem Fersenbereich auf der unsichtbaren Innenseite verlaufen. Der eigens verwendete Zwirn wird dazu mit Pech eingestrichen, um die Haltbarkeit zu erhöhen.

Die Firma Dinkelacker wurde 1879 im baden-württembergischen Sindelfingen gegründet und fertigt seit den 1960er-Jahren sowohl die maßgeschneiderten Schuhe als auch die Konfektionsmodelle in einer kleinen Manufaktur im Budapester Vorort Budafok an. Dabei kann der Kunde zwischen 15 unterschiedlichen Leistenformen auswählen, die Modellnamen wie „Buda" oder „Oxford" tragen. Der absolute Klassiker ist das Modell „Rio" mit Dreifach-Besohlung, obwohl der schmal zulaufende Leisten „Luzern" mittlerweile auch ein Verkaufshit ist.

„EIN MEISTER, DER SIE FERTIGT. EIN KENNER, DER SIE TRÄGT."

So lautet das Motto des Familienunternehmens, das seine Modellvielfalt seit 2005 im exklusiven Showroom des neuen Firmensitzes in Bietigheim-Bissingen präsentiert. Nachdem Burkhardt Dinkelacker, der Enkel des Unternehmensgründers, die Firma aus Altersgründen zum Verkauf angeboten hatte, übernahmen sowohl der ehemalige Porsche-Chef Wendelin Wiedeking und dessen Pressesprecher Anton Hunger als auch der ehemalige IBM-Manager Norbert Lehmann die Geschäftsführung.

Der traditionsbewussten Handwerksphilosophie treu bleibend, erweiterten sie das Produktspektrum jedoch um einige Modellvariationen, die unter verstärkter Verwendung von Gummiprofilsohlen neue Formen und Schnitte aufgreifen. Ein Budapester aus dem Hause Dinkelacker verbindet Bewährtes mit modernem Esprit und verschafft dem jeweiligen Träger einen sanften und doch soliden Kontakt zum Boden.

Dafür sorgt die komplex aufgebaute Sohlenbeschichtung eines jeden Schuhs. In Handarbeit werden Laufsohle, Zwischensohle, die sogenannte Brandsohle, und schließlich die mit dem Dinkelacker-Logo versehene Decksohle miteinander vernäht. Wobei die Brandsohle die Basis des Schuhs darstellt. Sie wird nach der Form des Leistens zugeschnitten und besteht aus 4 mm starkem, grubengegerbtem Leder.

Rahmengenähte Dinkelacker-Schuhe überzeugen auch durch die Verarbeitung hochwertigen Leders. Die Auswahl für das Obermaterial des Schaftes reicht von französischem Boxcalf, über italienisches Wasserbüffelcalf und ockergelbes Kalbsleder bis hin zu Cordovan, einem Pferdeleder, das von der altehrwürdigen Horween Company aus Chicago stammt.

Das Traditionsunternehmen Dinkelacker leistet sich ein weiteres hohes Gut, um sein Schuhmacherhandwerk wie ein Kunstwerk zur Vollendung zu bringen:

"Rio", a Dinkelacker classic, on one of the seven bridges connecting the districts of Buda and Pest.
Der Dinkelacker-Klassiker „Rio" auf einer der sieben Brücken, welche die Stadtteile Buda und Pest miteinander verbinden.

Zeit. Auf 12 bis 15 Tage verteilt, vollzieht der Schuhmachermeister rund 300 Arbeitsschritte. Während dieser aufwendigen, fast ausschließlich manuellen Fertigung in der ungarischen Manufaktur verweilt der „gezwickte" Schuh gänzlich auf dem Leisten und hat genügend Zeit, in seine endgültige Form hineinzureifen. Das „Zwicken" ist einer der kraftaufwendigsten Arbeitsschritte. Nachdem der jeweilige Schaft über den Leisten gezogen wurde, wird das Oberleder mit sogenannten Zwickstiften angeheftet. Nach mehreren Tagen der Ruhe zwickt der Schuhmacher nach, um Formkorrekturen vorzunehmen.

Auch stellen weitere Arbeitsschritte wie das „Aushobeln" des Einstechdamms auf der Brandsohle oder das „Einhämmern" der 60 Messingnägel in den Absatz in ihrer sorgfältigen Ausführung einen bewusst gewählten Kontrapunkt zur Schnelllebigkeit der heutigen Zeit dar.

Den letzten Schliff erhält ein Dinkelacker-Schuh unter anderem durch das „Ablassen", wobei die Sohlenkante mit einem speziellen Messer abgeflacht wird. Zuvor „stuppt" der Meister den Schuhrahmen und prägt eine Kerbe nach der anderen in das Material hinein. Die im Innenbereich des Schuhs aufgebrachte Signatur des Schuhmachers bürgt dann für die einwandfreie Qualität, die jeder Träger eines Dinkelacker-Schuhs bei jedem Schritt spüren kann.

Hand-stitched: sole, shaft and welt are joined together by the inseam.

Handgenäht: Boden, Schaft und Rahmen werden durch die Einstechnaht miteinander verbunden.

*The shoemaker hammers the brass
nails into the heel one by one.
Per Hand schlägt der Schuhmacher jeden
Messingnagel einzeln in den Absatz.*

DUCHAMP

"Strong colours
experience a comeback
particularly in times
of crisis. They radiate
a feeling of sheer
optimism."
Marc Psarolis

COLOUR – A PHILOSOPHY OF LIFE

Any man teaming an aubergine-coloured velvet blazer, a red-and-black striped
shirt and a floral tie must have the optimum of confidence. Above his suede leather shoes, one catches a glimpse of lilac-coloured Paisley socks. Marc Psarolis,
owner of the British label Duchamp, is a walking advertisement for his own brand.
His brightly coloured outfit positively trumpets the slogan "keep it sharp, keep it
lively". However, anyone who thinks that Marc Psarolis dresses eccentrically purely
for business reasons would be mistaken. A native of Scotland, he is passionate about
his collection, believing that colours radiate a positive aura. He loves the striking
patterns of his silk ties and refers to himself as "a bit of a dandy", a style statement
that one would not necessarily expect from a man from the harsh North.
Prior to his career with Duchamp, this ambitious Scotsman worked for twelve
years as a buyer and co-designer for Mulberry, serving clients who included
Princess Diana and Sir Bob Geldof. His aim is to make Duchamp "the best

British menswear label". This has always been his goal since the company's former boss, Mitchell Jacobs, offered him the position of sales director in 2002. Under his instruction, Duchamp become one of the top accessory labels in the UK as well as globally. When Jacobs began to think about selling in 2006, Marc Psarolis stepped in and now manages Duchamp London in partnership with his wife, Alison. Meanwhile, this former family firm, which began with just one shop in the British capital, has become an internationally successful brand with three stores in London and collections in numerous outlets all over Europe, Asia, North America and the United Arab Emirates. One of his fans is known to be Sir Anthony Hopkins.

Marc Psarolis

INSPIRATION FROM THE WORLD OF ART AND ARCHITECTURE

Marc Psarolis gives his tie and pochette designs names such as "Lollipop Multi Stripe", "Papillon Forrest", "Blossom Jacquard" and "Harlequin", and vivid stripes, polka dots, graphic Op Art designs and psychadelic patterns are used to create vibrant styles which glow as if they are fresh from a brand new paintbox. Marc Psarolis and his team find inspiration for these dynamic designs in the world of art and architecture: the Price skyscraper in Oklahoma by architect Frank Lloyd Wright with its asymmetrical façade and the intense colours of its interior was the inspiration for the "Panache" collection. The idea for his "Relic" design came from photographer Robert Polidori, who visited remote but unexpectedly colourful places on his travels. "For a new season, we often spend over a month looking for new colour moods. London's famous Portobello market with its vintage fabrics, old paintings and photos is an inexhaustible source of inspiration", he comments, pushing up his distinctive spectacles. Marc Psarolis does not pay much attention to predictions of colour trends. "We make our own trends", he says with confidence, pointing to a range of jungle-green accessories which form part of the "Amazonica" collection, inspired by digital collages by Dutch artist Ruud van Empel. They became a best-selling line even though green is considered a difficult colour in the field of menswear.

Getting away from uniform grey is the aim. This does not, after all, have to apply to the entire outfit but it is better to add a cleverly chosen colour accent for festive occasions or for Sunday brunch with friends – for example, a vivid silk scarf or one of the 80 tie designs, which Duchamp launches each year and which are produced on Jacquard looms by the best manufacturers in Italy and England. More discreet, but just as effective, are the cufflinks, for which Duchamp is famous, such as the "Cosmic Cube", made from crystal, or those featuring elaborately finished enamel patterns.

In 2009, after years of many of his customers asking him for shirts suitable for office wear, Marc Psarolis developed a small collection of classic shirts in striped, check and self-coloured fabrics. He himself adheres to his conspicuous look. "Strong colours experience a comeback particularly in times of crisis. They radiate a feeling of sheer optimism", is his prediction, as he examines the newly arrived collection in the elegant Duchamp flagship store in Regent Street, the wooden panelling of which is reminiscent of a treasure room or an elegant gentleman's club.

2012 sees an evolution for the Duchamp brand, bringing in new head designer Gianni Colarossi and producing its first ever ready-to-wear collection including knitwear, outerwear and of course, Duchamp's classic suiting.

COMPANY	UNTERNEHMEN
Duchamp	Duchamp
FOUNDED IN	GEGRÜNDET
1989	1989
FOUNDER	GRÜNDER
Mitchell Jacobs	Mitchell Jacobs
HEADQUARTERS	HAUPTFIRMENSITZ
London, Great Britain	London, Großbritannien
CEO	GESCHÄFTSFÜHRUNG
Marc Psarolis	Marc Psarolis
EMPLOYEES	MITARBEITER
40	40
PRODUCTS	PRODUKTE
Men's Clothing	Herrenbekleidung
ANNUAL PRODUCTION	JAHRESPRODUKTION
250,000 units	250.000 Artikel
EXPORT COUNTRIES	EXPORTLÄNDER
Asia, Australasia,	Asien, Australasien,
Canada, Europe, USA	Europa, Kanada, USA

DUCHAMP

LONDON

Modern Dandy, Winter Collection 2012
Moderner Dandy, Winter-Kollektion 2012

FARBE ALS LEBENSPHILOSOPHIE

Jeder Mann, der zum auberginefarbenen Samtblazer und einem rot-schwarz gestreiften Hemd eine geblümte Krawatte kombiniert, beweist Mut. Vor allem, wenn aus den Velourslederschuhen lilafarbene Paisley-Strümpfe blitzen. Marc Psarolis, der das britische Label Duchamp 1989 ins Leben gerufen hat, ist selbst der beste Werbeträger seiner Marke. Das farbenfrohe Outfit scheint den Slogan des Labels hinauszuposaunen: „Keep it sharp, keep it lively." Wer nun glaubt, Marc Psarolis kleide sich nur aus geschäftlichem Interesse derart exzentrisch, der irrt. Der gebürtige Schotte ist geradezu vernarrt in seine Kollektion, glaubt an die positive Strahlkraft der Farben, begeistert sich für die ausgefallenen Muster der Seidenkrawatten und bezeichnet sich selbst „a bit of a dandy", ein Stil-Statement, das man von einem Mann aus dem rauen Norden eher nicht erwarten würde.

Vor seiner Karriere bei Duchamp war Psarolis zwölf Jahre lang Einkäufer und Co-Designer bei Mulberry, wo er Kunden wie Prinzessin Diana und Sir Bob Geldorf bediente. Als ihm der damalige Chef, Mitchell Jacobs, 2002 die Position des Verkaufsdirektors anbot, war sein erklärtes Ziel, Duchamp „zur besten britischen Herrenbekleidungsmarke zu machen". Und in der Tat gelang es dem engagierten Schotten binnen kurzer Zeit, das Unternehmen in Großbritannien und auch global in eines der führenden Accessoire-Labels zu verwandeln. Als Jacobs 2006 an den Verkauf seines Unternehmens dachte, schlug Marc Psarolis zu. Heute führt er Duchamp London gemeinsam mit seiner Frau Alison. Das einstige Familienunternehmen mit nur einem Shop in der britischen Metropole ist mittlerweile zu einer weltweit erfolgreichen Marke avanciert – mit Läden in London und Dubai, Kollektionen in zahlreichen Boutiquen Europas und begeisterten Kunden in Amerika, wie Sir Anthony Hopkins.

INSPIRATIONEN AUS DER WELT DER KUNST UND ARCHITEKTUR

Seinen Einstecktüchern und Krawattenmodellen gibt Marc Psarolis Namen wie „Lollipop Multi Stripe", „Papillon Forrest", „Blossom Jacquard" und „Harlequin". Knallbunte Streifen, Polka Dots, grafische Op-Art-Muster und psychedelische Dekore werden eingesetzt, um lebendige Muster zu schaffen, die leuchten wie reine, unbenutzte Tuschkastenfarben. Inspirationen für die impulsiven Designs finden Marc Psarolis und sein Team in der Welt der Kunst und Architektur: So regte sie der Price-Wolkenkratzer in Oklahoma, ein Entwurf des Architekten Frank Lloyd Wright, mit seiner asymmetrischen Fassadengestaltung und seinem farbintensiven Interieur zur Kollektion „Panache" an. Auf die Idee für das „Relic"-Design brachte Psarolis der Fotograf Robert Polidori, der auf seinen Reisen vergessene, aber dennoch überraschend farbenfrohe Orte dokumentiert. „Für eine neue Saison suchen wir oft über einen Monat lang nach neuen Farbstimmungen. Eine unerschöpfliche Inspirationsquelle ist Londons berühmter Portobello-Markt mit seinen Vintage-Stoffen, alten Gemälden und Fotos", sagt Psarolis und rückt sein markantes Brillengestell zurecht. Um Farbprognosen kümmert sich der Firmenchef nicht. „Wir machen die Trends", sagt er selbstbewusst und zeigt auf eine Reihe regenwaldgrüner Accessoires der „Amazonica"-Kollektion, angeregt von den Digitalcollagen des holländischen

DESIGN
ROOM

Design archive dating from the 18th century
Das Design Archiv aus dem 18. Jahrhundert

Künstlers Ruud van Empel. Sie wurden zum Bestseller, obwohl die Farbe Grün in der Herrenbekleidungsbranche als schwierig gilt.

Raus aus dem Einheitsgrau, lautet das Ziel. Es muss ja nicht gleich ein komplettes Outfit sein, lieber ein clever ausgewählter Akzent zu festlichen Anlässen oder zum Sonntagsbrunch mit Freunden: Etwa ein leuchtender Seidenschal oder einer der 80 Krawattendekore, die Duchamp pro Jahr lanciert und die auf den Jacquard-Webstühlen der besten Manufakturen Italiens und Englands entstehen. Noch dezenter, aber ebenso effektvoll sind die Manschettenknöpfe, für die Duchamp bekannt ist, etwa „Cosmic Cube", aus Kristall gearbeitet, oder jene mit aufwendigen Email-Verzierungen.

Weil viele Kunden ihn nach bürotauglichen Hemden fragten, entwickelte Marc Psarolis 2009 eine kleine klassische Hemdenkollektion in gestreift, kariert und uni. Der Firmenchef selbst bleibt seinem auffälligen Look treu. „Gerade in Krisenzeiten erleben kräftige Farben ein Comeback. Sie verbreiten puren Optimismus", prophezeit er und begutachtet die neu eingetroffene Kollektion im eleganten Duchamp-Flagship-Store in der Regent Street, der mit seiner dunklen Holzvertäfelung an eine Schatzkammer oder einen gediegenen Gentlemen's Club erinnert. 2012 erfährt die Marke Duchamp eine weitere Entwicklung: Mit dem neuen Chefdesigner Gianni Colarossi kommt auch die allererste Kollektion an Konfektionskleidung heraus, mit Strickwaren, Oberbekleidung und natürlich Duchamps klassischen Anzügen.

91

It takes two weeks to tie by hand the 10,000 threads on the exclusive warp-beam.
Es dauert zwei Wochen, um die 10.000 Fäden per Hand in diesen Kettbaum einzuknüpfen.

Gentlemen's Club store concept
Ladenkonzept Gentlemen's Club

EAGLE
— SINCE 1893

"We have accepted the challenge of ensuring that traditions handed down from the past are given a future."
Christian Hagen &
Barbara Sprinzl

FOURTH GENERATION IN HOF

Barbara Sprinzl and her brother, Christian Hagen, are now the fourth generation to be running the family firm in Hof, a Franconian town in northern Bavaria. The firm has had its headquarters here since 1904 although the old building has been extended several times over the years. The two managing directors believe that the firm's loyalty to this location is one of the cornerstones for its success. "This is the only way we can offer the service and quality which our customers rightly expect of us." Upper Franconia, with its old-established textile industry, has a rich infrastructure of related branches, ranging from machine builders to textile home workers. The quality seal "Made in Germany" is the result of the many generations of experience which has been absorbed into every single Eagle product. The core of the factory consists of about 35 permanent employees working in design, administration, quality control and operations. Most of the production is handled by a large number of affiliated small businesses and contractors. A commitment to tradition is by no means incompatible with the firm's stated aim of keeping step with current trends. "We have accepted the challenge of ensuring that traditions handed down from the past are given a future", declared the young entrepreneurs. Shortly after taking over the helm in 1997, this undertaking meant abandoning the firm's old name and renaming the company "Eagle Products Textil GmbH". The old textile company had been producing scarves, plaids and blankets since 1893 under the founder's name of "Franz Barth", a name which gave no hint of the firm's own label of "Adler Fabrikate" (Eagle Products). The renaming was therefore aimed at raising awareness of the brand name.

COMMITMENT TO NATURAL FIBRES

The real key to this traditional company's secret lies in its commitment to natural fibres. Only the finest materials, such as cashmere, mohair and silk, etc., are acceptable. Anyone who has ever experienced the unsurpassable qualities of these natural fibres in terms of softness, lightness, warmth, durability, not to mention the flattering sheen and attractive texture, will probably already be a lifetime convert to the attractions of such high-quality raw materials. Furthermore, these natural products also meet the most stringent ecological requirements since supplies are being constantly replenished.

On the other hand, a sure instinct is absolutely essential when it comes to purchasing and processing these luxury yarns in a way that takes full advantage of their exceptional qualities. Only wool with extremely fine fibres does not scratch and only genuine cashmere with the right staple length produces a beautiful, wavy watermark-type sheen. The lengthy process of creating a perfectly finished silk scarf or fleecy cashmere plaid from silk or wool threads represents a considerable amount of work, much of which has to be carried out by hand. This is partly because the properties of natural fibres never remain completely constant. It takes specialised expert knowledge to balance out these natural fluctuations and achieve the unique suppleness which distinguishes luxury products from inferior ones. Constant checks are absolutely essential. In some cases, alterations have to be made or else the item is removed. A scarf may therefore be demoted to a lower-grade product because it is not soft enough.

The vast product spectrum covers everything from classic or country style to crazy plaids featuring an interwoven map of the world on which personal "entries" can be made with yarn supplied with the product. Home textiles belong to the past; the fresh, young designs by Eagle Products are actually turning "cocooning" into a really attractive prospect. Gorgeous colours, stylistic confidence and, as always, the lustre and seductive feel of the fabrics add new dimensions to the primitive "cocooning" instinct. In this respect, fashion and interior design can be mutually stimulating. Each year, four new collections are launched in the areas of Home, Accessories, Eagle Mini and Promotion. Special commissions and individual single items are also welcomed, a service which is appreciated by customers all over the world. It goes without saying that these include prominent figures, such as Queen Margrethe II of Denmark, for example. All of them can rely on the quality of a product which has been manufactured with utmost care. When it undergoes its last check, it will be how it feels to the touch that determines whether it is premium quality or not.

Franz Barth

COMPANY
Eagle Products Textil
GmbH

UNTERNEHMEN
Eagle Products Textil
GmbH

FOUNDED IN
1893

GEGRÜNDET
1893

FOUNDER
Franz Barth

GRÜNDER
Franz Barth

HEADQUARTERS
Hof, Germany

HAUPTFIRMENSITZ
Hof, Deustchland

CEO
Christian Hagen,
Barbara Sprinzl

GESCHÄFTSFÜHRUNG
Christian Hagen,
Barbara Sprinzl

EMPLOYEES
Approx. 35

MITARBEITER
Ca. 35

PRODUCTS
Scarves, stoles, hats
(clothing accessories),
plaids, blankets,
scatter cushions
(Home Collection)

PRODUKTE
Schals, Tücher, Mützen
(Bekleidungsaccessoires),
Plaids, Decken, Kissen
für den Wohnbereich
(Home Collection)

EXPORT COUNTRIES
Australia, Europe, Japan,
USA

EXPORTLÄNDER
Australien, Europa, Japan,
USA

Textilmanufaktur seit 1893

*Double-sided plaids and stoles are only made to order
and produced by hand according to the individual wishes
of the client.*
*Abseitenplaids und -schals werden nur auf Bestellung
gefertigt und von Hand nach den individuellen Wünschen
des Kunden konfektioniert.*

IN VIERTER
GENERATION IN HOF

Hoch im Norden Bayerns, im fränkischen Hof, führen
die Geschwister Barbara Sprinzl und Christian Hagen
das Familienunternehmen in der vierten Generation.
Seit 1904 befindet sich dort der Firmensitz, wenn auch
der Altbau im Laufe der Jahre mehrfach erweitert werden musste. Die Treue zum Standort ist nach Meinung
der beiden Geschäftsführer einer der Grundpfeiler für
den Erfolg des Unternehmens: „Nur so können wir den
Service und die Qualität bieten, die unsere Kunden zu
Recht von uns erwarten." Die Region Hochfranken mit
ihrer alteingesessenen Textilindustrie verfügt über eine
reiche Infrastruktur mit branchenaffinen Berufszweigen,
vom Maschinenbauer bis zum Textil-Heimarbeiter. Das
Gütesiegel „Made in Germany" basiert hier auf den Er-
fahrungen vieler Generationen, die in jedes einzelne Produkt der heutigen Eagle-Manufaktur einfließen. Nur circa
35 feste Mitarbeiter in den Bereichen Design, Verwaltung, Qualitätskontrolle und Vertrieb gehören zum Kern
des Betriebs; der überwiegende Teil der Produktion wird
über die vielen angeschlossenen Klein- und Kleinstunternehmer abgewickelt.
Das Bekenntnis zur Tradition steht aber nicht im Widerspruch zum erklärten
Selbstverständnis, mit den aktuellen Entwicklungen Schritt zu halten. Die Devise
„Wir nehmen die Herausforderung an, dem Überlieferten eine Zukunft zu geben" bedeutete für die Jungunternehmer kurz nach der Geschäftsübernahme
im Jahr 1997 auch, sich mit der Neugründung des Unternehmens vom alten
Firmennamen zu verabschieden. Unter dem Namen des Firmengründers Franz
Barth produzierte das Textilunternehmen seit 1893 Schals, Tücher, Plaids und
Decken, ohne dass aus dem Firmennamen die Hausmarke „Adler Fabrikate" er-
sichtlich wurde. Die neue Gesellschaft Eagle Products Textil GmbH schafft nun
Bewusstsein für den Markennamen.

BEKENNTNIS ZUR NATURFASER

Der eigentliche Schlüssel zum Geheimnis des Traditionsunternehmens liegt
aber im Bekenntnis zur Naturfaser. Mit Kaschmir, Mohair, Seide & Co werden nur edelste Materialien verarbeitet. Wer einmal die unübertroffenen
Eigenschaften dieser Naturmaterialien in puncto Weichheit, Leichtigkeit,
Wärmeausgleich, Langlebigkeit in Verbindung mit dem schmeichelhaften
Glanz und der angenehmen Oberflächenstruktur kennengelernt hat, bleibt von
den Vorteilen dieser hochwertigen Produkte ein Leben lang überzeugt. Hinzu
kommt, dass diese Rohstoffe höchsten ökologischen Anforderungen genügen,
da sie immer wieder nachwachsen.
Auf der anderen Seite verlangen die luxuriösen Garne viel Fingerspitzengefühl im Einkauf und in der Verarbeitung, um ihre hervorragenden Qualitäten
voll zu entfalten. Allein Wolle mit extrem dünnen Fasern kratzt nicht und nur
echter Kaschmir mit der richtigen Stapellänge ergibt einen schönen Was-

serglanz. Auf dem langen Weg vom seidenen oder wollenen Faden bis zum perfekt konfektionierten Seidenschal oder flauschigen Kaschmirplaid ist viel Handarbeit gefragt, was auch darauf zurückzuführen ist, dass die Naturfasern in ihren Eigenschaften nie ganz konstant sind. Sehr spezielles Fachwissen ist nötig, um die natürlichen Schwankungen auszugleichen und diese besondere Geschmeidigkeit zu erreichen, die den Luxusartikel von einer schlechteren Qualität unterscheidet. Ständige Kontrollen sind unerlässlich. Gegebenenfalls wird nachgearbeitet oder aussortiert. Ein Schal kann auch deshalb zur 1b-Ware werden, weil er nicht die erforderliche Weichheit besitzt.

Die riesige Produktpalette bietet einfach alles, von klassisch über Country Style bis zu den verrücktesten Einfällen, so etwa Plaids mit eingewebter Weltkarte, auf der man mittels mitgeliefertem Garn selbst „Einträge" vornehmen kann. Heimtextilien, das war gestern, das junge und frische Design von Eagle Products macht Cocooning erst so richtig schön. Betörende Farben, Stilsicherheit und immer wieder der Glanz und die angenehme Griffigkeit des Materials eröffnen dem uralten Grundbedürfnis „schön schützen" ganz neue Dimensionen. Dabei befruchten sich Mode- und Einrichtungswelt gegenseitig. Jedes Jahr werden vier neue Kollektionen in den Bereichen Home, Accessoires, Eagle Mini und Promotion auf den Markt gebracht. Aber auch Sonderanfertigungen und individuelle Einzelstücke sind kein Problem. Kunden in aller Welt wissen das zu schätzen. Dass sich darunter auch prominente Persönlichkeiten finden wie beispielsweise Königin Margrethe II. von Dänemark versteht sich von selbst. Sie alle können sich auf die Qualität eines mit größter Sorgfalt hergestellten Produkts verlassen, bei dem in der Endabnahme die haptische Kontrolle darüber entscheidet, ob es die Premiumqualität erreicht oder nicht.

Classic wool scarves are part of the basic product range at Eagle Products – and part of the basic wardrobe of a well-dressed gentleman.
Klassische Wollschals gehören zum Basisprogramm bei Eagle Products – und zur Grundausstattung eines gutangezogenen Gentlemans.

All pattern books are carefully archived and serve as inspiration for new designs.
Alle Musterbücher werden sorgfältig archiviert und dienen als Inspiration für neue Designs.

Top left: The end threads of knitted articles are carefully woven in and made fast to prevent the scarf unravelling.
Oben links: Von Hand werden die Endfäden der Strickwaren sorgfältig eingezogen und vernäht, um ein Wiederauftrennen zu vermeiden.

Each item is individually checked and labelled – with the relevant "Made in Germany" label.
Jedes Teil wird einzeln geprüft und etikettiert – zu Recht mit dem Gütesiegel „Made in Germany".

As recently as the beginning of last century, home weavers using hand looms were still an integral part of northern Franconia's textile industry. Noch zu Beginn des letzten Jahrhunderts waren Heimweber mit Handwebstühlen fester Bestandteil der oberfränkischen Textilindustrie.

EDSOR
— SINCE 1909

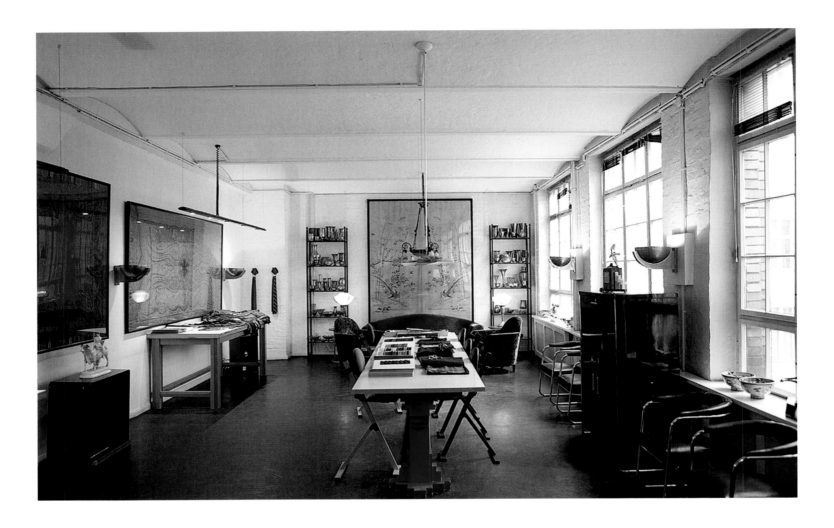

"Art Deco is my life!"
Jan-Henrik M. Scheper-Stuke

GUARDIAN OF TRUE ELEGANCE

The modest company plaque in an inner courtyard of Kreuzberg gives no hint of the unique world hidden behind the words "Edsor, 2nd floor". Those who find their way here find themselves on the threshold of what many believe to be a lost era. The rooms, decorated in elegant Art Deco style, radiate an atmosphere of exclusivity born of thoroughly refined tastes. Not a single detail is left to chance – and this same principle is also applied to the products which have been manufactured in these original Berlin premises for over 100 years. From drafting the original design to cutting out the fabric and packing the item in rustling silk paper before distributing it, the whole process, involving an annual production of around 100,000 ties, bow ties, scarves, cummerbunds and dressing-gowns, is watched over by a good spirit. Originally known as Kronen, the company was launched in 1909 by Jewish businessman Ildefons Auerbach in fashionable Berlin and situated next to the retail store. The brand experienced its first boom when it was appointed purveyor to the

Imperial Court. During the vibrant period of the "Golden Twenties", Auerbach's "innovations of the finest genre" also became very popular among the ladies. The modern woman of the day adopted an androgynous appearance and confidently wore her bobbed hair with a perfectly tailored man's suit accompanied by a tie or bow tie. However, the changing political situation in the early 1930s made it difficult for Ildefons Auerbach to continue running his business. Recognising the warning signals of the day, he sold the business to Fritz M. Tübke at the turn of 1934 / 35 and fled with his family to America. The company's fortunes did not revive until 1954 when Wilhelm Stelly joined the company. Together, Tübke and Stelly rebuilt the label's excellent reputation and devised an acronym from the first and second names of the renowned fashion icon, EDward WindSOR. Henceforth, the former Kronen label was known as Edsor, a name which reflects the timelessness and elegance of English style. It is thanks to the great talent of Wilhelm Stelly's son and successor that the Edsor label has become a synonym for stylistically confident creations. Since 1973, Günther H. Stelly has been the leading designer whose creations are turned into fabrics by Italian silk producers in Como. At the rate of 1,600 new fabrics per season, this means he has so far produced around 120,000 designs for ties, bow ties, scarves and cummerbunds.

Jan-Henrik M. Scheper-Stuke

DEDICATION AND A COMPANY BELIEF IN THE BRAND

Just as the company was celebrating its 100th anniversary in 2009, Jan-Henrik M. Scheper-Stuke appeared on the scene. This man with his eccentric name is the godson of the company's owner. Now aged 30, he works very hard at stimulating an appreciation in his contemporaries for exclusive, high-quality workmanship and an individual fashion style. As a gifted self-promoter, he is a walking advertisement for the label. He personifies a new type of dandy, reflecting a sense of the style of the 1920s, those glorious days of Berlin tailoring when a Kronen tie was an inherent part of an elegant outfit. This lively young entrepreneur, sporting his trademark bow-ties, is completely in his element guiding members of the press and celebrities through this inner sanctum in Kreuzberg. He never tires of making himself available for interviews and made it into the 2011 December issue of the magazine "Kulturspiegel". Collaboration with other fashion labels such as Michalsky, Wunderkind and Lala Berlin have also helped Scheper-Stuke to give a huge boost to the label's reputation. When he opened his own flagship store in the Hackeschen Höfe area of central Berlin, the opening speech was given by German Economics Minister Philipp Rösler, who – it goes without saying – was attired in evening dress since "black tie" is de rigueur at Edsor's. Politicians, from Konrad Adenauer to Helmut Kohl and Barack Obama, have always numbered among Edsor fans.

Günther H. Stelly retired from the company at the beginning of 2012. His departure was followed by a fundamental restructuring process. Kronen Manufaktur GmbH is now responsible for production whilst Edsor Berlin GmbH is in charge of distribution. As the new umbrella company, Edsor Holding GmbH now owns 100 per cent of the shares in the two companies. Jan-Henrik M. Scheper-Stuke is responsible for communication and marketing, Christian Brey is in charge of brand management and distribution and Marco Illbruck is responsible for business development. In the hands of these three partners, the company is well placed to continue its triumphal progress, producing an exquisite brand of ties in an incomparable range of designs, from classic to extravagantly magnificent, which epitomise the label's unique style.

COMPANY	UNTERNEHMEN
Edsor Berlin GmbH	Edsor Berlin GmbH
FOUNDED IN	GEGRÜNDET
1909 Kronen-Manufaktur	1909 Kronen-Manufaktur
1954 Edsor	1954 Edsor
FOUNDERS	GRÜNDER
Ildefons Auerbach	Ildefons Auerbach
(Kronen-Manufaktur);	(Kronen-Manufaktur);
Fritz M. Tübke,	Fritz M. Tübke,
Wilhelm Stelly (Edsor)	Wilhelm Stelly (Edsor)
HEADQUARTERS	HAUPTFIRMENSITZ
Berlin, Germany	Berlin, Deutschland
CEO	GESCHÄFTSFÜHRUNG
Jan-Henrik M. Scheper-	Jan-Henrik M. Scheper-
Stuke, Marco Illbruck	Stuke, Marco Illbruck
PRODUCTS	PRODUKTE
Ties, bow ties, scarves,	Krawatten, Schleifen,
cummerbunds, dressing-	Tücher, Kummerbunde,
gowns	Hausmäntel
ANNUAL PRODUCTION	JAHRESPRODUKTION
100,000 items	100.000 Artikel
EXPORT COUNTRIES	EXPORTLÄNDER
Asia, North and Central	Asien, Nord- und Mittel-
Europe	europa

Edsor also makes ties for SØR.
Edsor fertigt auch Krawatten für SØR.

HÜTER WAHRER ELEGANZ

Das nüchterne Firmenschild in einem Kreuzberger Hinterhof lässt kaum er-
ahnen, welches Kleinod sich dahinter verbirgt. „Edsor, 2. Etage" ist darauf
zu lesen. Wer den Weg hierher findet, tritt ein in eine vergangen geglaubte
Welt. Die mit feinstem Art déco ausgestatteten Räume atmen die Noblesse eines durch und durch erlesenen Geschmacks. Nicht das kleinste Detail
bleibt dem Zufall überlassen, und das gilt auch für die Produkte, die in dieser
original Berliner Manufaktur seit über 100 Jahren hergestellt werden: Vom
Entwurf der Dessins über den Zuschnitt bis zur Verpackung in raschelndes
Seidenpapier und dem Vertrieb wacht ein guter Geist über das Gelingen
der jährlichen Produktion von etwa 100.000 Krawatten, Schleifen, Schals,
Kummerbunden und Hausmänteln.
Anno 1909 eröffnete der jüdische Kaufmann Ildefons Auerbach im mondänen
Berlin die Kronen-Manufaktur nebst dazugehörigem Verkaufsladen. Die erste
Glanzzeit erlebte das Unternehmen als Hoflieferant des Kaisers. Im pulsie-
renden Leben der Goldenen Zwanziger erfreuten sich Auerbachs „Neuheiten
feinsten Genres" auch bei den Damen großer Beliebtheit. Die moderne Frau
gab sich androgyn und trug zu Bubikopf und perfekt geschnittenem Herren-
anzug selbstbewusst Krawatte oder Fliege. Mit dem veränderten politischen
Klima zu Beginn der 1930er-Jahre wurde es jedoch für Ildefons Auerbach
schwierig, seinen Betrieb weiterzuführen. Er erkannte früh die Zeichen der
Zeit, verkaufte zur Jahreswende 1934/35 an Fritz M. Tübke, um mit seiner
Familie ins amerikanische Exil zu fliehen. Den Anschluss an die glanzvollen
Zeiten fand das Unternehmen jedoch erst wieder, als 1954 Wilhelm Stelly
hinzukam. Gemeinsam brachten Tübke und Stelly die angeschlagene Marke
wieder in Hochform und entwickelten aus dem Namen der Stilikone EDward
WindSOR ein Akronym. So wurde die einstige Kronen-Manufaktur zur Marke
Edsor, die sich der Zeitlosigkeit und Eleganz des englischen Stils verschrieb.
Dem großen Talent von Wilhelm Stellys Sohn und Nachfolger ist es zu ver-
danken, dass Edsor zum Synonym für absolut stilsichere Kreationen wurde.
Günther H. Stelly entwarf seit 1973 als alleiniger Createur die Dessins, die
in den Seidenwebereien im italienischen Como in Stoffe verwandelt werden.
Bei 1.600 neuen Stoffen pro Saison sind das in seinem bisherigen Leben rund
120.000 Muster für Krawatten, Schleifen, Schals und Kummerbunde.

MIT ENGAGEMENT UND ÜBERZEUGUNG FÜR DIE MARKE

Pünktlich zum 100-jährigen Firmenjubiläum erscheint 2009 Jan-Henrik M.
Scheper-Stuke auf der Bildfläche. Der Mann mit dem exzentrischen Namen ist
der Patensohn des Firmeninhabers. Der heute 30-Jährige arbeitet hart daran,
bei seinen Zeitgenossen das Bewusstsein für hochwertige Qualitätsarbeit und
individualistischen Kleidungsstil anzukurbeln. Als begnadeter Selbstdarsteller
gibt er der Marke ein Gesicht. Er verkörpert einen neuen Typus des Dandys mit
gewissen Anleihen an den Stil der 1920er-Jahre, jenen glanzvollen Zeiten der
Berliner Konfektion, als die Kronen-Krawatte selbstverständlich zur gehobenen Ausstattung dazugehörte. Der quirlige Schleifen-Träger ist ganz in seinem
Element, wenn er Presse und Prominenz durch das Kreuzberger Allerheiligste
führt. Er steht unermüdlich für Interviews bereit und schafft es 2011 in die
Dezember-Nummer des „Kulturspiegel". Auch über Kooperationen mit den

Each year, Italy's finest silk-weaving factories manufacture 1,600 new fabrics for Edsor.
1.600 neue Stoffe werden pro Jahr in den besten italienischen Seidenwebereien für Edsor gefertigt.

Mode-Labels Michalsky, Wunderkind oder Lala Berlin kann Scheper-Stuke den Bekanntheitsradius der Marke enorm erweitern. Als er in den Hackeschen Höfen seinen eigenen Flagship-Store einrichtet, hält der deutsche Wirtschaftsminister Philipp Rösler die Eröffnungsrede, selbstverständlich im Smoking, denn bei Edsor ist „black tie" angesagt. Politiker gehören schon lange zur Riege der bekennenden Edsor-Träger, von Konrad Adenauer über Helmut Kohl bis zu Barack Obama.

Mit Beginn des Jahres 2012 zog sich Günther H. Stelly aus dem Unternehmen zurück. Darauf erfolgte eine grundsätzliche Umstrukturierung. Heute ist die Kronen Manufaktur GmbH für die Fertigung und die Edsor Berlin GmbH für den Vertrieb zuständig. Als neue Dachgesellschaft hält die Edsor Holding GmbH 100 Prozent der Anteile beider Gesellschaften. Jan-Henrik M. Scheper-Stuke zeichnet verantwortlich für Kommunikation und Marketing, Christian Brey für Markenführung und Vertrieb, Marco Illbruck für Business Development. Mit diesen drei Gesellschaftern ist das Unternehmen gut gerüstet für den weiteren Siegeszug der exquisiten Krawattenmarke, die mit ihrem unvergleichlichen Sortiment von klassisch bis extravagant hervorragend geeignet ist, den eigenen Stil wirkungsvoll zu unterstreichen.

Each tie is carefully produced by hand in a series of steps.
Jede Krawatte wird in mehreren Arbeitsschritten sorgfältig
von Hand gearbeitet.

EDUARD DRESSLER
— SINCE 1929

"A label must have the
self-confidence to be
creative and yet still
remain true to itself."
Eduard Dressler

A LABEL
WITH SELF-CONFIDENCE

The difference is visible and tangible. Customers enjoy wearing suits by Eduard
Dressler, the successful menswear specialist, because of their perfect fit, sleek
elegance and the high-quality fabrics which clothe the wearer like a second
skin. The headquarters of the firm, which was established over 80 years ago,
are situated in Großostheim, Aschaffenburg district. To this day, it has remained
true to the company's original aim of dressing men in clothes which exhibit
elegant restraint. A suit bearing the Eduard Dressler label is notable for its
understatement. Consistent quality has won over a large number of customers
who wish to enjoy the luxury of perfect craftsmanship and outstanding hand-
tailoring in clothing that reflects all contemporary lifestyles.
"A label must have the self-confidence to be creative and yet still remain true to
itself", comments Eduard Dressler, founder of the firm. There is good reason why

Eduard Dressler is called "The Gentleman's Tailor". It presents two main collections each year based on the individual lifestyles of its customers and features dinner jackets for gala dinners, business suits, notable for their meticulous detail and perfect for business meetings, and products from the elegant "casual wear" range, designed for various leisure activities, all of which were introduced into the range of products in 2007. Eduard Dressler offers the customer an opportunity to choose from a wide range of options, thereby allowing him a strong sense of personal freedom.

ELEGANT APPEARANCE, WIDE RANGE OF CHOICE

When the firm's founder, Eduard Dressler, began to produce clothes for men in 1929, this freedom of personal choice became an important criterion in the company's approach to creativity. Eduard Dressler also revolutionised traditional hand-tailoring practices by introducing an industrially produced, so-called "tailor's suit". His "tailormade" line encompasses suits and jackets as well as trousers and coats, not to mention a complementary line which comprises exclusive shirts, elegant ties and scarves.

The firm's casual wear production sites are situated in Bosnia and Poland. The industrially manufactured, "tailormade" ready-to-wear collection as well as the "made to measure" line of custom-made suits, which was established in the 1960s, are produced in Turkey although the final checks on all product lines are carried out at the Großostheim headquarters.

Eduard Dressler is also extremely quality-conscious when it comes to fabrics. The firm insists on the highest quality and only uses fabrics from the world's leading weaving mills, which are mainly situated in Italy. The firm's long-term partners include Loro Piana, Guabello, Cerruti and Ermenegildo Zegna.

The industrial production of a suit bearing the Eduard Dressler label involves more than 200 individual steps which are carried out by hand as part of an exclusive production process. One of the most important steps in creating a "tailormade" suit is fixing the outer fabric. To ensure the suit keeps its shape, the stabilising interfacing material is provided with adhesive points using extremely high-tech procedures and joined to the outer fabric in a fixing machine involving dry heat and pressure.

The jacket is constructed by building up layers of so-called "facing materials", consisting of wool, goat- or horsehair. The chest facing is not attached with adhesive but is invisibly stitched to the outer material using fine, loose stitches. During the ensuing finishing process, the outer fabric of the jacket is shaped by means of humidity, pressure and cooling.

The carefully constructed shape of an Eduard Dressler jacket embodies – in the truest sense of the word – the company's philosophy. The main focus is on fashion which radiates reliability, continuity and determination. It is no coincidence, therefore, that the firm's logo features an ibex. As a symbol of the astrological sign of Capricorn, under which Eduard Dressler was born, the ibex also represents the self-confident entrepreneurial spirit which is the basis of the firm's international success.

Lars Kröckel, Dieter Reinert

COMPANY	UNTERNEHMEN
Dressler Bekleidungs-werke Brinkmann GmbH & Co. KG	Dressler Bekleidungs-werke Brinkmann GmbH & Co. KG
FOUNDED IN 1929	GEGRÜNDET 1929
FOUNDER Eduard Dressler	GRÜNDER Eduard Dressler
HEADQUARTERS Großostheim, Germany	HAUPTFIRMENSITZ Großostheim, Deutschland
CEO Lars Kröckel, Dieter Reinert	GESCHÄFTSFÜHRUNG Lars Kröckel, Dieter Reinert
EMPLOYEES 110	MITARBEITER 110
PRODUCTS Suits, jackets, trousers, coats, waistcoats, casual wear, shirts, ties, scarves, pocket handkerchiefs	PRODUKTE Anzüge, Sakkos, Hosen, Mäntel, Westen, Casualwear, Hemden, Krawatten, Schals, Einstecktücher
EXPORT COUNTRIES Austria, Belgium, Moldova, Russia, Scandinavia, Switzerland, The Netherlands, UK, Ukraine	EXPORTLÄNDER Belgien, Moldawien, Niederlande, Österreich, Russland, Schweiz, Skandinavien, UK, Ukraine

EINE MARKE MIT SELBSTBEWUSSTSEIN

Es ist sichtbar und fühlbar. Anzüge des erfolgreichen Herrenausstatters Eduard Dressler bestechen durch den perfekten Sitz, ihre geschmeidige Eleganz und die hochwertigen Stoffe, die sich wie eine schützende Hülle um den Körper des jeweiligen Trägers legen. Der Sitz des seit über 80 Jahren bestehenden Unternehmens befindet sich in Großostheim im Kreis Aschaffenburg, wo man dem ursprünglichen Vorsatz bis heute treu geblieben ist: den Mann in stilvoller Zurückhaltung zu kleiden. Denn ein Anzug der Marke Eduard Dressler glänzt durch Understatement. Beständige Qualität überzeugt eine große Käuferschar, die den Luxus handwerklicher Perfektion und höchster Schneiderkunst in jeder Lebenslage genießen möchte.

„Eine Marke muss das Selbstbewusstsein haben, kreativ zu sein und sich dennoch stets treu zu bleiben", so Firmengründer Eduard Dressler. Und nicht umsonst versteht sich Eduard Dressler als „The Gentleman's Tailor" und präsentiert jährlich zwei Hauptkollektionen, die auf den individuellen Lifestyle der Kunden abgestimmt sind. Sei es der Smoking für ein Galadiner, sei es der durch feine Details ins Auge fallende Businessanzug für ein Geschäftsmeeting oder die lässig-elegante „Casualwear"-Linie für diverse Freizeitunternehmungen, die im Jahr 2007 zur Produktpalette hinzukam. Eduard Dressler bietet ein großes Spektrum an konfektionsimmanenten Kombinationsmöglichkeiten, damit sich der Mann gänzlich frei fühlen kann.

STILVOLL IM AUFTRITT, FREI IN DER KOMBINATION

Als Firmengründer Eduard Dressler 1929 damit begann, den Mann zu kleiden, wurde dieses Freiheitsgefühl zum ausschlaggebenden Kriterium innerhalb der schöpferischen Unternehmenskultur. Eduard Dressler revolutionierte zudem das traditionelle Schneiderhandwerk, indem er den industriell gefertigten, sogenannten Tailor-Anzug etablierte. Die „Tailormade"-Linie umfasst neben Anzügen und Sakkos auch Hosen und Mäntel sowie eine ergänzende Linie, welche exklusive Hemden, elegante Krawatten und Schals beinhaltet.

Die Produktionsstätten des Unternehmens befinden sich für die Casualwear in Bosnien und Polen. Sowohl die industriell gefertigte „Tailormade"-Konfektion als auch die seit Mitte der 1960er-Jahre etablierte Maßanzuglinie „Made to Measure" werden in der Türkei produziert, wobei die Endkontrolle aller Produktlinien im Großostheimer Mutterhaus vorgenommen wird.

Auch bei der Stoffauswahl ist Eduard Dressler qualitätsbewusst. Das Unternehmen setzt auf feinste Qualität und verwendet ausschließlich Stoffe der weltbesten Webereien, die schwerpunktmäßig in Italien angesiedelt sind. Zu den langjährigen Partnerunternehmen zählen Loro Piana, Guabello, Cerruti und Ermenegildo Zegna.

Um einen Anzug der Marke Eduard Dressler industriell zu fertigen, bedarf es mehr als 200 Arbeitsschritte, die per Hand und ausschließlich an exklusiven Produktionsbändern ausgeführt werden. Bei der Herstellung eines „Tailormade"-Anzugs ist die Fixierung des Oberstoffs besonders wichtig. Um die Formbeständigkeit eines Anzugs zu gewährleisten, wird der stabilisierende Einlagestoff mit hoch technisierten Klebepunkten versehen und in einer Fixiermaschine bei trockener Hitze und Druck mit dem Oberstoff verbunden. Das Sakko wird aus einer Zusammenschichtung verschiedener sogenannter Plackmaterialien aus Woll-, Ziegen- und Rosshaar in Form gebracht. Dabei wird der Brustplack nicht aufgeklebt, sondern mit feinen und losen Pikierstichen mit dem Oberstoff unsichtbar vernäht. Bei der abschließenden „Dressur" wird der Oberstoff des Sakkos mittels Feuchtigkeit, Hitze, Druck und Kühlung in Form gebracht.

Die mit äußerster Sorgfalt herausgearbeitete Passform eines Eduard-Dressler-Sakkos verkörpert im wahrsten Sinne des Wortes die Philosophie des Unternehmens. Man setzt auf Mode, die Zuverlässigkeit, Kontinuität und Bestimmtheit ausstrahlt. So ist es kein Wunder, dass der Steinbock das Wappentier des Unternehmens ist. Das Sternzeichen des Firmengründers Eduard Dresslers symbolisiert überdies den selbstbewussten Unternehmergeist, der die Basis des internationalen Erfolgs darstellt.

Eduard Dressler's first industrially-tailored suit revolutionised traditional, hand-tailoring without loss of quality.
Mit dem ersten industriell gefertigten Tailor-Anzug revolutionierte Eduard Dressler das traditionelle Schneiderhandwerk ohne Qualitätsverlust.

SINCE 1929

EDUARD DRESSLER

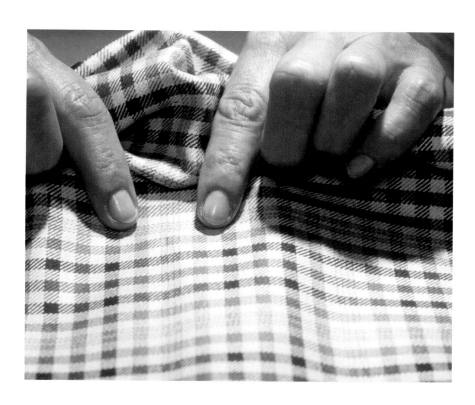

Even today, every single garment
is a masterpiece of perfection.
Noch heute veredelt handwerkliche
Perfektion jedes einzelne Stück.

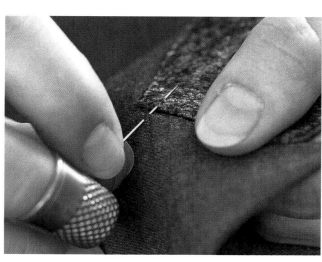

ELLEN PAULSSEN

— SINCE 1991

"I design hats for women who wear cosmetics, take care of themselves, dress well, wear hats and want to reward themselves."
Ellen Paulssen

WELL PROTECTED EVERY DAY

A pink bast hat, girlishly decorated with corded ribbons, brightly coloured fabric flowers and silver anchors. A velours felt hat of hare fur with a slight sheen and decorated with a bunch of feathers and a brooch pin in the shape of a gentian flower. Or a sporty-casual masculine style of hat in a leopard-print fabric, decorated with a decorative gingham bow and a silver hat pin. Ellen Paulssen's hat creations are anything but run-of-the-mill. Every fulled cap and every hat is a small millinery masterpiece made from unusual material combinations and daring details.

Ellen Paulssen has been making distinctive, handmade hats in her Aachen premises since 1991. In partnership with her husband, Volker Lauven, who runs the business, and with the help of eleven staff, she is now creating around 12,000 models a year – and certainly not with the aid of machines. "Every model is pulled, steamed, modelled and sewn by hand using traditional craftmanship techniques", says Ellen Paulssen, pinning a catwalk photo of a behatted model to the wall of inspiration in her studio. Her creative rooms are part of an old building with a modern extension in the protected conservation area of the Aachen Soer, a short walk from the famous cathedral. Not only is this her home but she also works here with her team producing two collections a year. It's hardly surprising that the atmosphere tends to be rather informal. However, Ellen Paulssen never loses sight of the competition or her own ambitious goals. She has specialised in producing hats and berets from a single piece of fabric, with the basic hat body being pulled into shape around hat blocks or fashioned from straw and felt cape-lines – a procedure which ensures a very snug fit without any awkward seams. The most important aspect of wearing a hat, after all, is that it fits comfortably. Ellen Paulssen began by showing her early collections at various avant-garde shows, which is where she met the design team of Wolfgang Joop, for whom she was soon designing hats for collections and catwalk shows. Top designers like Sônia Bogner, Joseph Janard, Annette Görtz, Luis Trenker and Toni Gard likewise accessorise their fashions with Ellen Paulssen hats. Well-known retailers, such as Beck und Lodenfrey in Munich, Schnitzler in Münster, SØR, Bailly Diehl in Frankfurt on the Main and Eder in Kitzbuehel, have stocked her hats for years.

Volker Lauven & Ellen Paulssen

HATS WITHOUT ECCENTRICITY

Meanwhile, Ellen Paulssen has been concentrating on expanding her own label. Depending on the season, her studio is piled high with wintry warm styles in fleecy melousine, a shaggy type of felt "which is slightly ragged looking ", and others in a matt wool felt, decorated with thick tufts of fur, long pheasant feathers or old walking-stick badges. Hikers used to decorate their walking-sticks with colourful badges depicting famous views and sights, like Salzburg, Kitzbuehel, Cologne Cathedral and the Loreley. "These little badges are best-sellers, the customers go mad for them", enthuses Ellen Paulssen. Another trend which she created is the so-called "cap hat" which is cut and shaped from felted new wool and feels as soft as a knitted hat. One of the major autumn lines is "Oktoberfest hats" with amusing little vintage badges depicting beer mugs, edelweiss flowers and pretzels. "We like playing with details", remarks Ellen Paulssen, holding up a lilac hat, glinting with half a dozen silver badges. Despite all this playful creativity, she is absolutely uncompromising when it comes to quality, claiming to be "almost boringly meticulous" when selecting materials and creating perfect shapes offering maximum comfort to the wearer.

The most popular summer models include hats with wide, sometimes fringed, brims, made from Panama straw, crocheted raffia or green-tinged sea grass from the Philippines. To prevent scratching, Ellen Paulssen lines the natural materials with brightly coloured, viscose straw which shimmers through.

In contrast to the eccentric creations designed by London hatmaker, Philip Treacy, who designs hats for the fashionable elite at major events like the wedding of Prince William to Kate, Duchess of Cambridge, this Aachen designer makes "hats for every day". She designs them for women "who wear cosmetics, take care of themselves, dress well, wear hats and want to reward themselves." Customers do indeed seem to become very attached to their hats: "We sometimes receive desperate emails from clients who have left their hat in some taxi or other", relates Ellen Paulssen with a smile. "In which case, we will just make last season's hat all over again!"

COMPANY	UNTERNEHMEN
Ellen Paulssen Hüte e. K.	Ellen Paulssen Hüte e. K.
FOUNDED IN	**GEGRÜNDET**
1991	1991
FOUNDERS	**GRÜNDER**
Ellen Paulssen,	Ellen Paulssen,
Volker Lauven	Volker Lauven
HEADQUARTERS	**HAUPTFIRMENSITZ**
Aachen, Germany	Aachen, Deutschland
CEO	**GESCHÄFTSFÜHRUNG**
Volker Lauven	Volker Lauven
EMPLOYEES	**MITARBEITER**
11	11
PRODUCTS	**PRODUKTE**
Hats and caps	Hüte und Mützen
ANNUAL PRODUCTION	**JAHRESPRODUKTION**
Approx. 12,000 models	Ca. 12.000 Modelle
EXPORT COUNTRIES	**EXPORTLÄNDER**
Austria, Belgium, Italy,	Belgien, Italien, Korea,
Korea, Luxembourg,	Luxemburg, Niederlande,
The Netherlands,	Österreich, Schweden,
Sweden, Switzerland, USA	Schweiz, USA

ELLEN PAULSSEN
• Hüte von Hand gearbeitet •

JEDEN TAG GUT BEHÜTET

Ein rosa Basthut, mädchenhaft geschmückt mit gewebten Ripsbändern, bunten Stoffblumen und silbernen Ankerbroschen. Ein Veloursfilzhut mit leichtem Glanz aus weichem Hasenhaar, besetzt mit Federbüschel und Enzian-Anstecker. Oder eine sportlich-lässige Herrenhutform, gezogen aus mit Leopardendesign bedruckten Stumpen, verziert mit Vichykaroschleife und einer silbernen Hutnadel. Die Hutkreationen von Ellen Paulssen sind alles andere als durchschnittlich. Jede gewalkte Mütze, jeder Hut ist ein kleines Kunstwerk aus ungewöhnlichen Materialkombinationen und gewagten Details.

Seit 1991 fertigt die Hutmacherin in ihrer Aachener Manufaktur handgemachten Kopfschmuck, der im Gedächtnis bleibt. Gemeinsam mit ihrem Mann Volker Lauven, der die Geschäfte leitet, und elf Mitarbeitern kreiert sie mittlerweile rund 12.000 Modelle pro Jahr – und das keinesfalls maschinell. „Jedes Modell wird in traditioneller Handwerkskunst von Hand gezogen, gedämpft, modelliert und genäht", sagt Ellen Paulssen und pinnt ein Laufstegfoto mit einem behüteten Modell an ihre Inspirationswand im Atelier. Die Kreativräume sind Teil eines Altbaus mit modernem Anbau im Landschaftsschutzgebiet der Aachener Soers, einen kurzen Spaziergang vom berühmten Dom entfernt. Hier wohnt sie und tüftelt zugleich mit ihrem Team an zwei Kollektionen pro Jahr. Da wundert es nicht, dass die Atmosphäre geradezu familiär anmutet. Dennoch verliert Ellen

Paulssen die Mitbewerber und die eigenen ehrgeizigen Ziele nie aus den Augen. Sie hat sich darauf spezialisiert, Hüte und Mützen aus einem Guss herzustellen, indem sie die Materialien aus Stumpen und Capelines aus Stroh und Filz zieht – ein Verfahren, das hohen Tragekomfort ohne drückende Nähte verspricht. Das Wichtigste bei einem Hut ist schließlich die bequeme Passform.

Bereits ihre ersten Kollektionen präsentierte Ellen Paulssen auf verschiedenen Avantgardeschauen. Dabei entstand auch der Kontakt zum Designteam von Wolfgang Joop, für den sie bald darauf Hüte für Kollektionen und Defilés entwarf. Auch Top-Designer wie Sônia Bogner, Joseph Janard, Annette Görtz, Luis Trenker und Toni Gard zeigten ihre Mode mit Ellen-Paulssen-Hüten. Namhafte Einzelhändler wie Beck und Lodenfrey in München, Schnitzler in Münster, SØR, Bailly Diehl in Frankfurt a. M. und Eder in Kitzbühel führen seit Jahren ihre Modelle.

KOPFSCHMUCK OHNE EXZENTRIK

Mittlerweile konzentriert sich Ellen Paulssen auf die Expansion der eigenen Marke. Je nach Saison stapeln sich dann im Atelier winterlich wärmende Modelle aus flauschigem Melousine, einer zotteligen Filzart, „die nicht so fein gemacht aussieht", und aus matterem Woll-Schurfilz mit dicken Fellbuscheln, langen Fasanenfedern und immer wieder alten Stocknägeln. Mit den bonbonbunten Miniansichten von Orten und Sehenswürdigkeiten wie Salzburg, Kitzbühel, dem Kölner Dom oder der Loreley schmückten Wanderer früher ihre Spazierstöcke. „Die kleinen Plaketten sind der Renner, da flippen die Kunden total aus", freut sich Ellen Paulssen. Einen weiteren Trend schuf sie mit sogenannten Hut-Mützen: Der Kopfputz wird aus gewalktem Strick zugeschnitten und geformt und fühlt sich weich wie eine Mütze an. Ein großes Herbstthema sind die „Oktoberfest-Hüte" mit witzigen Vintage-Ansteckern wie Maßkrügen, Edelweiß und Brezeln. „Wir haben Lust am Spiel mit Details", sagt Ellen Paulssen und hält ein lila Modell hoch, an dem gleich ein halbes Dutzend Anstecker blitzen. Bei aller verspielten Kreativität ist sie bei der Qualität kompromisslos: „Fast spießig sorgfältig" sei sie bei der Auswahl der Materialien und der Fertigung perfekter Formen für den bestmöglichen Tragekomfort. Im Sommer gehören Hüte mit Schatten spendendem, manchmal fransigem Rand aus Panama-Stroh, gehäkeltem Raffia oder grünlichem Seegras von den Philippinen zu den beliebtesten Modellen. Damit sie nicht kratzen, unterlegt Ellen Paulssen die Naturmaterialien mit knallfarbenem, durchschimmerndem Viskosestroh.

Im Unterschied zu den exzentrischen Kreationen, wie sie beispielsweise der Londoner Hutmacher Philip Treacy für die Mode-Elite zu Großereignissen wie der Hochzeit von Prinz William und Herzogin Kate designte, fertigt die Aachener Designerin „Hüte für jeden Tag". Sie entwirft sie für Frauen „die sich schmücken, schützen, stylen, behüten und belohnen wollen". Die Bindungen, die Kunden zu ihren Hüten aufbauen, scheinen jedenfalls stark zu sein: „Ab und zu bekommen wir verzweifelte Emails von Kunden, die ihren Hut oder ihre Mütze in irgendeinem Taxi liegen gelassen haben", erzählt Ellen Paulssen und lächelt. „Dann fertigen wir ihnen den Hut aus der vorletzten Saison eben einfach noch einmal!"

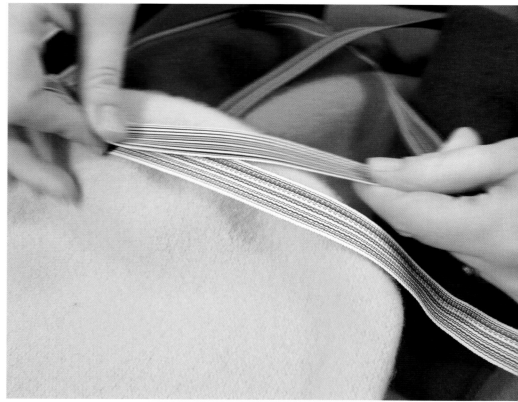

ELLEN PAULSSEN   SINCE 1991

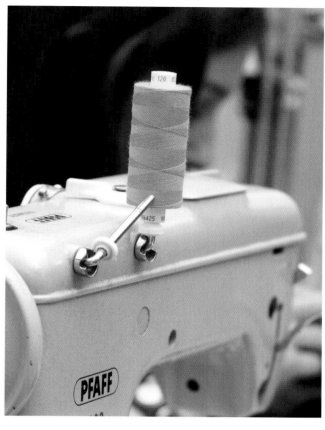

Impressions of the workshop
Impressionen aus der Werkstatt

EMANUEL BERG

— SINCE 1989

"Live a bespoke
lifestyle!"
Petra & Jaroslaw Szychulda

THE "IN" THING WITH STYLE ENTHUSIASTS

Tailoring a shirt is on a par with preparing a gourmet menu: a perfect result will only be achieved using the finest ingredients, prepared with skilful finesse and loving attention to detail. Emanuel Berg shirt manufacturers have been following this successful formula since 1989. At the production workshop in Dirschau, near Gdansk, experienced seamstresses with a flair for the art of hand-stitching, produce perfect shirts and blouses. The brand has recently become the "in" thing with style enthusiasts, who delight, not least, in the subtle details which go into the making of an Emanuel Berg shirt. For instance, the extremely fine workmanship which comprises nine stitches per centimetre. Or the barely discernible "single-needle seam" down the side of each shirt. The interfacing in the collar is not glued in: consequently, the shirt still feels comfortable even after a long day at the office. In addition, each shirt is designed with an additional allowance in the collar width to prevent it becoming tight after the garment has been washed a few times. The fabric remains pleasant to touch and crease-resistant. "The outstanding quality of Emanuel Berg shirts is highlighted by the meticulous detail, as demonstrated, for example, in the solid buttons made of Australian mother-of-pearl, which are – it goes without saying – properly sewn on with a shank or stem", explains Gabriele Semmerling, head of production, "and the labels, which are particularly gentle on the skin, are made on old looms."

When Jaroslaw Szychulda established the Emanuel Berg label in 1989 in Cologne, he never dreamed that this family-run business would be so successful. Nowadays, around 200,000 shirts and blouses are produced each year by the company's own factory in Dirschau and distributed all over the world to discerning customers with a sense of style and elegance. At a time when more and more firms are shifting production to the Far East, Emanuel Berg is particularly proud of the fact that their shirts and blouses are all made in Europe and being exported in increasing numbers to China and Japan. The collections are developed by the firm's owner and his wife Petra Szychulda. The latter designs new collars and styles and likes to advise his international clients and retail partners personally – including on their choice of top-quality fabrics sourced from famous, traditional weaving firms such as Thomas Mason, Albini, Testa or the Swiss luxury brand of Alumo. Jaroslaw Szychulda has been fascinated by luxury fabrics and the art of tailoring since childhood. Both he and his wife derive their inspiration from their travels to different cities, from international fairs and from 1950s films, in which the male stars were always correctly and elegantly attired.

DISTINCTIVE ORIGINALITY FOR DISTINCTIVE PERSONALITIES

Anyone who orders a bespoke Emanuel Berg shirt faces a serious dilemma as he leafs through the thick pattern books since these contain patterns for more than 700 different twill fabrics, including Sea Island cotton and two-ply twill weaves. There seems to be a virtually unlimited choice of striped patterns, which, thanks to a special weaving process, appear slightly blurred and somewhat less "sharp" than is the case with other premium labels in order to avoid the "flickering" effect. Every season, the choice of colours and patterns is augmented by new trends. In addition, the brand offers more than 60 different collar shapes and, if desired, embroidered monograms. Emanuel Berg also offers a dozen different types of cuff, including French cuffs, which are fastened with cuff links. Once everything has been decided, the individually fashioned shirt is produced within a maximum of four weeks. The uniqueness of a made-to-measure shirt emphasises the wearer's own distinctive personality by its precise fit. A shirt is simply more than just a shirt.

Petra & Jaroslaw Szychulda

COMPANY Emanuel Berg	UNTERNEHMEN Emanuel Berg
FOUNDED IN 1989	GEGRÜNDET 1989
FOUNDER Jaroslaw Szychulda	GRÜNDER Jaroslaw Szychulda
HEADQUARTERS Roesrath, Germany	HAUPTFIRMENSITZ Rösrath, Deutschland
CEO Petra and Jaroslaw Szychulda, Leszek Bystry	GESCHÄFTSFÜHRUNG Petra und Jaroslaw Szychulda, Leszek Bystry
EMPLOYEES 300	MITARBEITER 300
PRODUCTS Shirts and blouses: ready-to-wear and made-to-measure	PRODUKTE Hemden und Blusen: Konfektion und Maßanfertigung
ANNUAL PRODUCTION Approx. 200,000 shirts and blouses	JAHRESPRODUKTION Ca. 200.000 Hemden und Blusen
EXPORT COUNTRIES China, Europe, Japan, USA	EXPORTLÄNDER China, Europa, Japan, USA

Emanuel Berg
SUPERFINE SHIRTING

Jaroslaw Szychulda takes Bernhard Roetzel's measurements.
Jaroslaw Szychulda nimmt Maß bei Bernhard Roetzel.

GEHEIMTIPP FÜR
STIL-ENTHUSIASTEN

Das Fertigen eines Hemdes ist vergleichbar mit dem Zubereiten eines Sterne-Menüs: Nur unter Verwendung der besten Zutaten, durch meisterliche Verarbeitung und mit Liebe zum Detail entsteht ein überzeugendes Spitzenprodukt. Die Hemdenmanufaktur Emanuel Berg arbeitet seit 1989 nach diesem Erfolgsrezept. In Dirschau, nahe Danzig, fertigen erfahrene Weißnäherinnen mit Gespür für die hohe Schule des feinen Handstichs Hemden und Blusen in Perfektion. Die Marke hat sich in jüngster Zeit zum Geheimtipp für Stil-Enthusiasten entwickelt, die sich nicht selten auch für die subtilen Details interessieren, die ein fertiges Emanuel-Berg-Hemd ausmachen. Zum Beispiel die Tatsache, dass es mit neun Stichen pro Zentimeter äußerst sauber verarbeitet wird. Oder dass jedes Hemd an den Seiten mit einer kaum spürbaren „single-needle-Naht" versehen ist. Die Einlage im Kragensteg ist nicht verklebt – so bleibt das Tragegefühl auch nach einem langen Geschäftstag noch angenehm. Außerdem wird jedes Hemd mit einer Einlaufzugabe bei der Kragenweite konzipiert, die verhindert, dass der Kragen nach einigen Wäschen zu eng wird. Die Stoffe bleiben griffig und knitterarm. „Qualität bis ins kleinste Detail erkennt man bei Emanuel Berg auch an den massiven Knöpfen aus Australia-Perlmutt, die natürlich auf Stiel genäht sind", erklärt Produktionsleiterin Gabriele Semmerling, „und die extra hautfreundlichen Etiketten werden auf alten Webstühlen gefertigt."

Als Jaroslaw Szychulda 1989 die Marke Emanuel Berg in Köln gründete, hatte er nicht im Traum daran gedacht, dass sein familiär geführter Betrieb einmal so erfolgreich sein würde. Heute verlassen jährlich etwa 200.000 Hemden und Blusen die eigene Produktionsstätte in Dirschau und erreichen weltweit Kunden mit Sinn für Stil und Eleganz. In Zeiten, in denen immer mehr Firmen ihre Produktionen nach Fernost verlegt haben, ist man bei Emanuel Berg besonders stolz, dass die Hemden und Blusen aus der eigenen europäischen Manufaktur in immer größeren Zahlen nach China und Japan exportiert werden. Die Kollektionen entwickelt der Firmeninhaber gemeinsam mit seiner Frau Petra. Er entwirft neue Kragen- und Passformen und berät seine internationalen Kunden und Retail-Partner am liebsten persönlich – auch bei der Auswahl der hochwertigen Stoffe, die aus renommierten Traditionswebereien wie Thomas Mason, Albini, Testa oder der Schweizer Luxuskollektion Alumo kommen. Jaroslaw Szychulda, der schon als Kind von edlen Stoffen und der Schneiderarbeit fasziniert war, und seine Frau finden Inspiration auf ihren Reisen in die Metropolen, auf Messen und auch in den Filmen der 1950er-Jahre, in denen die männlichen Stars immer korrekt und elegant gekleidet waren.

UNVERWECHSELBARE UNIKATE
FÜR UNVERWECHSELBARE PERSÖNLICHKEITEN

Wer sich ein Emanuel-Berg-Hemd nach Maß anfertigen lässt, hat, wenn er in die dicken Musterbücher eintaucht, die Qual der Wahl. Darin befinden sich Muster von über 700 unterschiedlichen Vollzwirn-Stoffen, darunter die Sea-Island-Baumwolle mit zweifädigem Vollzwirn-Gewebe, genannt „two ply". Schier grenzenlos scheint auch die Vielzahl von Streifenmustern zu sein, die durch die spezielle Webung leicht verschwommen und weniger „scharf" als bei anderen hochwertigen Labels wirken, damit sie vor dem Auge nicht „flimmern". Zu jeder Saison werden die Farben und Muster durch neue Trends ergänzt. Dazu kommen mehr als 60 Kragenformen und auf Wunsch gestickte Monogramme. Natürlich bietet Emanuel Berg auch ein Dutzend Manschettenformen an, darunter die französische Variante, die mit Manschettenknöpfen geschlossen wird. Hat der Kunde alle Entscheidungen getroffen, wird das individuell gestaltete Hemd innerhalb von maximal vier Wochen hergestellt. Getragen unterstreicht das maßgefertigte Hemd als Unikat die unverwechselbare Persönlichkeit durch seine exakte Passform. Ein Hemd ist eben mehr als nur ein Hemd.

A seamstress stitching on a collar by hand
Eine Weißnäherin beim Annähen eines Kragens von Hand

Page/Seite 128:
White shirt made from the finest Thomas Mason poplin
Weißes Hemd aus feinstem Thomas-Mason-Popeline

FALKE

"We are fanatical about quality; innovation is high on our list of priorities."
Franz-Peter Falke

THE SECRET IS IN THE STITCHING

Soft and silky, discreet and seductive, self- or multi-coloured, patterned, elegant, trendy or even extravagant – there is nothing boring about our passion for socks. Roofer Franz Falke-Rohen may not yet have been aware of the full extent of this back in 1895 when he laid the cornerstone for what is now the internationally famous Falke label. Although he later became an entrepreneur, he once earned a living during the winter months as a seasonal knitter and very quickly recognised the potential of delicate hosiery. He was convinced that fine stitching had great future potential and without further ado set up his own small knitting business. Each of his eight employees produced just two dozen socks a day. However, a pioneer spirit, hard work and diligence paid off and in 1918, in partnership with his son, Franz Falke-Rohen bought the old Carl Meisenburg spinning mill in Schmallenberg.

The quality of Falke products soon became increasingly popular and the small spinning company rocketed to success. Just two years later, father and son, Franz Junior, built a modern, new factory in Schmallenberg which is still home to the Falke group's headquarters. Franz Senior died in 1928, leaving his son with a very respectable business and a workforce numbering 800 employees. The unmistakeable Falke logo was developed and a new generation took over running of the company. Brothers Paul and Franz-Otto Falke, spurred on by the economic miracle in the 1950s, were keen to expand and cultivated export markets in Europe and overseas. The manufacture of nylon and cotton tights marked a new chapter in the firm's success story. During the 1970s, Falke production groups were established in South Africa, Portugal, Austria and Hungary. Famous designers, such as Kenzo, Boss and Joop were impressed by the quality of Falke products and henceforth, this Sauerland enterprise found itself producing hosiery for the big names in the fashion industry. The secret of Falke's success lies in the stitching, the interplay of colours and patterns, a sensitive instinct for elegance and trendy looks and, not least, the expert know-how, which are valued by both male and female fans of Falke's products.

Franz Falke-Rohen

BASIC, HIGH-TECH, LUXURY

Since the mid-90s, the company has been run by the fourth generation of the family. Cousins Franz-Peter Falke and Paul Falke seek inspiration in the spirit of the times and, in that respect, are following entirely in their predecessors' footsteps. The company has had considerable success, in particular, in developing new materials: in 1994, Falke Garne was awarded an environmental protection prize by the Federation of German Industry (BDI) for its "Climate Wool", an insulating material made from sheep's wool.

In 2005, Falke introduced an entire new line of functional sportswear, the Falke Ergonomic Sport System, which elevated the company to the position of market leader in high-tech sportswear. The firm was soon opening elegant flagship stores and selling its wide-ranging assortment of fashionable knitwear, knitted socks, ladies' fine hosiery, as well as knitting accessories, via the modern shop-in-shop concept, to leading department stores all over the world. The Falke Cotton Touch line, silky smooth and pure matt tights, have meanwhile become a basic item for every fashion- and quality-conscious woman. These Sauerland specialists are also setting new benchmarks in the sector of exclusive leg wear by introducing the Falke "Luxury Collection". This range is made from the world's finest materials and processed in a manufacturing process in the traditional Schmallenberg knitting business.

In 2010, Falke experienced a particular triumph, succeeding where other sock producers have always failed and manufacturing socks from the world's most expensive and coveted wool. Vicuña wool puts all other types of luxury wool in the shade and is so light and fine that other manufacturers' earlier attempts to produce it met with failure. It is best not to ask the price but it does at least demonstrate that Falke can offer the perfect sock to go with even the most elegant outfit.

A total of more than 3,000 employees now work for this internationally famous firm, each day fulfilling the highest expectations in design and material. For Falke customers, purist elegance combined with the unconditional quality of Falke products represents a daily dose of luxury.

COMPANY	UNTERNEHMEN
Falke KGaA	Falke KGaA
FOUNDED IN	GEGRÜNDET
1895	1895
FOUNDER	GRÜNDER
Franz Falke-Rohen	Franz Falke-Rohen
HEADQUARTERS	HAUPTFIRMENSITZ
Schmallenberg,	Schmallenberg,
Germany	Deutschland
CEO	GESCHÄFTSFÜHRUNG
Franz-Peter Falke,	Franz-Peter Falke,
Paul Falke	Paul Falke
EMPLOYEES	MITARBEITER
3,081	3.081
PRODUCTS	PRODUKTE
Socks and tights	Beinbekleidung
(knitted and denier), Falke	(Strick und Fein), Falke
Ergonomic Sport System	Ergonomic Sport System
(sport function socks,	(Sportfunktionsstrümpfe
sport function underwear),	und -unterwäsche),
menswear	Menswear
ANNUAL PRODUCTION	JAHRESPRODUKTION
6,700,000 men's socks	6.700.000 Herrenstrümpfe
EXPORT COUNTRIES	EXPORTLÄNDER
Worldwide,	Weltweit,
over 30 countries	über 30 Länder

F A L K E

Perfection in handcraftsmanship
Handarbeit in Perfektion

DIE MASCHE MIT DER MASCHE

Zart und seidig, dezent und verführerisch, uni, farbenfroh, gemustert, elegant, modisch oder auch extravagant – die Strumpfleidenschaft kennt keine Langeweile. Das mag dem Dachdecker Franz Falke-Rohen noch gar nicht in diesem Ausmaß bewusst gewesen sein, als er 1895 im Sauerland den Grundstein für das heute weltweit bekannte Unternehmen Falke legte. Der spätere Unternehmer verdiente in den Wintermonaten sein Geld als Saisonstricker und erkannte schon früh das Potenzial der zarten Beinkleider. Er glaubte, die feinen Maschen seien zukunftsträchtig und gründete kurzerhand seine eigene kleine Strickerei. Jeder der acht Mitarbeiter produzierte zur damaligen Zeit gerade einmal zwei Dutzend Socken pro Tag. Doch Pioniergeist, Fleiß und Mühe zahlten sich aus, und 1918 kaufte Franz Falke-Rohen gemeinsam mit seinem Sohn die alte Spinnerei Carl Meisenburg in Schmallenberg.

Die Qualität der Falke-Produkte gewann schnell an Popularität und die kleine Spinnerei ging auf Erfolgskurs. Nur zwei Jahre später bauten Vater und Sohn Franz junior eine neue moderne Fabrik in Schmallenberg, wo noch heute der Firmensitz der Falke-Gruppe beheimatet ist. 1928 verstarb der Senior und hinterließ seinem Sohn ein mittlerweile stattliches Industrieunternehmen mit 800 Mitarbeitern. Das unverkennbare Falke-Logo wurde entwickelt, und eine weitere Generation übernahm das Führungsruder im Unternehmen. Die Brüder Paul und Franz-Otto Falke setzten, befeuert vom Wirtschaftswunder der 1950er-Jahre, auf Expansion und erschlossen Exportmärkte in Europa und Übersee.

Mit der Herstellung der Nylon- und der Baumwoll-Strumpfhose wurde ein neues Kapitel in der Erfolgsgeschichte des Unternehmens geschrieben. In den 1970er-Jahren entstanden Falke-Produktionsgesellschaften in Südafrika, Portugal, Österreich und Ungarn. Namhafte Designer wie Kenzo, Boss oder Joop überzeugte die Qualität der Falke-Produkte und fortan fertigte das Unternehmen aus dem Sauerland auch für die großen Namen der Modewelt. Es ist die Masche mit der Masche, das Spiel mit Farben und Mustern, das sensible Gespür für Eleganz und trendigen Look und nicht zuletzt das fachliche Know-how, die Frauen wie Männer gleichermaßen schätzen, wenn sie sich von Falke umgarnen lassen.

BASIC, HIGHTECH, LUXURY

Seit Mitte der 1990er-Jahre wird das Unternehmen in vierter Generation geführt. Auch die Cousins Franz-Peter Falke und Paul Falke lassen sich vom Zeitgeist inspirieren und handeln damit ganz im Sinne ihrer Ahnen. Insbesondere bei der Entwicklung neuer Materialien läuft die Entwicklung im wahrsten Sinne des Wortes ausgezeichnet: Für ihre „Clima Wool", ein Dämmstoff aus Schafwolle, erhalten die Falke-Garne 1994 den Umweltschutzpreis des BDI.

2005 präsentiert Falke eine komplette Linie funktionaler Sportbekleidung und avanciert mit dem Falke Ergonomic Sport System zum Marktführer im

Bereich Hightech-Sportswear. Das Unternehmen eröffnet schon bald elegante Flagship-Stores und präsentiert durch das moderne Shop-in-Shop-Konzept das breitgefächerte Sortiment an modischer Strickbekleidung, Strickstrümpfen, Damenfeinstrümpfen und -strumpfhosen sowie Strickaccessoires weltweit auch in führenden Kaufhäusern. Die Falke-Cotton-Touch-, Seidenglatt- und Pure-Matt-Strumpfhosen sind mittlerweile ein Basic jeder mode- und qualitätsbewussten Frau. Neue Maßstäbe im Segment der exklusiven Strumpfbekleidung setzen die Experten aus dem Sauerland mit der Falke „Luxury Collection". Die weltweit erlesensten Materialien werden in der Schmallenberger Traditionsstrickerei im Manufakturverfahren verarbeitet.

2010 landet Falke einen besonderen Coup, der zuvor noch keinem Strumpfproduzenten glückte: aus der teuersten und begehrtesten Wolle der Welt Strümpfe herzustellen. Die Vicuna-Wolle stellt alle anderen Luxus-Wollqualitäten in den Schatten und ist so leicht und fein, dass bisherige Produktionsversuche von anderen Herstellern scheiterten. Über den Preis sollte man freilich schweigen, aber der Strumpfproduzent Falke beweist damit, dass er auch zum edelsten Outfit den passenden Strumpf anbieten kann.

Die mehr als 3.000 Mitarbeiter des international aufgestellten Unternehmens arbeiten jeden Tag daran, den höchsten Ansprüchen an Design und Material gerecht zu werden. Für viele Kunden ist die puristische Eleganz in Verbindung mit der bedingungslosen Qualität der Falke-Produkte ihre tägliche Dosis Luxus.

The changing face of sock advertisements
Strumpfwerbung im Wandel der Zeit

FAME

"Not only does the
market give rise to new
ideas but sometimes the
inspiration for new looks
comes from old films or
illustrated books."
Fabian Flötotto

YOUNG, DYNAMIC, HIGH-QUALITY

Relax and unwind, enjoy the wind and weather but look good at the same time:
this is the message behind the photos in the "Fame meets Sylt" campaign.
And it's true that Fame outdoor jackets are the perfect choice for this uncomplicated, unspoilt landscape which symbolises both all that is genuine as well
as straightforward simplicity. These jackets feel like a second skin and give the
wearer a sense of security and protection against the challenges of everyday
life, the buffeting winds of which can sometimes be even harsher than those that
sweep across this North Sea island. The fact that a Fame jacket will withstand
anything and, at the same time, give its wearer a youthful, slender silhouette
makes it an absolute favourite amongst a dynamic generation which is self-
confident and independent enough of current trends to prefer a clothing style
which, in terms of style and comfort, is ideally suited to the wearer's individual
personality. This is one of the reasons why these jackets are so popular in creative circles – fans of Fame jackets include celebrities, such as representatives of
the modern German film industry.

A GOOD INSTINCT, A SENSE OF PURPOSE AND RESPONSIBILITY

Fabian Flötotto

How does a young designer acquire the kind of fundamental knowledge necessary to – in Fabian Flötotto's words – "impart a soul" to the jacket, which will distinguish it from other jackets? This young entrepreneur comes from a family which has been involved in the clothing industry for generations – and should not be confused with the furniture manufacturer of the same name. Carefully selected materials, meticulous finishing and a combination of timeless, classic styles and youthful charm: Fabian Flötotto has, since childhood, cultivated his passion for all these elements which distinguish an elegant clothing culture. There can be no other explanation for such extraordinary, single-mindedness of purpose. After graduating from high school, he started off with a few designs and his own label. He seemed to know exactly what he wanted, adding the very traditional touch of a coat-of-arms as the brand's logo, which incorporated not only the firm's name but also his date of birth and the heraldic symbol of a bellowing stag. This logo can be found on the left sleeve of every Fame jacket. Soon after the firm was established in 2005, he joined forces with the elegant Munich chain of Ludwig Beck, a move which attracted the attention of the fashion industry. Meanwhile, Fame F.F.C.C. now sells several thousand outdoor jackets a year throughout Europe. The small team of people who run the company is located in the firm's Bielefeld office whilst production currently takes place in Asia in order to keep the price-performance ratio at an attractive level. The company works solely with CSR-certified production workshops in this respect and is punctilious about operating responsibly, not only with regard to its own domestic workers but also towards its suppliers. By making a deliberate commitment to Corporate Social Responsibility, this new firm remains in tune with the spirit of the times on an issue which is also important to its clientele. Quite apart from their delight in the high-quality feel of the fabric, in the feather-light weight of the jackets, the excellent finishing and elegant details, such as zips, corded ribbon trim, unusual collars and pocket designs, many clients also want to know where the genuine duck feathers come from? What the properties of the fabrics are and under what conditions are the garments produced? In contrast to the fast pace of our modern world, Fame attaches considerable importance to values such as transparency and sustainability and the beautiful things in life. The ultra soft polyamide fabrics are made from the finest Italian nylon whilst the somewhat more robust cotton and polyurethane mix also comes from Italy. The colours are inspired by nature and are dominated by sand and earth tones, interspersed with the occasional light blue to reflect the vastness of the northern skies. With just 10 to 15 new styles each season, the product range remains manageable with Fabian Flötotto consequently attaching all the more importance to the exquisite quality – involving a large amount of hand-finishing – of each individual garment. Each jacket is a valuable product which reflects the younger generation's expectations in terms of durability and economic responsibility.

COMPANY Fame F.F.C.C.	UNTERNEHMEN Fame F.F.C.C.
FOUNDED IN 2005	GEGRÜNDET 2005
FOUNDER Fabian Flötotto	GRÜNDER Fabian Flötotto
HEADQUARTERS Gütersloh, Germany	HAUPTFIRMENSITZ Gütersloh, Deutschland
CEO Fabian Flötotto	GESCHÄFTSFÜHRUNG Fabian Flötotto
PRODUCTS Outdoor jackets	PRODUKTE Outdoor-Jacken
EXPORT COUNTRIES Europe	EXPORTLÄNDER Europa

JUNG, DYNAMISCH, QUALITÄTVOLL

Die Seele baumeln lassen, Wind und Wetter genießen und dabei einfach gut aussehen: Genau das vermitteln die Bilder der Kampagne „Fame meets Sylt". Und in der Tat, die Outdoor-Jacken von Fame passen gut in diese unkomplizierte, unverfälschte Landschaft, die für das Echte steht, für eine schnörkellose Geradlinigkeit. Man schlüpft in diese Jacken wie in eine zweite Haut, fühlt sich geschützt und gerüstet für die Herausforderungen des Alltags, bei denen manchmal ein rauerer Wind weht als auf der Nordseeinsel. Dass eine Fame-Jacke alles mitmacht und dabei ihrem Träger eine junge und schlanke Silhouette verleiht, macht sie zur absoluten Lieblingsjacke einer dynamischen Generation, die selbstbewusst und unabhängig von gängigen Trends einen Kleiderstil bevorzugt, der sich der eigenen Persönlichkeit in Schnitt und Tragekomfort optimal anpasst. Das erklärt auch ihre Beliebtheit in der kreativen Szene – bisweilen finden sich unter den Fame-Trägern wirkliche Berühmtheiten, so etwa einige Protagonisten des jungen deutschen Films.

MIT GUTEM GESPÜR, ZIELSTREBIGKEIT UND VERANTWORTUNG

Wie kommt ein junger Designer zu diesen fundierten Kenntnissen, die so wichtig sind, um einer Jacke „eine Seele einzuarbeiten", wie es der Firmengründer Fabian Flötotto ausdrückt, und die sie vor anderen Jacken auszeichnet? Der Jungunternehmer stammt aus einer Familie, die seit Generationen in der Kleiderbranche tätig ist – und nicht verwechselt werden sollte mit dem gleichnamigen Möbelhersteller. Ausgesuchte Materialien, sorgfältigste Verarbeitung und die Kombination zeitlos klassischer Schnitte mit jugendlichem Charme: Fabian Flötotto hat seine Leidenschaft für das, was eine gehobene Kleiderkultur ausmacht, von Kindesbeinen an entwickelt. Nur so lässt sich diese ungewöhnliche Zielstrebigkeit erklären. Direkt nach dem Abitur ging er mit eigenen Entwürfen und seinem eigenen Label an den Start. Er schien genau zu wissen, was er wollte, kreierte sehr traditionsbewusst ein Wappen als Markenzeichen, auf dem außer dem Firmen-Schriftzug sein Geburtsdatum und als Wappentier der typisch deutsche „röhrende Hirsch" prangt. Dieses Wappen ist auf dem linken Ärmel einer jeden Fame-Jacke zu finden.
Schon kurz nach der Firmengründung 2005 wurde Fabian Flötotto mit der Münchner Nobel-Kette Ludwig Beck handelseinig und damit für die Branche interessant. Inzwischen verkauft die Firma Fame F.F.C.C. jährlich mehrere Tausend Outdoor-Jacken in ganz Europa. Im Bielefelder Büro sitzt die Verwaltung mit einem kleinen Team, produziert wird derzeit in Asien, um das Preis-Leistungs-Verhältnis auf einem attraktiven Niveau zu halten. Dabei arbeitet das Unternehmen ausschließlich mit CSR-zertifizierten Betrieben zusammen und setzt auf diese Weise auf verantwortliches unternehmerisches Handeln, nicht nur in Bezug auf die eigenen Mitarbeiter, sondern auch auf die Zulieferer. Mit dem bewussten Einsatz für die Corporate Social Responsibility zeigt sich der Newcomer ganz auf der Höhe der Zeit. Und das interessiert auch die Kunden.

Showroom, Düsseldorf 2012
Showroom, Düsseldorf 2012

Bei aller Freude an der edlen Griffigkeit des Materials, dem federleichten Gewicht der Jacken, der guten Verarbeitung und den raffinierten Details wie Reißverschlüssen, Ripsbandeinsätzen, überraschenden Kragen- und Taschenformen möchten viele Kunden auch wissen: Wo kommen die echten Entendaunen her? Welche Eigenschaften haben die Stoffe und unter welchen Bedingungen wurde produziert? Als Kontrast zu unserer schnelllebigen Zeit setzt Fame auf Werte wie Transparenz und Nachhaltigkeit und auf die schönen Dinge des Lebens. Bei den hauchzarten Stoffen aus Polyamid handelt es sich um feinstes italienisches Nylon und auch das etwas robustere Baumwoll-Polyurethan-Gemisch kommt aus Italien. Die Farben sind von der Natur inspiriert – Sand- und Erdtöne dominieren, dazwischen erinnert ein lichtes Blau an die Weite des nordischen Himmels. Bei 10 bis 15 neuen Modellen pro Saison bleibt die Produktpalette überschaubar. Desto mehr Gewicht legt Fabian Flötotto auf die exquisite, mit viel Handarbeit verbundene Qualität jedes einzelnen Stücks. Jede dieser Jacken ist ein wertvolles Produkt, in dem sich das Bedürfnis einer jungen Generation nach Beständigkeit und ökonomischer Verantwortung widerspiegelt.

FRANCO BASSI
— SINCE 1972

"Fashion is underestimated identity."
Francesca Bassi

FAMILY TIES WITH AN INTERNATIONAL PROFILE

The creative philosophy behind the Italian label Franco Bassi is based on "family ties". The clever play on the word "ties" in English (which can mean both "necktie" and "bond") led the firm to adopt this English phrase as its motto. The closely knit Bassi family attributes the firm's success both to the family and its passion for ties and scarves. The family's instinctive and delicate approach to stylish elegance and top-quality materials has been handed down from generation to generation. Bassi accessories, designed and finished with considerable creative flair and outstanding workmanship, fall into place around the neck almost spontaneously and can be tied in a variety of ways to create a personal bond with the respective wearer. The firm was founded by Franco Bassi in 1972, since which time its headquarters have been based in the town of Como. In the meantime, the running of the com-

Francesca Bassi

pany has been passed on to the next generation. The firm continues to remain true to its origins under the leadership of its current general manager, Franco Bassi's daughter, Francesca. Ties and scarves from the House of Bassi are synonymous with the excellence, first-class design and distinction.

Men's ties and scarves with the "Franco Bassi" label are designed by Cesare Bassi, son of the former founder. The "Francesca Bassi" label is devoted to women's scarves and accessories, designed by Francesca personally. She is also responsible for distribution in Japan, Spain and Germany. A breath of British design flair is added by Francesca Bassi's husband, Richard Allen, who looks after clients in his native Great Britain, as well as in the USA and Korea. The company's 15-strong team produces approximately 100,000 items each year. Sixty-two per cent of the ties, scarves and accessories are exported to Japan, the USA and Germany.

THE MOST BEAUTIFUL

Only the most beautiful and top-quality products leave the fashion house of Bassi, which sources fabrics, such as wool and cashmere, entirely from the Como area and from Biella in Piedmont. Overall production also takes place in Como, only the embroidery work is carried out in India. The finished fabrics for ties consist of 60 per cent silk. Cotton, wool and linen are woven into the silk to prevent them looking too shiny and to ensure the finished tie or scarf conforms with current fashion trends.

A Bassi tie is produced in a series of steps carried out by machine and by hand. The fabric is first cut out manually. Next, an inlay is inserted, which is made of a firmer material such as wool. This forms the "interno", or body of the tie. The additional "fodera" – or inner lining – produces a subtle, silky sheen in places, including on the back of the tie. Whilst the signature in the "Franco Bassi" menswear collection consist of various shades of blue and brown, the women's collection comprises a captivatingly beautiful range of floral and multi-coloured designs. The mink and fox appliqué, which are mainly reserved for winter, enhance this already exclusive look even further.

Roland Barthes, the French semiologist, said that a necktie reflects the personality of its wearer. Francesca Bassi agrees and adds that a necktie can lend to the wearer a requisite confidence and professionalism in business situations. A cravat (an ascot, as the Americans call it) does not fulfil the same criteria and is therefore inappropriate for business situations. As attached as a person may be to their cravat, it is considered a casual wear item and should not be worn to any business meeting.

The Franco Bassi label is characterised by an awareness of beauty, quality and good taste. Francesca and Cesare Bassi, as well as Richard Allen, have all adopted this underlying principle of the firm's founder as their own.

COMPANY	UNTERNEHMEN
BB Cravatte Srl	BB Cravatte Srl
FOUNDED IN	**GEGRÜNDET**
1972	1972
FOUNDER	**GRÜNDER**
Franco Bassi	Franco Bassi
HEADQUARTERS	**HAUPTFIRMENSITZ**
Como, Italy	Como, Italien
CEO	**GESCHÄFTSFÜHRUNG**
Francesca Bassi	Francesca Bassi
(General manager,	(Geschäftsführerin,
designer of the ladies'	Designerin der
collection)	Damenkollektion)
Cesare Bassi (Sales	Cesare Bassi
manager, designer of	(Vertriebsleiter, Designer
the men's collection)	der Herrenkollektion)
Richard Allen (Inter-	Richard Allen (Vertriebs-
national sales manager)	leiter international)
EMPLOYEES	**MITARBEITER**
15	15
PRODUCTS	**PRODUKTE**
Ties, men's scarves,	Krawatten, Damen-
ladies scarves,	und Herrentücher und
accessories	-schals, Accessoires
ANNUAL PRODUCTION	**JAHRESPRODUKTION**
100,000 items	100.000 Artikel
EXPORT COUNTRIES	**EXPORTLÄNDER**
Europe, Japan, South	Europa, Japan, Südkorea,
Korea, UK, USA	UK, USA

Scarf with murmansky fur, Fall/Winter 2012/13
Schal mit Waschbärenpelz, Herbst/Winter 2012/13

FAMILIENBANDE MIT INTERNATIONALER PRÄSENZ

Das kreative Fundament des italienischen Labels Franco Bassi basiert auf Familienbanden. „Family ties"– so lautet passenderweise das Motto des Unternehmens im Englischen. Ein schönes Wortspiel, denn „Tie" bedeutet auch „Krawatte". Derart „zusammengebunden" gründen die Bassis ihren Erfolg sowohl auf die Familie als auch auf die Liebe zu Krawatte und Schal. Der selbstverständliche und leichtfüßige Umgang mit modischer Eleganz und mit feinen Stoffen wird von Generation zu Generation weitergegeben. Die von den Bassis mit viel schöpferischem und handwerklichem Know-how entworfenen und gefertigten Accessoires schmiegen sich ganz selbstverständlich um den Hals und gehen durch verschiedene Knotungen mit dem jeweiligen Träger eine Verbindung ein. 1972 wurde das Unternehmen von Franco Bassi gegründet. Der Firmensitz befindet sich seitdem in Como. Mittlerweile hat die erste Generation die Unternehmensleitung an die nachfolgende übertragen. Auch unter der aktuellen Geschäftsführung von Franco Bassis Tochter, Francesca, bleibt die Firma ihren Ursprüngen treu. Die Krawatten und Schals aus dem Hause Bassi stehen für höchste Qualitätsansprüche, erstklassiges Design und Distinguiertheit.

Unter dem Labelnamen „Franco Bassi" firmiert die Produktion der Herrenkrawatten und -schals, die von Cesare Bassi, dem Sohn des Seniorchefs, entworfen werden. Die Linie „Francesca Bassi" widmet sich Damenschals und Accessoires, die nach Designentwürfen der gleichnamigen Geschäftsleiterin entstehen. Francesca Bassi kümmert sich auch um den Vertrieb in Japan, Spanien und Deutschland. Für einen Hauch an britischem Flair im Design sorgt Francesca Bassis Mann, Richard Allen, der die Kunden in seinem Heimatland Großbritannien, in den USA und in Korea betreut. Das Unternehmen mit seinem insgesamt 15-köpfigen Team stellt jährlich rund 100.000 Artikel her. Wobei die Krawatten, Schals und Accessoires zu 62 Prozent nach Japan, in die USA und nach Deutschland exportiert werden.

NUR DIE SCHÖNSTEN

Nur die schönsten und qualitativ hochwertigsten Produkte verlassen das piemontesische Modehaus Bassi, das Stoffe wie Wolle oder Kaschmir ausschließlich aus der Umgebung von Como und aus Biella im Piemont bezieht. Auch die gesamte Produktion findet in Como statt, nur die Stickereiarbeiten werden in Indien angefertigt. Die verarbeiteten Stoffe für Krawatten bestehen zu 60 Prozent aus Seide. Damit sie nicht zu stark glänzt und das finale Krawatten- oder Schaldesign den aktuellen modischen Trends entspricht, wird die Seide mit Baumwolle, Wolle und Leinen verwebt.

Die Herstellung einer Bassi-Krawatte erfolgt in maschinellen und manuellen Arbeitsschritten. In den mit der Hand zugeschnittenen Stoff wird eine Einlage

Book of samples for necktie designs
Musterbuch für Krawattendessins

eingesetzt, die aus einem stabileren Material wie Wolle besteht und das „Interno", das Innenleben, den Körper der Krawatte bildet. Das zusätzlich angebrachte Innenfutter, „Fodera" genannt, lässt die Krawatte an gewissen Stellen auch auf der nach innen gewandten Seite seidig glänzen. Während die Herrenlinie „Franco Bassi" sich durch unterschiedliche Blau- und Brauntöne auszeichnet, erscheinen die Dessins der Damenschal-Kollektion in wunderschönen blumigen, verspielten Mustern. Die meist im Winter verwendeten Nerz- und Fuchsapplikationen erhöhen den an sich schon exklusiven Look.

Eine Krawatte spiegele die Persönlichkeit ihres Trägers wider, so meinte einst der Philosoph Roland Barthes. Das sagt auch Francesca Bassi und ergänzt, dass die Krawatte in offiziellen Geschäftskontexten die nötige Sicherheit verleihe und Seriosität ausstrahle. Ein Halstuch erfülle diese Funktion nicht, weswegen es bei offiziellen Anlässen nichts zu suchen habe. Es gehe zwar auch eine Verbindung mit dem Träger ein, gehöre aber definitiv in den elegant-sportlichen Freizeitbereich.

Die Identität des Labels Franco Bassi ist geprägt durch das Bewusstsein für Schönheit, Qualität und guten Geschmack. Dieses Selbstverständnis des Firmengründers haben Francesca und Cesare Bassi sowie Richard Allen auch zu ihrem Credo gemacht.

Pages/Seiten 148–149:
A loom weaving a check, silk
fabric for ties
Ein karierter Seidenstoff für
Krawatten auf dem Webstuhl

GANT
— SINCE 1949

"My passion is American sportswear and Gant."
Christopher Bastin

"ONLY THOSE WHO RESPECT TRADITION...

... will still be classics tomorrow!" As is so often the case with American success stories, the Gant label grew from modest beginnings. Ukrainian immigrant Bernard Gant set up a tailoring business manufacturing men's shirts in New Haven, Connecticut, on the US East coast. In 1941, he began making classic shirts for leading American brands and introduced new styles with an interwoven "G" as his logo. A passionate "shirtmaker" and keen observer, he realised that professors and students at the elite Yale University were in need of high-quality, comfortable shirts. In 1949, having observed baseball players, yachtsmen and rowers in their team outfits, he and his sons, Marty and Elliot, launched the first Gant collection aimed at the smart eleven and their casual, sporty lifestyle. Encouraged by his early success, he went on to introduce elegant details, such as the button on the back of the collar designed to keep the necktie and collar firmly in place, and incorporated a casual pleat into the back of the shirt to ensure unrestricted movement.

FROM SHIRT TO STATUS SYMBOL

It was not long before Gant shirts became an integral part of a student's wardrobe. It was claimed in campus circles that "if a Yale student possesses a button-down Oxford and a broadcloth shirt in white, blue, cream or striped, then he has pretty well got all he needs". A Gant shirt became a cult garment at Yale University. Students began to use this status symbol as a discreet indicator signalling a different kind of status: when you started "going steady" with a girlfriend, you removed the loop at the back of the shirt to show that you were taken. The most famous Yale shirt, the so-called Yale co-op shirt, is still produced to this day – as a seasonal shirt in smooth Madras cotton in distinctive Yale blue or in lightweight, broad-striped Oxford cotton or Tattersall check. Still styled and packed as it was in the 60s, it is only available for sale in selected Gant shops. During the 1950s and 60s, Gant college shirts developed a distinctive preppy look, which inspired a growing number of new fashion trends for men, such as the Club blazer. The "American East Coast Style" was born. During the years that followed, Gant became one of the biggest selling men's shirt brands in the USA. Ever since the company was first founded by Bernard Gant, the sight of Gant striped polo shirts, rugby shirts, sweaters, Oxford shirts, Club blazers, or chinos etc. has always conjured up associations of high school days, beaches in the Hamptons, sailing parties, happy families, adventure and freedom. Gant-collections are not concerned with fast-changing trends. The firm's ethos of "American casualness with European elegance" remains its guiding principle to this day.

Meanwhile, responsibility for creating the distinctive Gant look has now passed to Christopher Bastin, Director of Design. He likes clothes to be colourful, comfortable and casual. American sportswear is his passion. Today, Gant is one of the oldest collections in the history of American premium sportswear with 700 shops worldwide. Over the course of six decades, this former shirt manufacturer has developed into a comprehensive brand of casual and sports clothing for "men, women, girls, boys and babies". The company meanwhile also produces a home collection featuring living accessories and bed linen, as well as watches, shoes, glasses and perfumes. After the Gant family sold the company, it was initially taken over by Pyramid Sportswear, a Swedish firm, which ran the business from Stockholm. At the time, the world's biggest luxury consortium of Louis Vuitton Moët Hennessy (LVMH) was also involved in Gant. In 2008, the label was taken over 100 per cent by the Geneva Maus Frères Group – with a good deal of success! Within a year, Gant models were on show at Berlin's Mercedes-Benz and New York Fashion Week – and Gant also provided the kit for the German Hockey Association (DHB).

As far as Gant is concerned, outdoor fashion and a commitment to the environment go hand in hand,: the company has recently been involved in environmental protection projects, including cooperation with environmental activist and lawyer Robert F. Kennedy Jr., nephew of former US President John F. Kennedy, Jean-Michel Cousteau, son of legendary marine biologist, Jacques Cousteau, Mattis Klum, world-famous National Geographic Photographer and Dr. Jane Goodall, the famous behavioural scientist.

Since fall/winter 2011/12, a further testimonial has been added to the ranks of these famous celebrities: Elettra Rossellini, the extremely attractive daughter of Isabella Rossellini and granddaughter of Ingrid Bergman, has become the new face of the "Gant collection", a high-end womenswear collection.

Bernard Gant

COMPANY	UNTERNEHMEN
GANT AB	GANT AB
FOUNDED IN	GEGRUNDET
1949	1949
FOUNDER	GRUNDER
Bernard Gant	Bernard Gant
HEADQUARTERS	HAUPTFIRMENSITZ
Stockholm, Sweden	Stockholm, Schweden
CEO	GESCHÄFTSFUHRUNG
Dirk-Jan Stoppelenburg	Dirk-Jan Stoppelenburg
EMPLOYEES	MITARBEITER
Approx. 3,500 worldwide	Ca. 3.500 weltweit
PRODUCTS	PRODUKTE
American Sportswear	American Sportswear
(Men, Women, Kids),	(Herren, Damen, Kinder),
living accessories, watches,	Wohnaccessoires, Uhren,
shoes, glasses, perfumes	Schuhe, Brillen, Parfüms
ANNUAL PRODUCTION	JAHRESPRODUKTION
Approx. 10 million items	Ca. 10 Millionen Artikel
EXPORT COUNTRIES	EXPORTLÄNDER
Worldwide, 60 countries	Weltweit, 60 Länder

GANT

„NUR WER SEINE TRADITION PFLEGT…

… wird morgen noch ein Klassiker sein." Wie es amerikanische Erfolgsgeschichten oft an sich haben, begann auch der Aufstieg der Marke Gant bescheiden. In New Haven, Connecticut, an der amerikanischen Ostküste, machte sich der ukrainische Immigrant Bernard Gant mit einer Schneiderei für Herrenhemden selbstständig. Ab 1941 schneiderte er klassische Hemden für die führenden Marken Amerikas, etablierte neue Schnitte und ein eingewebtes „G" als Logo. Als leidenschaftlicher „Shirtmaker" und aufmerksamer Beobachter fiel ihm das Bedürfnis der Professoren und Studenten der ortsansässigen Elite-Universität Yale für hochwertige und zugleich komfortable Hemden auf. Er schaute den Baseballspielern, Seglern und Ruderern in ihren Mannschaftsoutfits zu und entwickelte 1949 unter dem Namen Gant gemeinsam mit seinen Söhnen Marty und Elliot eine erste Kollektion für die smarten Eleven und ihren sportlich-legeren Lebensstil. Motiviert durch den schnellen Erfolg, ließ er sich raffinierte Details wie den Knopf an der Rückseite des Kragens einfallen, der Krawatte und Kragen am richtigen Platz hält und sorgte mit einer lässigen Rückenfalte für uneingeschränkte Bewegungsfreiheit.

VOM HEMD ZUM STATUSSYMBOL

Bald gehörten Gant-Hemden zum festen Bestandteil der Studentengarderobe. „Wenn ein Yale-Student ein ‚Button-Down-Oxford'- und ein ‚Broadcloth'-Hemd in Weiß, Blau, Crème und gestreift besitzt, dann ist er ziemlich gut ausgestattet", hieß es in Campus-Kreisen. Das Gant-Hemd wurde Kult an der Yale-Universität. Die Studenten gaben mit diesem Statussymbol auf subtile Weise sogar noch einen anderen Status bekannt: Wer sich in „festen Händen" befand, entfernte die Aufhängeschlaufe des Hemdes, um zu zeigen, dass er vergeben war. Das wohl berühmteste Yale-Shirt, das sogenannte „Yale Co-op"-Shirt wird noch heute gefertigt – und zwar als Saison-Hemd aus glatt gewebter Madras-Baumwolle im charakteristischen Yale-Blauton oder aus leichtem Oxford-Cotton mit breiten Streifen oder Tattersall-Karos. Geschnitten und verpackt wie in den 1960er-Jahren, geht es nur in ausgewählten Gant-Shops über den Tresen. Aus den College-Hemden entwickelte sich in den 1950er- und 1960er-Jahren der für Gant typische Preppy-Look, der immer wieder neue Fashiontrends für Herren wie den Club-Blazer hervorbrachte. Der „American East Coast Style" war geboren. In den Folgejahren stieg Gant zu einer der meist verkauften Hemdenmarken der USA auf. Seit der ersten Gant-Kollektion denkt man beim Anblick von gestreiften Polos, Rugby-Shirts, Sweatern, Oxford-Hemden, Club-Blazern, Chinos & Co. sofort an High-School-Zeiten, die Strände der Hamptons, Segelturns, Familienglück, Abenteuer und Freiheit. Die Kollektionen von Gant kümmern sich wenig um schnelllebige Trends. Das Credo der Firma „American casualness with european elegance" ist bis heute maßgebend.

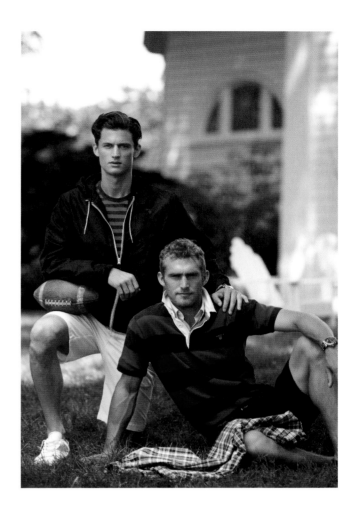

Den typischen Gant-Look kreiert inzwischen Christopher Bastin, Director of Design. Er liebt es farbenfroh, bequem und lässig. American Sportswear ist seine Leidenschaft. Heute ist Gant eine der ältesten Kollektionen in der Geschichte der amerikanischen Premium-Sportswear mit weltweit 700 Shops. Aus der einstigen Herrenhemden-Kollektion hat sich im Laufe von sechs Jahrzehnten eine umfangreiche Casual- und Sportswear-Marke für „men, women, girls, boys and babies" entwickelt. Auch eine Home-Kollektion mit Wohnaccessoires und Bettwäsche, aber auch Uhren, Schuhe, Brillen und Parfüms gehören mittlerweile zum Konzern, der nach dem Verkauf durch die Familie Gant zunächst von der schwedischen Firma Pyramid Sportswear von Stockholm aus betrieben wurde. Damals beteiligte sich auch die weltgrößte Luxus- Unternehmensgruppe, Louis Vuitton Moët Hennessy (LVMH), an Gant. 2008 übernahm die Genfer Maus Frères Group zu 100 Prozent die Marke – mit Erfolg! Ein Jahr später liefen Gant-Models bei der Berliner Mercedes-Benz und bei der New Yorker Fashion Week – und Gant stattete den Deutschen Hockey-Bund (DBH) aus.

Outdoor-Fashion und das Bekenntnis zur Umwelt gehören für Gant zusammen: In jüngerer Vergangenheit engagiert sich das Unternehmen auch für Umweltschutzprojekte, darunter Kooperationen mit dem Umweltaktivisten und Rechtsanwalt Robert F. Kennedy Jr., Neffe des ehemaligen amerikanischen Präsidenten John F. Kennedy, mit Jean-Michel Cousteau, Sohn des legendären Meeresforschers Jacques Cousteau, mit dem weltbekannten National-Geographic-Fotografen Mattias Klum und der berühmten Verhaltensforscherin Dr. Jane Goodall. Neben diesen bekannten Persönlichkeiten steht seit Herbst/Winter 2011/12 ein weiteres Testimonial für Gant: Elettra Rossellini, bildhübsche Tochter von Isabella Rossellini und Enkelin von Ingrid Bergman. Sie ist das neue Gesicht der hochwertigen Damenkollektion „Gant Collection".

Gant's headquarters in New Haven in the 1950s
Gants Firmensitz in New Haven, 1950er-Jahre

Elliot and Marty Gant, sons of Bernard Gant, who founded the company
Elliot und Marty Gant, die Söhne des Unternehmensgründers Bernard Gant

GIMO'S
— SINCE 1968

"Leather is definitely embedded in our DNA."
Renzo Girardin

LEATHER DE LUXE

The story of Gimo's Italiana, the Italian leather manufacturer, begins in 1968 with a single tailor working in the garage of the Girardin family in Monastiero. This is the year in which Adriano Celentano remained at Number 1 in the charts for more than seven weeks with his hit "Azzurro" while the world went completely topsy-turvy with student protests, the hippy movement, the Vietnam war and rock'n'roll. Leather jacket became a symbol of freedom. The firm's name was derived from combining the first two letters of each surname of the firm's two founders, Renzo Girardin and Antoni Moschini, whose interest focused on leather and who concentrated on producing top quality goods in terms of material and finishing. Their aim was to produce individu products which would be coveted for their timeless design. Since it was first estab lished, this family-run firm has specialised in high-end leather clothing for men ar women. When Moschini left the firm in 1985, Girardin upheld the company's poli of combining top-quality raw materials with modern designs and innovative styles

CLOTHES ARE A STATEMENT

Since 1975, the firm's headquarters have been situated in San Martino di Lupari in the Italian province of Padua. Nowadays, its goods are produced in Europe, India and China. After 40 years, Gimo's has secured an established place in international stores and is a symbol of Italian elegance and quality. "The advantage we have is that we are not a 'Total Look' label. We are a designer firm with an instinct for new trends. We offer exceptional jackets made from first-class materials. We love all our products but leather is definitely embedded in our DNA", comments Girardin. And this is exactly what the clientele loves: hand-finished favourites which last a lifetime. Soft to touch, perfectly formed and timelessly elegant. The efforts which go into manufacturing these garments are reflected in their exceptional durability. Hardly surprising that 90 per cent of the firm's clientele are regular customers.

Gimo's has remained a family firm to this day. Girardin's children, Sabrina and Massimo, have joined the family business. In addition to the main menswear line Gimo's daughter Sabrina is responsible for Gimo's women's collection, which is dedicated to the modern business woman. An elegant women's blazer worn with a pair of jeans emphasises femininity, whilst the perfect silhouette of the ever popular suede, epaulette trenchcoat is equally flattering.

The GMS-75 men's and women's line is managed by Massimo, Girardin's son. The clothes in this range are designed with the modern city dweller and individualist in mind and feature unusual textures and innovative finishing processes. Be it a lambskin or motorcycle jacket, clothes are a statement. Whenever possible, Massimo likes to spend his leisure time on the water, sailing up the Italian and Croatian coasts in his motorised yacht. Salt water, seafood and simply relaxing – the kind of Italian lifestyle depicted in films of the 1950s. Although Gimo's has not, as yet, upholstered any boats in leather, it has, however, been responsible for covering several cars.

In 2005, Gimo's hit the headlines when the firm's trade stand at the famous Pitti Uomo fashion fair in Florence exhibited a Smart car, covered inside and out with leather. The calf leather used for the purpose was treated with special oils to make the leather waterproof. In 2006, it was the turn of an MG Cabrio Oldtimer, a legend of the 1950s, to be covered with leather. Two years later, Gimo's presented an exclusive python leather collection, which was advertised by a Fiat 500, likewise completely covered in python leather. Other vehicles in this repertoire included a Vespa and a city bike, designed for the modern dandy – yet another proof that Gimo's loves and lives for individuality.

Gimo's extensive "Fabric" line of mens- and womenswear was introduced in the fall/winter season of 2011/2012. This range is characterised by easy-to-wear designs, which defy the ordinary with their simple elegance and exclusivity. Leather details provide a reminder of this label's original focus.

Three external designers create two new collections a year of each line. These are produced by an in-house team of twelve people. Gimo's meanwhile employs a total of 60 workers. What once began in a small garage has since developed into an international company with an annual turnover of 15 million Euros. It is not surprising, therefore, that the motto of company boss Girardin is: "Never stop pursuing your goals".

Sabrina, Renzo & Massimo Girardin

COMPANY	UNTERNEHMEN
Gimo's Italiana S.p.A.	Gimo's Italiana S.p.A.
FOUNDED IN	GEGRÜNDET
1968 (1975)	1968 (1975)
FOUNDER	GRÜNDER
Renzo Girardin	Renzo Girardin
HEADQUARTERS	HAUPTFIRMENSITZ
San Martino di Lupari	San Martino di Lupari
(Padua), Italy	(Padua), Italien
CEO	GESCHÄFTSFÜHRUNG
Renzo Girardin	Renzo Girardin (Vorstands-
(President), Massimo	vorsitzender), Massimo
Girardin (CEO),	Girardin (Geschäftsfüh-
Sabrina Girardin	rer), Sabrina Girardin
(CEO)	(Geschäftsführerin)
EMPLOYEES	MITARBEITER
60	60
PRODUCTS	PRODUKTE
Men's and Ladies'	Damen- und Herren-
leather / Shearling	oberbekleidung aus
and fabric outerwear	Leder, Fell und Stoff
ANNUAL TURNOVER	JAHRESUMSATZ
15 million Euros	15 Millionen Euro
EXPORT COUNTRIES	EXPORTLÄNDER
Canada, Europe, Japan,	Europa, Japan, Kanada,
Russia, USA	Russland, USA

Gimo's jackets are famous for their outstanding quality and excellent finishing.
Höchste Qualität und beste Verarbeitung zeichnen Gimo's Jacken aus.

LEDER DE LUXE

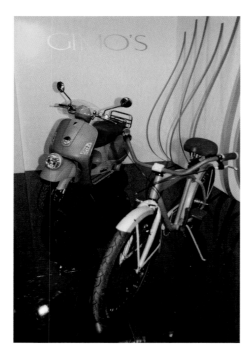

Vespa and city bike finished in leather by Gimo's, "Pitti Uomo", Florence, 2006
Vespa und City-Bike in Lederausstattung von Gimo's, „Pitti Uomo", Florenz 2006

Die Geschichte der italienischen Ledermanufaktur Gimo's Italiana beginnt im Jahre 1968 mit nur einem Schneider in der Garage der Familie Girardin in Monastiero. Es ist das Jahr, in dem Adriano Celentano sich in Italien mit seinem Hit „Azzurro" über sieben Wochen auf Platz eins hält, während die Welt Kopf steht – Studentenaufstände, Hippiebewegung, Vietnamkrieg, Rock'n'Roll. Lederjacken werden zum Symbol für Freiheit. Die beiden Firmengründer, Renzo Girardin und Antonio Moschini, aus deren jeweils ersten beiden Anfangsbuchstaben ihrer Nachnamen sich der Firmenname ergibt, investieren in Leder und legen den Fokus auf höchste Qualität in puncto Material und Verarbeitung. Ihr Ziel: einzigartige Produkte, die durch ihren zeitlosen Charakter bestechen. Der Familienbetrieb ist seit jeher spezialisiert auf High-End-Lederbekleidung für Damen und Herren. Als Moschini 1985 die Firma verlässt, behält Girardin die Strategie bei, qualitativ hochwertige Rohmaterialien mit modernen Schnitten und innovativen Styles zu verbinden.

Seit 1975 hat das Unternehmen seinen Sitz in San Martino di Lupari in der italienischen Provinz Padua. Produziert wird heute in Europa, Indien und China. Nach über 40 Jahren hat sich Gimo's einen festen Platz in den internationalen Stores gesichert und steht für italienische Eleganz und Qualität. „Unser Vorteil ist es, dass wir keine Total-Look-Marke sind. Wir sind eine Designfirma mit Gespür für neue Trends. Wir bieten außerordentliche Jacken aus First-Class-Materialien an. Wir lieben alle unsere Produkte, aber Leder ist definitiv in unserer DNA verankert", so Girardin. Und das ist es, was die Kunden lieben: handgearbeitete Lieblingsstücke, die einen ein Leben lang begleiten. Anschmiegsam, formvollendet, zeitlos schön. Der Aufwand, der in die Fertigung der Kleidungsstücke investiert wird, macht sich durch eine extrem lange Lebensdauer bemerkbar. Kein Wunder, dass 90 Prozent der Kunden Stammkunden sind.

Bis heute ist Gimo's ein Familienunternehmen geblieben. Girardins Kinder, Sabrina und Massimo, sind ins Familiengeschäft hineingewachsen. Neben der Hauptlinie „Gimo's" ist Tochter Sabrina Girardin verantwortlich für die „Gimo's-Women's"-Kollektion, die eine Hommage an die moderne Businessfrau ist. Ein eleganter Damenblazer zur Jeans getragen unterstreicht die Weiblichkeit, der beliebte Wildleder-Trenchcoat mit Epauletten schmeichelt durch seine perfekte Silhouette.

KLEIDUNG IST STATEMENT

Die „GMS-75-Men's-and-Women's"-Linie wird von Sohn Massimo betreut. Die Entwürfe zeichnen sich durch ungewöhnliche Texturen und innovative Verarbeitungsprozesse aus. Zielgruppe ist der moderne Stadtmensch, ein Individualist. Ob Lammfell- oder Motorradjacke – Kleidung ist Statement. Massimo selbst verbringt seine Freizeit am liebsten auf dem Wasser. Mit seiner Motorjacht schippert er entlang der italienischen und kroatischen Küsten. Salzwasser, Sonne, Meeresfrüchte und süßes Nichtstun. Italienischer Lifestyle wie man ihn aus den Filmen der 1950er-Jahre kennt. Ein Boot hat Gimo's noch nicht mit Leder bezogen. Dafür aber schon mehrere Autos.

Im Jahr 2005 sorgte Gimo's genau damit für Schlagzeilen. Auf dem Messestand der berühmten Modemesse „Pitti Uomo" in Florenz wurde ein von innen und außen mit Leder bezogener Smart präsentiert. Das verwendete Kalbsleder wurde mit speziellen Ölen behandelt, um das Leder wasserundurchlässig zu machen. 2006 folgte ein Oldtimer, ein MG Cabrio, der Mythos der 1950er-Jahre, mit Leder bezogen. Zwei Jahre später zeigte Gimo's eine exklusive Kollektion aus Pythonleder, die gemeinsam mit einem komplett mit Pythonleder bezogenen Fiat 500 präsentiert wurde. Auch eine Vespa sowie ein City-Bike für den modernen Dandy gehören zum Repertoire. Ein Zeichen mehr dafür, dass Gimo's Individualität liebt und lebt.

Seit der Saison Herbst/Winter 2011/2012 präsentiert Gimo's die umfangreiche „Fabric"-Linie für Damen und Herren, die sich durch ihre Easy-to-wear-Designs auszeichnet und dem Alltag mit schlichter Eleganz und Exklusivität trotzt. Lederdetails schaffen den Bezug zur ursprünglichen Ausrichtung der Marke. Drei externe Designer entwerfen jährlich zwei Kollektionen je Linie. Die Umsetzung erfolgt durch ein firmeninternes Team von 12 Mitarbeitern. Insgesamt beschäftigt Gimo's heute 59 Mitarbeiter. Was einst in einer kleinen Garage begann, hat sich zu einem weltweit agierenden Unternehmen mit einem Jahresumsatz von 15 Millionen Euro etabliert. Kein Wunder, lautet doch das Motto des Firmenchefs Girardin: „Höre niemals auf, deine Ziele zu verfolgen."

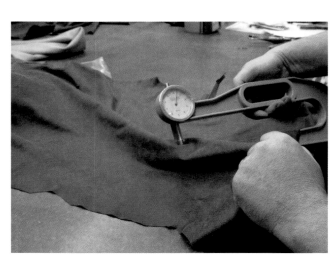

A garment consists of hundreds of separate pieces.
Ein Kleidungsstück besteht aus hunderten Teilen.

GRÄFIN V. LEHNDORFF

"As far as work is concerned, I grew up in Prussia and take after my father when it comes to discipline."
Catharina Gräfin von Lehndorff

WHEN A GOLDSMITH'S ART IS APPLIED TO BELTS

The belts made by the famous goldsmith Catharina Gräfin von Lehndorff are internationally coveted, luxury goods and collector's items made from exclusive leather with elegant buckles of Palladium silver or a gold finish. If you once become the proud owner of one of these belts, you will simply end up wanting more of them even though, in practical terms, more than one is unnecessary since the quality is such that they will last an entire lifetime.

The story of Catharina Gräfin von Lehndorff resembles one of those great family sagas around which novels and films are often based. On 21 July 1944, Catharina's father, Heinrich Graf von Lehndorff, was arrested by the Gestapo at the family seat of Schloss Steinort in East Prussia. He had been exposed as a member of the "Operation Valkyrie" resistance group involved in the previous day's assassination attempt on Adolf Hitler. The untroubled childhood of the Lehndorff sisters, Gabriele, Nona and Veruschka, came to an abruptly violent end. Their pregnant mother, Gottliebe von Lehndorff, was imprisoned. The three older sisters were bundled off to the Borntal NS children's home in Bad Sachsa. Their father was executed on 3 September 1944. When Gottliebe Gräfin von Lehndorff and her new-born baby, Catharina, were united with her other three daughters a few months later, it marked the start of a very different and far more modest lifestyle since they had lost all their possessions and were vilified as traitors to the fatherland. Gottliebe urged her daughters to learn a trade and be creative. Catharina decided to train as a goldsmith. Around this time, her older sister Veruschka von Lehndorff was starting a career as an international model. She frequently took Catharina along to important photo shoots for "Vogue" or "Harper's Bazaar". Shy Catharina travelled with her sister around the world, fashioning artistic costume jewelery for her out of paper and other unusual materials. She found the kind of small, filigree pieces traditionally produced by goldsmiths uninspiring – it had to be big and be born of spontaneity. During photo shoots in Africa and Brazil, she became fascinated by the symbolism of primitive peoples. She tirelessly recorded her impressions in sketchbooks. Her designs are mostly entirely made from metal, for example, series of metal plates joined together, decorated with ornaments or animals. Her older sister, Veruschka, became a fashion icon of the 1970s and a well-known member of the jet set. Wherever she appeared, she wore jewelery created by her sister. However, Catharina had no interest whatsoever in high society. This reserved young woman was happiest spending her time in her subterranean workshop, which echoed until late in the night to the sound of hammering and tapping. During busy periods, Catharina von Lehndorff would work in her basement alongside a staff of 15 young women and even now she still spends much of her time in her studio where she fashions a prototype of each of her designs.

Catharina Gräfin von Lehndorff & Sebastian Spehr

WITH PASSION, HARD WORK AND CREATIVITY

Catharina describes herself in the beginning as a "freelance designer in the hippie look with a mixed array of products". There is a certain element of understatement in this remark as even back in 1979, a young Hamburg designer, who opened a shop in the Milchstrasse, became completely captivated by Catharina's work. So it was that each week, with Prussian reliability, Catharina delivered her latest pieces to the small shop run by an as yet unknown Jil Sander.

Business was soon booming. This single-minded goldsmith set off with her hand-crafted prototypes to Florence where she had her designs turned into substantial quantities of belt buckles, appliqué and decorative work by master craftsmen. Back in her Hamburg workshop, these individual pieces were assembled into belts. The calfskin, reptile skin and ostrich leather for the belts comes from Germany whilst these exclusive pieces are produced in Italy. Her irresistibly eye-catching collection includes belt tips edged in silver, clasps incorporating the letters "CL", buckles in the shape of Indian heads, wings or timeless classics in traditional form. It is precisely because Catharina von Lehndorff is not swayed by short-term fashion trends that her collections are regarded as collector's items and cult objects. Her bestselling product and "must-have" accessory is the belt with the Jaguar motif. It is a favourite worn by Gunter Sachs, Udo Jürgens and Marlon Brando. When the Hollywood star first commissioned his belt from the young designer, she was astonished: "Seven women could easily fit into a belt this size!" Men's belts still constitute the bulk of the business and are sold all over the world in top-class boutiques. It is thanks to Catharina Gräfin von Lehndorff that the belt, once sadly underestimated, has become one of the most important and attractive fashion accessories.

COMPANY Schuchard & Friese GmbH & Co. KG	UNTERNEHMEN Schuchard & Friese GmbH & Co. KG
FOUNDED IN 1896	GEGRÜNDET 1896
FOUNDERS Fam. Schuchard & Fa Friese	GRÜNDER Fam. Schuchard & Fa. Friese
HEADQUARTERS Löhne, Germany	HAUPTFIRMENSITZ Löhne, Deutschland
CEO Peter Beck, Sebastian Spehr	GESCHÄFTSFÜHRUNG Peter Beck, Sebastian Spehr
EMPLOYEES 75	MITARBEITER 75
PRODUCTS Leather belts, i. e. under licence for Gräfin von Lehndorff	PRODUKTE Ledergürtel, u. a. Lizenz für Gräfin von Lehndorff
ANNUAL TURNOVER 15 million Euros	JAHRESUMSATZ 15 Millionen Euro
EXPORT COUNTRIES Austria, Benelux, Russia, Switzerland	EXPORTLÄNDER Benelux, Österreich, Russland, Schweiz

GRÄFIN v. LEHNDORFF
HAMBURG

WENN GOLDSCHMIEDEKUNST ZUM GÜRTEL WIRD

Die Gürtel der Goldschmiedin Catharina Gräfin von Lehndorff sind international begehrte Luxusobjekte und Liebhaberstücke, die aus exklusiven Ledern und mit edlen Schließen mit Palladium-Silber- und Goldfinish gearbeitet sind. Wer einmal so einen Gürtel besitzt, möchte einfach noch mehr davon, obwohl es praktisch gesehen nicht nötig wäre, denn die Gürtel sind von so beständiger Qualität, dass sie einen ein Leben lang begleiten.

Die Geschichte der Catharina Gräfin von Lehndorff erinnert an die großen Familiensagen, die wir unter anderem aus Erzählungen, Romanen und Verfilmungen kennen. Am 21. Juli 1944 wurde Catharinas Vater, Heinrich Graf von Lehndorff, auf dem Familiensitz Schloss Steinort in Ostpreußen von der Gestapo verhaftet – enttarnt als einer der Widerstandskämpfer der „Operation Walküre", des am Tage zuvor gescheiterten Attentats auf Adolf Hitler. Mit brachialer Gewalt endete für die Lehndorff-Schwestern Gabriele, Nona und Veruschka eine unbeschwerte Kindheit. Die schwangere Mutter Gottliebe von Lehndorff wurde inhaftiert. Die drei älteren Schwestern verschleppte man in das NS-Kinderheim Borntal nach Bad Sachsa. Ihr Vater wurde am 3. September 1944 hingerichtet. Als Gottliebe Gräfin von Lehndorff mit der neugeborenen Catharina einige Monate später ihre drei anderen Töchter wieder in die Arme schließen konnte, beginnt ein neues, sehr bescheidenes Leben, denn sie hatten alle Besitztümer verloren und wurden als Vaterlandsverräter geächtet.

Mutter Gottliebe ermutigte ihre Töchter, einen Beruf zu erlernen und kreativ zu sein. Catharina absolvierte eine Ausbildung zur Goldschmiedin. Zu der Zeit begann die Karriere ihrer älteren Schwester Veruschka als international gefragtes Model. Oft nahm sie Catharina mit zu den großen Fotoshootings für die „Vogue" oder „Harper's Bazaar". Die zurückhaltende Catharina reiste mit ihrer Schwester um die Welt und kreierte für sie künstlerischen Modeschmuck aus Papier und anderen ungewöhnlichen Materialien. Kleine filigrane und typische Goldschmiede-Arbeiten fand sie langweilig, groß musste es sein und spontan entstehen. Während der Shootings in Afrika und Brasilien entbrannte ihr Interesse für die Symbolik der Naturvölker. Unermüdlich hielt Catharina ihre Impressionen in Skizzenblöcken fest. Ihre Entwürfe sind meistens komplett aus Metall, viele Platten aneinandergesteckt, verziert mit Ornamenten oder Tiergestalten. Ihre große Schwester Veruschka, die zur Fashion-Ikone der 1970er-Jahre wurde und der der Jetset zu Füßen lag, trug bei all ihren Auftritten die Kreationen der Schwester. Catharina hingegen ließ die High Society kalt. Am liebsten verbrachte die zurückhaltende junge Frau ihre Zeit in ihrer Souterrain-Werkstatt, aus der man bis spät in die Nacht das Hämmern und Nieten hören konnte. In Hochzeiten saß Catharina von Lehndorff mit 15 jungen Frauen in dem Souterrain, und noch heute verbringt sie viel Zeit in ihrem Atelier, denn von jedem ihrer Entwürfe fertigt sie dort den Prototypen an.

MIT BEGEISTERUNG, FLEISS UND KREATIVITÄT AN DIE WELTSPITZE

Sich selbst beschreibt Catharina in ihren beruflichen Anfängen als „freischaffende Gestalterin im Hippielook mit Bauchladenverkauf". Etwas Understatement gehört zu dieser Aussage dazu, denn schon 1979 war eine junge Hamburger Designerin, die einen Laden in der Milchstraße eröffnete, ganz angetan von Catharinas Arbeiten. Und so brachte diese mit preußischer Verlässlichkeit wöchentlich die neuesten Stücke in den kleinen Laden der damals noch unbekannten Jil Sander. Das Geschäft lief bald auf Hochtouren. Mit ihren handgefertigten Prototypen macht sich die eigenwillige Goldschmiedin auf nach Florenz, um dort nach ihrer Vorlage Gürtelschließen, Applikationen und Verzierungen von Kunsthandwerkern in größeren Mengen anfertigen zu lassen. In der Hamburger Werkstatt werden die Einzelteile anschließend zu Gürteln zusammengesetzt. Das Kalbs-, Reptilien- und Straußenleder für die Gürtel kommt aus Deutschland, produziert werden die erlesenen Stücke in Italien. Eingefasste Gürtelspitzen in Silber, Schließen mit den Initialen CL, Schließen in Form von Indianerköpfen, Flügeln oder in zeitlos klassischer Form ziehen unweigerlich den Blick auf sich. Gerade weil sich Catharina von Lehndorff nicht von kurzweiligen Moden beeinflussen lässt, gelten ihre Kollektionen als Sammler- und Kultobjekte.

Zum Must-Have avanciert und das meistverkaufte Modell ist der Gürtel mit den Jaguar-Applikationen. Er schmückte schon die Hüften von Gunter Sachs, Udo Jürgens und Marlon Brando. Als der Hollywood-Star damals seinen Gürtel bei der jungen Designerin in Auftrag gab, versetzte er sie in großes Staunen: „In diese Umfanglänge hätten locker sieben Frauen reingepasst!"

Herrengürtel sind bis heute das Hauptgeschäft und werden weltweit in den nobelsten Boutiquen verkauft. Es ist Catharina Gräfin von Lehndorff zu verdanken, dass der bis dato eher unbeachtete Gürtel zu einem der wichtigsten und schönsten Mode-Accessoires geworden ist.

HABSBURG
— SINCE 1992

"People wear the Habsburg label before, during and after hunting."
Katharina Schneider

NOBLESSE OBLIGE

When the luxury Habsburg label was launched in 1992 – aptly enough at Schloss Blühnbach, a former hunting lodge in Salzburg province – the illustrious guests naturally included His Imperial and Royal Majesty Karl von Habsburg, after whom the brand was named. The idea for this label, which converts the rich historical traditions of the world of hunting parties into high-end fashion was the brainchild of purveyor to the imperial court Zapf in Werfen. He was given permission to use the "Habsburg" name for a hat collection and was looking for someone to manufacture a corresponding clothes collection. Hans Zapf and Alfons Schneider, head of Schneiders, a traditional Salzburg clothing company, knew each other – as one might have guessed – from their hunting activities.

Katharina Schneider, the middle of the three Schneider daughters, has now assumed responsibility for the Kleidermanufaktur Habsburg label. This exclusive label, which is designed to appeal to the stylish clientele of elegant society, is at the heart of the Schneider group. For over 60 years, the family-run firm in Salzburg has been manufacturing elegantly casual fashion with a subtle Austrian touch under the Schneiders and Habsburg labels. "Made in Austria" luxury has been shaped by the practical and social dictates of imperial and royal monarchy. Lovingly crafted, elaborate details such as piped buttonholes, embroidery stitching, rolled and finely finished seams, proper sleeve slits and hand-sewn fastenings show off the quality of the individual material, be it linen, loden, cashmere or fur, to its best advantage. The same care is lavished on accessories such as buttons made from natural materials, including buffalo horn, deer horn or mother-of-pearl. The in-house furrier's workshop is not only involved in producing "stylish formal attire for men and women from the world of hunting parties, gala dinners, tea ceremonies, polo tournaments, garden parties, countryside outings, luxury travel, horse rides and drives" but also supplies a range of garments to delight the huntsman: the outstanding craftsmanship of Wallsee hunting trousers, for example, will guarantee a touch of huntsman-style elegance whether in rural or urban surroundings. Noblesse oblige, a philosophy which is clearly demonstrated by the label's consistent individuality – from the production stage to the firm's image. In 2002, the firm celebrated its 10th anniversary not only by holding an appropriately Habsburg-style party but also by launching a special catalogue campaign. Since then, aristocratic ladies and gentlemen have been appearing in this exclusive catalogue as models for Habsburg. With a good dash of elegant irony, the natural elegance of celebrities such as Katharina von Garzuly-Hohenlohe, Baron Lukas Pius von Geusau and Wello von Wallsee (hunting dog) is showcased in words and pictures. The impressive photographs set against such princely backgrounds are the work of top Austrian photographer Elfie Semotan.

AN UNDERSTANDING OF LIVING TRADITIONS

It goes without saying that the exclusive Habsburg shops, Shop in Shops and showrooms are also run according to the same company philosophy, which is "to enhance the lives of our esteemed customers with the ultimate in exclusive hunting and social clothing". The first Habsburg shop was opened in 2004 in a prominent part of in Kitzbühel in collaboration with a long-standing Habsburg client, the Eder family. In 2008, a second shop was opened in the Old Town of Bad Tölz; this has since been followed by similar cooperative ventures in Vienna, Hamburg, Düsseldorf and Salzburg. Selected specialist retail stores in altogether 12 countries also stock the Habsburg label. The modern-day interpretation of the Imperial look is particularly popular outside Austria.

It is this understanding of living traditions which appeals not only to members of European royal families but also to prominent personalities in show business and the worlds of sport and politics, who enjoy appearing in stylishly elegant outfits bearing this Austrian label. Have you ever wondered where Thomas Gottschalk buys his distinctive wardrobe? Leading lights of elegant society, from Queen Noor of Jordan to Valery Giscard d'Estaing, love that special quality which radiates an Imperial aura and perfectly enhances the individuality of the wearer.

Kaiser Franz Joseph I. hunting in Bad Ischl
Kaiser Franz Joseph I. auf der Jagd in Bad Ischl

COMPANY Kleidermanufaktur Habsburg Ges.m.b.H.	UNTERNEHMEN Kleidermanufaktur Habsburg Ges.m.b.H.
FOUNDED IN 1992	GEGRÜNDET 1992
FOUNDER Alfons Schneider	GRÜNDER Alfons Schneider
HEADQUARTERS Salzburg, Austria	HAUPTFIRMENSITZ Salzburg, Österreich
CEO Katharina Schneider	GESCHÄFTSFÜHRUNG Katharina Schneider
EMPLOYEES 210 (including those at the mother company of Schneiders)	MITARBEITER 210 (zusammen mit der Muttermarke Schneiders)
PRODUCTS "Elegant social clothing" – In- and outdoor clothing for men and women	PRODUKTE „Feine Gesellschaftsbeklei- dung" – In- und Outdoor- bekleidung für Damen und Herren
ANNUAL PRODUCTION Womenswear: approx. 35,000 items Menswear: approx. 20,000 items	JAHRESPRODUKTION Damenoberbekleidung: ca. 35.000 Artikel Herrenoberbekleidung: ca. 20.000 Artikel
EXPORT COUNTRIES Belgium, France, Germany, Italy, Japan, Russia, Spain, Switzerland, The Netherlands, UK, Ukraine, USA	EXPORTLÄNDER Belgien, Deutschland, Frankreich, Italien, Japan, Niederlande, Russland, Schweiz, Spanien, UK, Ukraine, USA

Kleider
Manufaktur
HABSBURG
Feine
Gesellschaftskleidung

In-house furrier's workshop
Hauseigene Kürschnerei

NOBLESSE OBLIGE

Coated cotton canvas bag with deer print
Tasche aus beschichtetem Baumwoll-Canvas mit Hirschdruck

Als die Nobelmarke Habsburg 1992 standesgemäß auf dem ehemaligen Jagd-schloss Blühnbach im Salzburger Land aus der Taufe gehoben wurde, befand sich unter den illustren Gästen selbstverständlich auch der Namenspatron, sei-ne kaiserlich-königliche Hoheit Karl von Habsburg. Die Idee zu einem Label, das den feudalen Glanz einer Jagdgesellschaft in hochwertige Mode umsetzt, kam vom Hutmacher und k. und k. Hoflieferanten Zapf in Werfen. Der hatte die Genehmigung für eine Hutkollektion namens „Habsburg" erhalten und such-te nach einem Hersteller für die dazu passende Kleiderkollektion. Hans Zapf und Alfons Schneider, der Firmenchef des Salzburger Traditionsunternehmens Schneiders, kannten sich – wie sollte es anders sein – von der Jagd.

Katharina Schneider, die mittlere der drei Schneider-Töchter, hat inzwischen die Leitung der Kleidermanufaktur Habsburg übernommen. Die ganz auf eine stilbewusste Klientel der feinen Gesellschaft zugeschnittene Linie ist das Herzstück der Schneider-Gruppe. Seit über 60 Jahren fertigt das Familienun-ternehmen in Salzburg unter den beiden Marken Schneiders und Habsburg sportlich-elegante Mode mit dem diskreten „Austrian touch". Luxus „Made in Austria" ist geschult an den praktischen und gesellschaftlichen Anforderungen der k. und k. Monarchie. Liebevoll gearbeitete, aufwendige Details wie paspelierte Knopflöcher, Stick-Stiche, rollierte und sauber verarbeitete Nähte, echte Ärmelschlitze und handgenähte Handriegel bringen den Materialcharakter von Leinen, Loden, Kaschmir oder Pelz vollendet zur Geltung. Dieselbe Sorgfalt gilt dem Zubehör wie Knöpfen aus Naturmaterialien, Büffelhorn, Hirschhorn oder Perlmutt. Die hauseigene Kürschnerei hat nicht nur ihren Anteil an der Verfeinerung der „Gesellschaftskleidung für Damen und Herren aus der Welt der Jagdgesellschaften, Galadiners und Teezeremonien, Poloturniere, Gartenfeste, Landpartien, Luxusreisen, Ausritte und Ausfahrten", sondern auch an einem Paradestück des Waidmannsglücks: Die mit handwerklichen Details versehene Jagdhose „Wallsee" sorgt nicht nur im ländlichen, sondern auch im städtischen Revier für Waidmannschic. Noblesse oblige. Dieses Motto äußert sich in der Konsequenz des Unternehmensstils – von der Produktion bis zum Firmenauftritt. 2002 wurde das 10-jährige Firmenjubiläum nicht nur mit entsprechendem Habsburger Gepräge gefeiert; man ließ sich dazu auch eine besondere Katalog-Kampagne einfallen. Seither posieren in dem feinen, edel gestalteten Katalog adelige Damen und Herren für Habsburg. Mit einem guten Schuss feiner Ironie inszenieren Bilder und Texte die natürliche Vornehmheit von Akteuren wie Katharina von Garzuly-Hohenlohe, Baron Lukas Pius von Geusau und Jagdhund Wello von Wallsee. Die eindrucksvollen Aufnahmen in fürstlicher Kulisse stammen von der österreichischen Starfotografin Elfie Semotan.

MIT EINEM SELBSTVERSTÄNDNIS FÜR GELEBTE TRADITION

Selbstverständlich sind auch die exklusiven Habsburg-Shops, Shop in Shops und Showrooms auf die Firmenphilosophie ausgerichtet, die also lautet, „mit der nobelsten Jagd- und Gesellschaftsgarderobe das Leben der werten Kunden zu veredeln". Der erste Habsburg-Shop wurde 2004 in Kooperation mit dem langjährigen Habsburg-Kunden Familie Eder in Kitzbühel in prominenter Lage eröffnet. 2008 kam der zweite Shop in der Altstadt von Bad Tölz hinzu; bis heute haben sich entsprechende Kooperationen in Wien, Hamburg, Düsseldorf und Salzburg dazugesellt. Ausgewählte Fachhandelskunden in insgesamt 12 Ländern führen Habsburg-Mode. Gerade im Ausland kommt die moderne Neuinterpretation des imperialen Looks gut an.
Es ist dieses Selbstverständnis der gelebten Tradition, das nicht nur Mitglieder der europäischen Königshäuser überzeugt. Auch die Prominenz aus Showgeschäft, Sport und Politik glänzt gerne in einem stilsicheren Outfit der österreichischen Kleidermanufaktur. Haben Sie sich schon einmal gefragt, woher Thomas Gottschalks ausgefallene Garderobe stammt? Die Souveräne des glatten gesellschaftlichen Parketts, von Königin Nūr von Jordanien bis Valéry Giscard d'Estaing, lieben dieses gewisse Etwas einer imperialen Aura, das die eigene Persönlichkeit aufs Vorteilhafteste umschmeichelt.

Patched frock coat in top-quality Habsburg suede leather
Gepatchter Gehrock aus feinstem Habsburg-Veloursleder

169

Impressions from the factory in Salzburg
Impressionen aus der Manufaktur in Salzburg

Gusswerk showroom, Salzburg
Showroom Gusswerk, Salzburg

HILTL

"430 metres of sewing
thread in every pair of
trousers."
Franz Josef Wolf

PERFECT FIT,
PERFECT FINISH

If trousers had a problem area, then it would be in the knees. After a long day of
sitting behind a desk or spent in meetings, trousers often lose their shape, become baggy and bulge at the knee. The Hiltl company has long since consigned
this problem to history. This Bavarian family firm in Sulzbach-Rosenberg manufactures trousers with a viscose front lining which is 75 centimetres long and
therefore substantially longer than usual. This helps retain their shape in the knee
area. The Hiltl company, which has concentrated exclusively on trouser manufacture since its establishment in 1955, sometimes even receives fan mail in praise
of this and many other sophisticated touches. This is hardly surprising given that
the Hiltl family themselves describe themselves as "quality freaks".
These high standards were set by the company's founder, Fritz Hiltl and his wife
Hedwig, who has taken over the management of the firm since her husband's death:
"We never wanted to be the biggest, just the very best", is the family maxim. To
this end, Hiltl spares no expense when it comes to fabric nor is any manufacturing detail too much trouble. With sales currently topping 600,000 pairs of

trousers to four continents, the company has demonstrated its commitment to this philosophy time and time again. At Hiltl, each production step is governed by five principles: quality, innovation, creativity, individuality and flexibility.

Loyal fans of Hiltl trousers appreciate the label's unmistakeable distinguishing qualities: the front and back pockets are embellished with a meticulously worked, decorative band whilst the waistband has a supple, elastic finish to ensure nothing pinches or constricts the wearer. The pockets are meticulously edged with decorative bar tacks. The so-called eye buttonhole with cross bar tack ensures that the distinctive, Hiltl-specific, genuine horn buttons, which are attached by a special machine specifically designed for the purpose of preventing them from becoming loose, sit in precisely the right place. And, finally, Hiltl trousers also feature nickel-free metal zippers with extra fine teeth. Anyone tempted to kneel in the presence of so much quality can feel reassured in the knowledge that the extra long lining will prevent the fabric from bagging at the knee. At Hiltl, the cutting and sewing is still done by hand. Genuine Hiltl trousers are a masterpiece of precision, requiring meticulous skill. Some 430 metres of sewing thread goes into every pair of trousers "with four to five stitches per centimetre to be on the safe side", boasts Franz Josef Wolf, managing director at Hiltl, adding that "three is the usual number".

"TOP QUALITY AND THE LATEST NANO TECHNOLOGY"

Hiltl's extensive trouser collections are only supplied to the most exclusive men's outfitters. The trousers range from casual, lightweight, linen summer trousers to classic jeans and stretch microcord as well as exclusive business trousers made from pure new wool or the new superfine, carded yarn flannel. In addition to this unmatched fabric quality, Hiltl also sets great store on design and innovative materials. Examples of this include the natural stretch, fashioned for Hiltl by the famous Ermenegildo Zegna, the wool-and-silk mix "Light Dream" by Loro Piana and the superfine cotton trousers by Hiltl which incorporate a windproof concept based on nanotechnology: in extremely windy conditions, these trousers keep the wind out more efficiently than normal trousers made of winter cotton, yet retain good breathability at the same time. The trousers get their velvety smooth finish thanks to a highly sophisticated, emery-based production procedure.

Most quality fabrics are made from Giza cotton, a long-staple Egyptian cotton with an "air-conditioning feeling". The fabric is so light and airy that it keeps the wearer pleasantly cool in summer. With a view to expanding its wool and cotton product range, Hiltl has also delved into the company archives – where old pattern books have revealed some fantastic fabric structures. New additions to the Hiltl collection are cotton chinos, hard-wearing trousers made from triple-twisted yarn, which offer a perfect alternative to denim. For those who are unable to forego their jeans, Hiltl offers a luxury version: a cotton and cashmere stretch denim in blue, black or grey. The range of colours in leisurewear trousers, which in many cases are non-iron and "ready to go", is already greater than ever before. Subtle natural tones and shades of grey have been augmented by strong greens, reds and purples.

"For decades, we have hung onto details which other manufacturers have long since rationalised out of existence thanks to price pressure in the textile industry", comments Franz Josef Wolf, who likes to demonstrate some of the advantages of his product by pouring a few drops of coffee onto a leg of his trousers and watching it run off the material. "Our strength lies in consistently first-rate quality and the latest nanotechnology." It is with this attitude that this trouser-manufacturing stronghold in the Upper Palatinate defies all national and international competition.

Franz Josef Wolf & Ingrid Scharf

COMPANY	UNTERNEHMEN
Fritz Hiltl Hosenfabrik	Fritz Hiltl Hosenfabrik
GmbH & Co.	GmbH & Co.
FOUNDED IN	GEGRÜNDET
1955	1955
FOUNDERS	GRÜNDER
Hedwig and Fritz Hiltl	Hedwig und Fritz Hiltl
HEADQUARTERS	HAUPTFIRMENSITZ
Sulzbach-Rosenberg,	Sulzbach-Rosenberg,
Germany	Deutschland
CEO	GESCHÄFTSFÜHRUNG
Hedwig Hiltl (Proprietor),	Hedwig Hiltl (Inhaberin),
Ingrid Scharf (Managing	Ingrid Scharf (Geschäfts-
Director), Franz Josef Wolf	führerin), Franz Josef Wolf
(Managing Director)	(Geschäftsführer)
EMPLOYEES	MITARBEITER
120	120
PRODUCTS	PRODUKTE
High-class men's trousers	Hochwertige Herrenhosen
ANNUAL PRODUCTION	JAHRESPRODUKTION
Approx. 600,000 pairs of	Ca. 600.000
trousers	Hosen
EXPORT COUNTRIES	EXPORTLÄNDER
Worldwide, 45 countries	Weltweit, 45 Länder

Hiltl

HOSEN VOM BESTEN

Hedwig Hiltl, proprietor
Hedwig Hiltl, Inhaberin

PERFEKT IM SITZ.
PERFEKT IM DETAIL

Wenn Hosen Problemzonen hätten, dann wären es die Knie. Nach einem langen Tag hinter dem Schreibtisch oder im Meeting verlieren sie häufig die Form, werden schlaff und beulen aus. Diese „Hosen-Tücke" ist beim Unternehmen Hiltl längst Vergangenheit. Denn in dem bayerischen Familienunternehmen aus Sulzbach-Rosenberg werden die Viskose-Vorderfutter der Hosenmodelle mit 75 Zentimetern wesentlich länger als üblich zugeschnitten. So bleibt die Kniepartie in Form. Dank dieser und vieler anderer Raffinessen kommt bei der Firma Hiltl, in der seit ihrer Gründung 1955 ausschließlich Hosen gefertigt werden, sogar ab und zu Fanpost an. Kein Wunder, denn die Mitglieder der Familie Hiltl bezeichnen sich selbst als „Qualitätsfreaks".
Die hohen Standards des Unternehmens setzten schon Firmengründer Fritz Hiltl und seine Frau Hedwig, die seit dem Tod ihres Mannes das Unternehmen leitet: „Wir wollen nicht die Größten sein, sondern die Besten", lautet das Credo. Dafür ist Hiltl kein Material zu kostbar und kein Arbeitsschritt zu viel. Das stellt die Hosenfabrik, die mittlerweile jährlich über 600.000 Hosen auf vier Kontinenten verkauft, immer wieder unter Beweis. Denn bei Hiltl bestimmen fünf Grundsätze jeden Arbeitsgang: Qualität, Innovation, Kreativität, Individualität und Flexibilität.
Liebhaber schätzen die Marke wegen ihrer unverwechselbaren Erkennungszeichen: Die Vorder- und Gesäßtaschen sind mit einem sorgfältig gearbeiteten

Zierriegel versehen, dabei wird der Bund geschmeidig und elastisch gehalten, damit beim Tragen nichts zwickt und einengt. Die Tascheneingriffe schmücken aufwendige und dekorative Zierriegel. Das sogenannte Augenknopfloch mit Querriegel gibt dem typischen Hiltl-Knopf aus echtem Horn, der mit einer eigens angefertigten Spezialmaschine nahezu unverlierbar angenäht ist, perfekten Halt. Und nicht zuletzt zeichnet sich der Hiltl-Reißverschluss durch extra feinzahniges und nickelfreies Metall aus. Wer bei so viel Qualität in die Knie geht, ist vor dem Ausbeulen des Stoffes durch das extralange Innenfutter geschützt.

Bei Hiltl wird auch heute noch von Hand geschnitten und genäht. Eine echte Hiltl ist Millimeterarbeit und erfordert Fingerspitzengefühl. 430 Meter Nähgarn werden in jeder Hose vernäht, „der Sicherheit wegen mit vier bis fünf Stichen pro Zentimeter", schwärmt Franz Josef Wolf, Geschäftsführer bei Hiltl, und ergänzt, üblich seien drei.

Tailored waistband with eye buttonhole
Schneiderbund mit Augenknopfloch

„TOP-QUALITÄT UND NEUESTE NANO-TECHNOLOGIE"

Mit seinen umfangreichen Hosenkollektionen beliefert Hiltl nur die besten Herrenausstatter. Das Angebot reicht von sportlichen Sommerhosen aus luftigem Leinen über klassische Jeans und Mikrocord mit Stretch bis hin zu exklusiven Businesshosen aus reiner Schurwolle und dem neuen superweichen Streichgarnflanell. Neben den bekannten Stoffqualitäten stellt Hiltl auch hohe Ansprüche an Design und innovative Stoffe. Dazu zählt beispielsweise der Naturstretch, den die Nobelmarke Ermenegildo Zegna für Hiltl herstellt, der Wolle-Seide-Mix „Light Dream" von Loro Piana oder die extrem weiche Baumwoll-Hose von Hiltl mit Windproof-Concept und Nano-Ausrüstung, die, wenn es kräftig stürmt, weniger durchlässt als eine normale Hose aus Winterbaumwolle und dennoch atmungsaktiv bleibt. Ihren seidigweichen Griff erhält die Hose übrigens durch das hochmoderne Schmirgel-Verfahren in der Stoffherstellung.

Die meisten Qualitätsstoffe sind aus Giza-Baumwolle gefertigt, einer langstapeligen, ägyptischen Baumwolle mit „Aircondition Feeling". Der Stoff ist so luftig, dass er im Sommer angenehm kühlt. Um den Woll- und Baumwollbereich zu erweitern, hat Hiltl außerdem einen Blick in die Firmenarchive gewagt – und dort in den alten Musterbüchern fantastische Stoffstrukturen wiederentdeckt. Newcomer bei Hiltl sind die Baumwoll-Chinos, robuste Hosen mit dreifach-gezwirntem Garn als perfekte Alternative zu Denim. Wer nicht auf Jeans verzichten möchte, dem bietet die Hosen-Manufaktur auch eine Luxusvariante: einen Baumwoll-Kaschmir-Stretch-Denim in Blau, Schwarz und Grau. Ohnehin ist die Farbvielfalt bei den Freizeithosen, den häufig bügelfreien „ready to go"-Hosen, so groß wie nie. Dezente Natur- und Grautöne werden durch kräftige Grün-, Rot- und Purpurtöne ergänzt.

High-rise storage for the merchandise
Hochlager für die Kundenwaren

„Wir halten seit Jahrzehnten an Details fest, die andere unter dem Preisdruck in der Textilwirtschaft längst wegrationalisiert haben", sagt Franz Josef Wolf, der gerne die Vorzüge seiner Ware demonstriert, indem er ein paar Tropfen Kaffee oder Cola auf ein Hosenbein gießt und sie abperlen lässt. „Unsere Stärke ist eben kontinuierliche Top-Qualität und neueste Nano-Technologie." Auf diese Weise trotzt die Oberpfälzer Hosen-Hochburg der nationalen und internationalen Konkurrenz.

Company headquarters in Sulzbach-Rosenberg, 1968
Der Hiltl-Firmensitz in Sulzbach-Rosenberg, 1968

Fritz Hiltl at the Men's Fashion Week, Cologne, 1958
Fritz Hiltl auf der Herrenmodewoche, Köln 1958

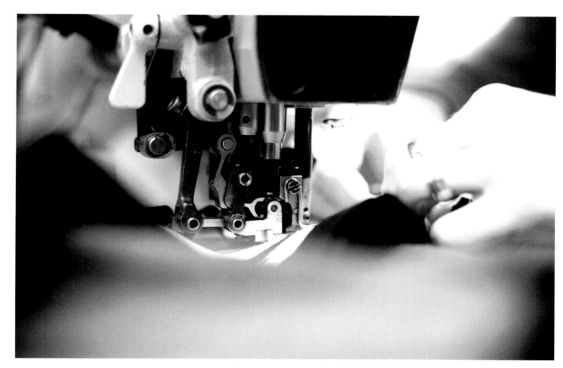

The waistband is carefully attached.
Sorgfältig wird der Hosenbund
aufgenäht.

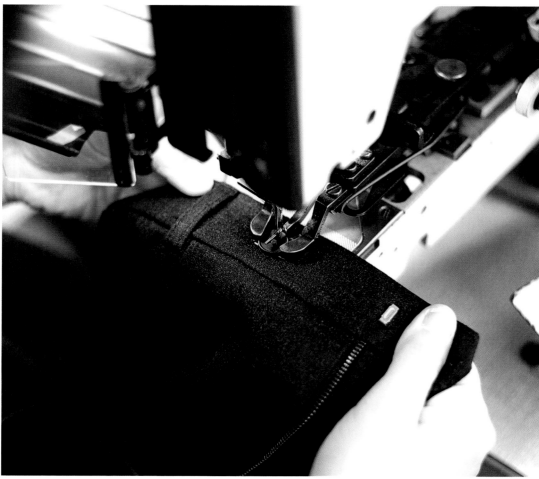

The buttons are sewn on by machine
with a shank.
Die Knöpfe werden mit der Maschine
auf Stiel genäht.

Raw materials warehouse
Rohwarenlager

179

HOHENBERGER

— SINCE 1884

"We aim to create exclusive products with a feel-good factor which are both light-weight and warm at the same time."

Thomas Hohenberger

THE STUFF OF DREAMS – DOWNY GOAT HAIR

To hear the passion with which Thomas Hohenberger, the firm's chief designer, talks about cashmere, one might almost think he had invented this luxury fabric. "We gently roughen the cashmere using the finest natural thistles, then carefully dye it", explains Weberei Hohenberger's creative director, stroking the fluffy texture of the newly woven fabric. "The plaids and scarves retain their incredible softness and feel-good character for many years." This traditional weaving mill can look back on a long history. It was founded in 1884 by Heinrich Hohenberger in the Bavarian town of Hof in Upper Franconia. For many decades, the precious wool was spun on hand looms until 1949 when the employees were trained to use mechanised looms. The family firm is now run by Sabine Weidner-Dietel and Thomas Hohenberger. Located in an old building in the centre of Hof, 20

Thomas Hohenberger & Sabine Weidner-Dietel

employees produce an annual 500,000 scarves, plaids, and super-soft blankets made from the finest cashmere and lambswool.

"Turning it into something special requires fashion creativity and long experience", comments Thomas Hohenberger, as he passes through the production hall where the weaving looms hum away, weaving the fine cashmere threads. The Hohenberger weaving mill has succeeded in applying years of accumulated knowledge of materials and manufacturing processes to contemporary fashions. In so doing, it is drawing on the experience of four generations. The downy hair of the cashmere goat is combed out by hand. Quantities of the wool, supplied by China and Mongolia, are stored on site in a large warehouse for raw materials. The fibres are gently roughened using thistles and worked into a fine, double-threaded yarn. It is not surprising that cashmere is regarded as the proud, beautiful queen of textiles when one considers how it is gathered: each floppy-eared, cashmere goat produces a mere 100 grams of wool during its annual moult – even a single scarf requires 150 grams.

"A SCARF IS NOT SIMPLY JUST A SCARF"

Once completed, these precious examples of weaving craftsmanship are subjected to one final check by an expert eye before being supplied to dozens of individual retailers. The spring / summer season is becoming increasingly important in this respect as cashmere is not only extremely light but also provides warmth on cool evenings. Scarves and shawls with a shimmery finish are particularly elegant. The material undergoes a process involving pressurised water which produces a wavy effect, causing it to shimmer like mother-of-pearl when the light hits it in a certain way. "The feel and silky finish must be absolutely right", explains Thomas Hohenberger, holding up a cashmere scarf, which is so soft and fluffy that it almost looks as if air has been whisked into it. "We want to create exclusive products with a feel-good factor which are both lightweight and warm at the same time."

Unlike the woven cashmere products, the knitted scarves are produced using knitting needles. The sheep's wool, imported from Australia, is knitted using flat or circular knitting techniques, sometimes loosely knit, sometimes finely knit, in cable knit or as a cablenet application, patterned with stripes, bobbles or diamonds or in classic, elegant single colours. The various processing methods also include what is probably the quickest and most traditional production technique for making lambswool scarves: open, lace-like "raschel" knitting. By combining different weaving and knitting techniques, it is possible to create silky, soft fringed scarves.

In addition to its wealth of expertise, the Hohenberger weaving company offers yet another special service which sets it apart from its competitors: "We design and produce cashmere and lambswool scarves or even elegant shawls which are individually made to order", says the creative director. "You can have your own private label reflecting your own personal requirements."

COMPANY	UNTERNEHMEN
Weberei Hohenberger GmbH	Weberei Hohenberger GmbH
FOUNDED IN	GEGRÜNDET
1884	1884
FOUNDER	GRÜNDER
Heinrich Hohenberger	Heinrich Hohenberger
HEADQUARTERS	HAUPTFIRMENSITZ
Hof, Germany	Hof, Deutschland
CEO	GESCHÄFTSFÜHRUNG
Sabine Weidner-Dietel, Thomas Hohenberger	Sabine Weidner-Dietel, Thomas Hohenberger
EMPLOYEES	MITARBEITER
20	20
PRODUCTS	PRODUKTE
Scarves, plaids and blankets	Schals und Tücher, Plaids und Decken
ANNUAL PRODUCTION	JAHRESPRODUKTION
500,000 items	500.000 Artikel
EXPORT COUNTRIES	EXPORTLÄNDER
Asia, Europe, North America	Asien, Europa, Nordamerika

HOHENBERGER
MANUFAKTUR SEIT 1884

TRÄUME AUS ZIEGENFLAUMHAAR

Wenn man hört, wie leidenschaftlich Chefdesigner Thomas Hohenberger über Kaschmir spricht, könnte man meinen, er hätte das Luxusmaterial erfunden. „Bei uns wird Kaschmir mit feinsten Naturdisteln behutsam angeraut und schonend gefärbt", sagt der kreative Kopf der Weberei Hohenberger und streicht mit der Hand über die flauschige Textur eines gerade gewebten Tuches. „So sind die Plaids und Schals noch nach Jahren extrem weich und behalten ihren Wohlfühlcharakter." Die Traditionsweberei kann auf eine lange Firmengeschichte zurückblicken: Gegründet wurde sie 1884 von Heinrich Hohenberger im oberfränkischen Hof. Dort wurde die edle Wolle jahrzehntelang auf Handwebstühlen verarbeitet, bevor die Mitarbeiter 1949 auf die maschinelle Fertigung umgeschult wurden. Heute leiten Sabine Weidner-Dietel und Thomas Hohenberger das Familienunternehmen. In einem Altbau im Zentrum von Hof produzieren sie mit 20 Mitarbeitern jährlich rund 500.000 Schals, Plaids, Tücher und kuschelweiche Decken aus feinstem Kaschmir und Lambswool.

„Um daraus etwas Besonderes zu machen, bedarf es modischer Kreativität und gereifter Erfahrung", sagt Thomas Hohenberger und läuft durch die Fertigungshalle, in der die Webstühle mit einem summenden „risch rasch risch" die feinen Kaschmirfäden umwälzen.

Die Weberei hat das Kunststück vollbracht, überliefertes Know-how über Material und Herstellungsverfahren zeitgemäß umzusetzen. Dabei macht sie sich die Erfahrung von vier Generationen zunutze: Das Flaumhaar der Kaschmirziege, das in einem großen Rohwarendepot mit Lieferungen aus China und der Mongolei ständig verfügbar vor Ort lagert, wird in Handarbeit ausgekämmt. Die Fasern werden anschließend mit Disteln leicht angeraut und zu einem feinen, zweifädigen Gewebe verarbeitet. Warum Kaschmir als die stolze, schöne Königin der Textilien gilt, wird deutlich, wenn man sich die „Gewinnung" vor Augen führt: Jede schlappohrige Kaschmirziege liefert während ihres jährlichen Fellwechsels nur rund 100 Gramm Wolle – für einen einzigen Schal werden jedoch schon 150 Gramm benötigt.

„EIN SCHAL IST NICHT EINFACH NUR EIN SCHAL"

Die fertig gewebten, handwerklichen Preziosen werden noch einmal mit Kennerblicken geprüft, bevor sie an Dutzende Einzelhändler ausgeliefert werden. Dabei wird die Frühjahr-/Sommersaison immer wichtiger, weil Kaschmir einerseits extrem leicht ist, andererseits an kühlen Abenden aber auch wärmt. Besonders exquisit wirken Schals und Tücher, die mit Wasserglanz veredelt sind. Dazu wird das Material mit unter Druck gesetztem Wasser behandelt und bekommt ein welliges Profil, was es je nach Lichteinfall wie Perlmutt schimmern lässt. „Der Griff und die Geschmeidigkeit müssen stimmen", erklärt Thomas Hohenberger und hält einen Kaschmirschal hoch, der so duftig und locker fällt, als wäre Luft untergeschlagen worden. „Wir wollen wertige Produkte mit Wohlfühlcharakter schaffen, leicht und zugleich wärmend."

Above: Wooden rollers of the fulling machine
Below: Threads on the loom
Oben: Holzwalzen der Walkmaschine
Unten: Fäden im Webstuhl

Im Unterschied zu den gewebten Kaschmirprodukten entstehen die Strickschals auf Nadeln. Die Schafwolle, die aus Australien kommt, wird im Flach- oder Rundstrickverfahren verarbeitet, mal grobmaschig, mal fein, mit Zopfmuster oder Cablenet-Applikationen, mit Streifen-, Tupfen- und Rhomben-Muster oder klassisch schick in uni. Auch das wohl schnellste und traditionellste Produktionsverfahren bei der Herstellung von Lambswool-Schals, das sogenannte maschenlose „Rascheln", zählt zu den Verarbeitungsmethoden. Durch die Mischung aus Web- und Stricktechnik gelingt es, geschmeidig-weiche Fransen-Schals herzustellen.

Neben der gewachsenen Expertise hebt sich die Weberei Hohenberger auch noch durch einen besonderen Service von ihren Wettbewerbern ab: „Wir designen und fertigen Kaschmir- und Lambswool-Schals oder sogar edle Tuche nach individuellen Wünschen", erklärt der Kreativchef. „So entsteht ein kleines ‚private label' nach den ganz persönlichen Vorstellungen eines Kunden."

Above: Preparing for the fulling process
Below: Roughing machine with natural thistles
Oben: Vorbereitung zum Walkprozess
Unten: Raumaschine mit Naturdisteln

Pages/Seiten 186–187:
Cashmere scarves after fulling
Kaschmirschals nach dem Walken

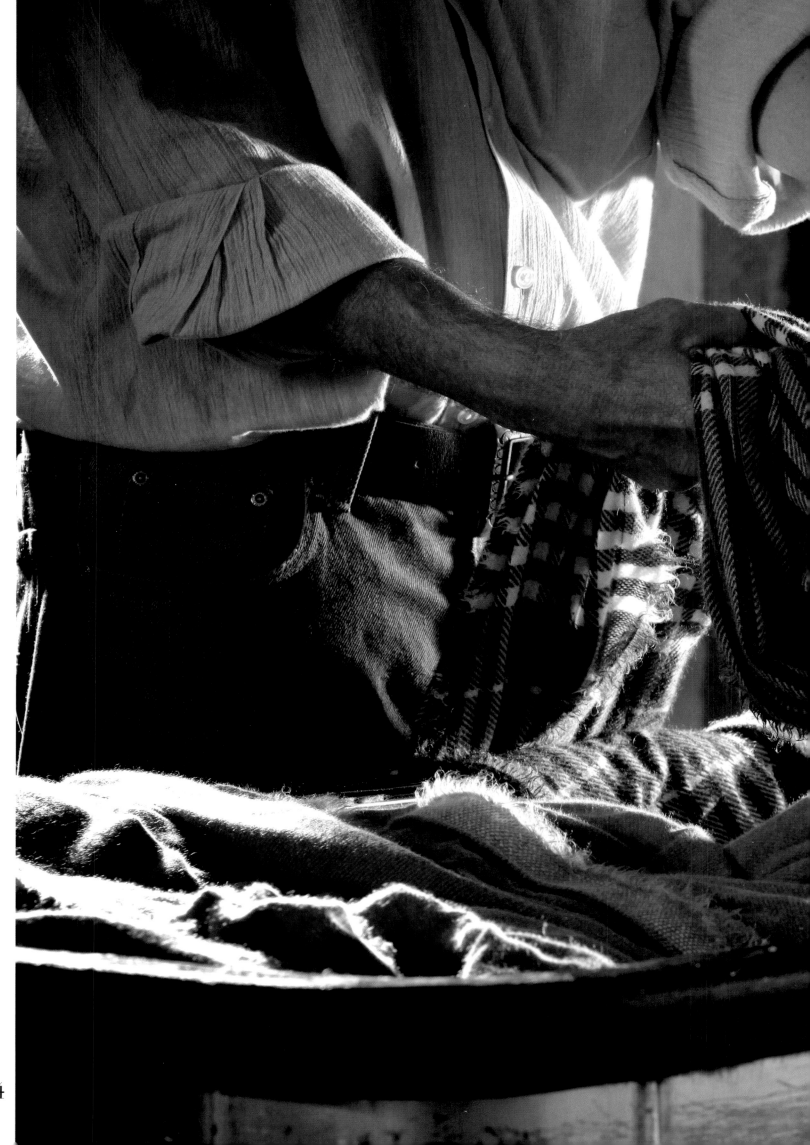

KAPRAUN
— SINCE 1961

"Leather manufacturing
is an art form."
Heinz Kapraun

EVERY PIECE IS UNIQUE

Not a scratch, not even the tiny mark left by a mosquito bite must be visible on the lamb- or goatskin since the selected piece of leather determines the quality of the jacket which is to be fashioned out of it. Armin Graeser, who runs the Kapraun leather goods businesses in Großostheim-Ringheim near Aschaffenburg with Herbert Schreier, is extremely particular about this. No two pieces of leather are alike which is why every leather garment is unique. "It is the slight variations which determine the character of the product," comments Armin Graeser.

FINEST QUALITY FROM ANTELOPE TO GOATSKIN

The finest leather comes from tanneries in Italy and Spain. As with a work of art, the provenance of the leather is an important factor when purchasing the raw

Heinz Kapraun

material. "Reindeer leather, for example, is only imported from Scandinavia, which produces the best raw material", he explained. "When it's available, we also use antelope and kangaroo leather. It goes without saying that we only use the hides of animals which are a by-product of food production."

So-called "neo-classics", in other words, classic styles which have incorporated various sophisticated details such as coloured lining and modern style variations to reflect current seasonal trends, are among Kapraun's best-selling lines. For instance, an azure-blue leather jacket may sometimes feature among the usual black or brown. Whatever the style, the key factor is the lightness of the material – be it glove-soft lamb nappa leather or feather-light goatskin suede leather. What distinguishes this company more than anything else is its manufacturing tradition: "We do everything ourselves, from buying the materials, such as genuine horn buttons and high-quality linings, to fashioning the templates and patterns." The clean look will stay, reveals the firm's managing director, but with the addition of some vintage touches, short styles and aviator-style blouson jackets with knitted waists. Even quilted down jackets are on the agenda. "The design department and technicians just have to make sure that the styles created by the Italian chief designer are actually workable", comments Armin Graeser with a grin.

From time to time, Heinz Kapraun, the firm's founder, stops by. He launched his first collection back in 1961. His sun-tanned face, scored by laughter lines, bears testimony to a full (professional) life. Quality was always paramount in his eyes. Well-defined lines, harmonious proportions, distinctive colours and first-rate materials were among his top priorities. And, during the course of numerous training sessions, he taught his staff everything there was to know about leather. No wonder that he is often nicknamed "the leather pope".

CONFIDENT UNDERSTATEMENT WITH A BIG IMPACT

Kapraun now ranks as one of Europe's top leather manufacturers. The company's excellent reputation is due to an in-depth knowledge of leather and a high level of expertise as well as sophisticated creative vision. Its unmistakeable classic / modern signature is still just as authentic after 50 years as it was at the beginning. Kapraun also leads the way in terms of technology: the label is renowned for its ultra-lightweight, quilted down jackets, as well as its waterproof leather "dry suit" and patented "hot seal" technique used to seal the seams.

The luxury element is in the detail. "Even the inner linings are made from top-quality materials, which others would use on the outside", remarks the managing director, "such as cashmere from Piacenza, one of the most exclusive wool spinning companies in the world". The Kapraun label attaches little importance to chasing after the latest trends since this brand of leather jacket is more about timeless classics. The focus is not on fleeting hype but on the wearer's personal attitude towards life: elegant understatement with a big impact is better than a brief moment in the limelight.

COMPANY	UNTERNEHMEN
Heinz Kapraun	Heinz Kapraun
Ledermoden GmbH	Ledermoden GmbH
und Co. KG	und Co. KG
FOUNDED IN	GEGRÜNDET
1961	1961
FOUNDER	GRÜNDER
Heinz Kapraun	Heinz Kapraun
HEADQUARTERS	HAUPTFIRMENSITZ
Großostheim-Ringheim,	Großostheim-Ringheim,
Germany	Deutschland
CEO	GESCHÄFTSFÜHRUNG
Herbert Schreier,	Herbert Schreier,
Armin Graeser	Armin Graeser
EMPLOYEES	MITARBEITER
50	50
PRODUCTS	PRODUKTE
Men's leatherjackets	Herrenlederjacken
ANNUAL PRODUCTION	JAHRESPRODUKTION
30,000 jackets	30.000 Jacken
EXPORT COUNTRIES	EXPORTLÄNDER
Worldwide, 43 countries	Weltweit, 43 Länder

KAPRAUN

FINEST LEATHER

JEDES STÜCK EIN UNIKAT

Kein Kratzer, nicht einmal das Pünktchen eines Mückenstiches darf auf dem Lamm- oder Ziegenleder zu sehen sein, denn das ausgewählte Leder entscheidet über die Qualität der Jacke, die daraus entstehen soll. Hierauf legt Armin Graeser, der gemeinsam mit Herbert Schreier die Geschäfte des Ledermodenherstellers Kapraun in Großostheim-Ringheim bei Aschaffenburg leitet, größten Wert. Keine Lederhaut gleicht der anderen, daher ist jedes Kleidungsstück aus Leder ein Unikat. „Die leichten Ledervarianten machen den Charakter des Produkts aus", sagt Armin Graeser.

BESTE QUALITÄT VON ANTILOPE BIS ZIEGE

Die besten Qualitäten liefern Gerbereien in Italien und Spanien. Wie bei einem Kunstwerk spielt beim Ledereinkauf auch die gute Provenienz eine Rolle. „Rentierleder etwa beziehen wir nur aus Skandinavien, dort gibt es die beste Rohware" erklärt Graeser. „Wenn der Markt es hergibt, verarbeiten wir auch Antilopen- oder Känguruleder. Selbstverständlich verwenden wir nur Felle von Tieren, die aus der Nahrungsproduktion stammen."
Sogenannte Neo-Klassiker, klassische Schnitte, die mit raffinierten Details wie farbigem Futter und zeitgemäßen Schnittvariationen die Trends der Saison auf-

greifen, gehören zu den Bestsellern von Kapraun. Da darf die Lederjacke statt schwarz oder braun auch mal azurblau glänzen. Stilübergreifend ist dabei die Leichtigkeit der Materialien – ob handschuhweiches Lammnappa oder federleichtes Ziegenvelours. Was das Unternehmen besonders auszeichnet, das ist sein Manufaktur-Charakter: „Wir machen alles selbst, vom Einkauf des Zubehörs, wie echter Hornknöpfe und hochwertiger Futterstoffe, bis hin zur Anfertigung der Schablonen und Schnittmuster." Die cleane Optik bleibe, verrät der Geschäftsführer, dazu kommen Vintage-Optiken, kurze Passformen und Fliegerblousons mit Strickbündchen. Selbst daunengefütterte Lederjacken sind im Programm. „Das Designgremium und die Techniker müssen nur darauf achten, dass sich die Schnitte des italienischen Chefdesigners auch realisieren lassen", sagt Armin Graeser und schmunzelt.

Ab und zu schaut der Firmengründer Heinz Kapraun vorbei. Bereits 1961 lancierte er die erste Kollektion. Sein gebräuntes Gesicht mit den Lachfalten verrät ein erfülltes (Berufs-)Leben. Qualität stand bei ihm immer an erster Stelle. Klare Linien, harmonische Proportionen, individuelle Farben und feinste Materialien gehörten auch zu seinen Prämissen. Er vermittelte seinen Mitarbeitern in zahlreichen Schulungen alles, was man über die Lederverarbeitung wissen sollte. Kein Wunder, dass ihn viele den „Lederpapst" nennen.

SOUVERÄNES UNDERSTATEMENT MIT GROSSER WIRKUNG

Inzwischen zählt Kapraun zur europäischen Spitzenklasse der Lederverarbeiter. Sein Renommee verdankt das Unternehmen neben einem profunden Leder-Know-how und hoher Handwerkskunst seiner souveränen kreativen Vision. Es ist die unverwechselbare klassisch-moderne Handschrift, die auch nach 50 Jahren noch so authentisch ist wie am ersten Tag. Zudem setzt Kapraun technologisch Maßstäbe: Bekannt ist die Marke u. a. für ihre ultraleichten Stepp-Daunenjacken, ihr wetterfestes Leder „Dry Suit" und die patentierte „Hot Seal"-Technologie zur Verschweißung der Nähte.

Prototypes are produced in the in-house studio and perfected down to the last detail.
Prototypen werden im hauseigenen Atelier von Hand erstellt und bis ins Detail perfektioniert.

Der Luxus steckt im Detail. „Selbst für Innenfutter verwenden wir feinste Materialien, die andere nach außen kehren würden", so der Geschäftsführer. „Etwa Kaschmir aus Piacenza, einer der exklusivsten Wollspinnereien der Welt." Die Jagd nach neuen Trends rückt bei Kapraun jedoch in den Hintergrund, denn das Lederlabel setzt auf zeitlose Wertigkeit. Betont wird nicht der flüchtige Hype, sondern das persönliche Lebensgefühl: Lieber ein gepflegtes Understatement mit großer Wirkung als ein kurzer Auftritt im Rampenlicht.

KLEMANN SHOES

— SINCE 1986

"A shoe must fit so well
that you forget you are
wearing it."
Benjamin Klemann

PRECIOUS AND DURABLE

We do not know what impelled Benjamin Klemann to take up a shoemaker's
apprenticeship in 1980 after graduating from high school and completing his
civilian service but he certainly has not lived to regret his decision. The beginning of his story reads like an excerpt from a book about the glorious days of
travelling craftsmen: having learnt his trade under Harai, the great Hungarian
master in the art of shoemaking, this young apprentice from the North Friesian
island of Föhr set forth into the wide world. He spent time in London where
he learnt from the traditional English school of craftsmanship and gradually
worked his way up in prestigious firms such as John Lobb, supplier to the Queen,
the Duke of Edinburgh and the Prince of Wales before setting up in business on
his own in 1986.

Klemann's exclusive shoes are the product of experiences gleaned from the two
main traditional schools of "shoe construction" and reflect the instinctive sensi-

tivity of a culture which provides style-conscious people with a sense of physical and mental well-being. Innumerable hours of patient manual work, fine leather, a perfect fit: all these are part of the firm's general philosophy and approach to life, which envelops the customer right from the start. The elegant building on Hamburg's Poolstrasse, which is now home to "Klemann Shoes" and incorporates living quarters, a workshop and showroom under one roof, is a symbol of the harmony between life and work. It seems entirely plausible when Benjamin Klemann claims that his company's philosophy revolves around taking pleasure in work (even on difficult days) and taking pleasure in creating something precious and lasting in the community.

DIALOGUE WITH THE CLIENT HAS TOP PRIORITY

His enthusiasm has also infected his wife and children. Magrit Klemann joined the family firm once the children were a little older and became a master shoemaker herself in 1997, thereby investing the firm with certified specialist status. Meanwhile, the two sons Lennert and Vincent have also joined the family firm as master shoemakers in their own right. The entire team consists of eight members. Even so, it is obviously still useful to have good allies: for the past 20 years, Benjamin Klemann and his shoes spend the first Saturday of every month doing the rounds of leading men's outfitters in Berlin, Münster and Düsseldorf. Discussions take place on the respective qualities of horsehide, calf leather and sharkskin, the advantages of welt-stitching and glazed edges and the superiority of Russia leather. These meetings serve to cultivate contacts and attract new clients.

This dialogue with the client has top priority in the development of a pair of shoes. These are always unique not only in shape but also in the choice of material, colour and style. The customer's individual style of dress must likewise be taken into account as the perfect shoe completes the wearer's overall appearance. Before work begins on constructing the shoe, a last must be fashioned from beech wood which replicates the individual foot. The last is the secret to creating the perfect fit – if this is not absolutely right, the shoe will not give its wearer any pleasure. This also explains why they cost around 2,000 Euros. First orders also incur an additional cost of 500 Euros for construction of the last.

The shelves in the workshop are piled to the ceiling with pairs of lasts; an individual last for each customer. They now total well over 1,000 pairs, all of them made single-handedly by Benjamin Klemann according to precise measurements. Each year, around 150 to 200 pairs of bespoke shoes are dispatched from here to clients in 19 countries: they include men's and women's shoes ranging from classic Oxfords to elegant ankle boots, sturdy golf shoes to comfortable hiking boots. Vincent Klemann is in charge of trainers for the younger market whilst his older brother, Lennert, specialises in bowling, cycling and boat shoes. Depending on the individual model, it takes around six months, or, in the case of first orders, up to eight months, to make a pair of shoes. Good things are simply worth waiting for! This is particularly true of shoes, considering that each pair is unique and will only fit one particular customer and no-one else. One cannot help thinking of Cinderella: on the night of the Prince's ball, she was obviously wearing custommade shoes, made by a master craftsman like Benjamin Klemann.

Vincent, Benjamin, Magrit & Lennert Klemann

COMPANY Klemann Shoes	UNTERNEHMEN Klemann Shoes
FOUNDED IN 1986	GEGRÜNDET 1986
FOUNDER Benjamin Klemann	GRÜNDER Benjamin Klemann
HEADQUARTERS Hamburg, Germany	HAUPTFIRMENSITZ Hamburg, Deutschland
CEO Benjamin Klemann	GESCHÄFTSFÜHRUNG Benjamin Klemann
EMPLOYEES 8	MITARBEITER 8
PRODUCTS Bespoke shoes	PRODUKTE Maßschuhe
ANNUAL PRODUCTION 150 – 200 pairs	JAHRESPRODUKTION 150 – 200 Paar
EXPORT COUNTRIES Worldwide, 19 countries	EXPORTLÄNDER Weltweit, 19 Länder

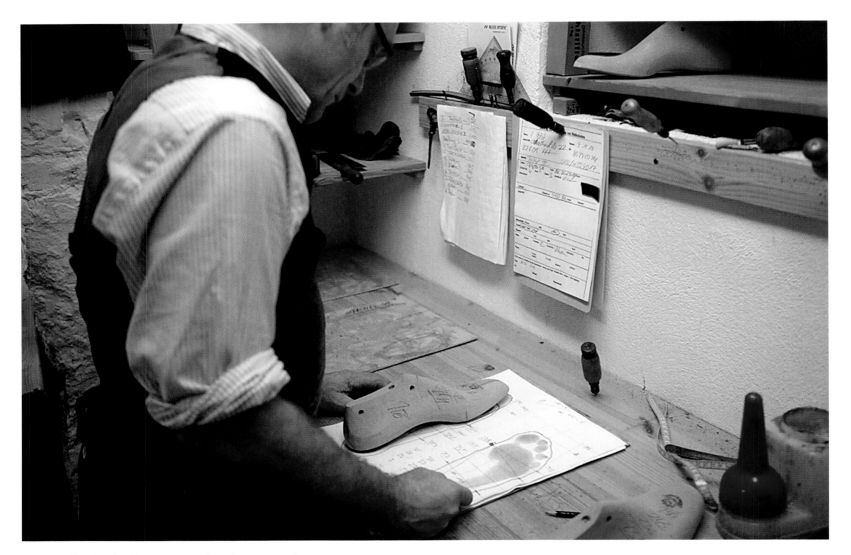

*Benjamin Klemann transfers the customer's
measurements to the last.
Benjamin Klemann überträgt die Kundenmaße
auf den Leisten.*

WERTVOLL UND DAUERHAFT

Wir wissen nicht, was Benjamin Klemann bewog, nach Abitur und Zivildienst –
das war 1980 – ausgerechnet eine Schuhmacherlehre zu beginnen. Bereut hat
er es jedenfalls nicht. Die Anfänge lesen sich wie aus einem Lehrbuch alter Hand-
werksburschen-Herrlichkeit: Nach einer Lehre bei Harai, dem großen Meister
ungarischer Schuhherstellungskunst, zog es den von der nordfriesischen Insel
Föhr stammenden Schuhmachergesellen in die weite Welt. Er verbrachte seine
Wanderjahre in London, wo er sich in die englische Traditionslinie des Hand-
werks einarbeitete. Er wurde Mitarbeiter so bedeutender Häuser wie John Lobb,
Hoflieferant der Queen, des Herzogs von Edinburgh und des Prinzen von Wales.
Dort machte er sich 1986 selbstständig.

In den noblen Maßschuhen aus seinem Haus stecken nicht nur die Erfahrun-
gen der zwei bedeutendsten stilistischen Traditionen des „Schuhbaus", so der
Fachausdruck, sondern auch die schwer erlernbare Sensibilität einer Kultur, die
Menschen mit Stil und Gefühl für Körper und Geist verbindet. Die endlosen
Stunden geduldiger Handarbeit, das feine Leder, die punktgenaue Passform:
All das ist eingebunden in eine umfassende Firmen-, ja Lebensphilosophie, die
sich dem Kunden von Anfang an vermittelt. Das stilvolle Stadthaus in der Ham-

burger Poolstraße, in der Klemann Shoes inzwischen residiert und das Wohn-
räume, Werkstatt und Ladengeschäft unter einem Dach beherbergt, steht für
eine harmonische Einheit von Leben und Arbeit. Dem Firmenchef nimmt man
es einfach ab, wenn er seine Unternehmenskultur mit den Worten beschreibt:
„Die Freude an der Arbeit (auch an harten Tagen) und die Freude, in der
Gemeinschaft etwas Wertvolles und Dauerhaftes herzustellen."

DAS KUNDENGESPRÄCH HAT OBERSTE PRIORITÄT

Diese Begeisterung hat sich auch auf seine Frau und die Söhne übertragen.
Magrit Klemann ist in den Familienbetrieb mit eingestiegen, als die Kinder aus
dem Gröbsten heraus waren, machte 1997 ihren Meister im Schuhhandwerk
und damit das Unternehmen zum Meisterbetrieb mit Brief und Siegel. Aber
auch die beiden Söhne Lennert und Vincent sind inzwischen als selbstständige
Schuhmachermeister mit dabei. Die ganze Belegschaft besteht aus acht Mitarbeitern. Doch offenbar geht es auch hier nicht ohne starke Verbündete: Seit
20 Jahren präsentiert Benjamin Klemann sich und seine Schuhe jeden ersten
Samstag des Monats bei führenden Herrenausstattern in Berlin, Münster oder
Düsseldorf. Beim Gespräch über die unterschiedlichen Eigenschaften von
Pferde-, Kalbs- und Haifischleder, die Vorzüge von Rahmenvernähung und „ge-
glasten" Kanten und die Erlesenheit von echtem Juchtenleder werden Kontakte
geknüpft und neue Kunden akquiriert.

A perfectly sewn welt seam
Eine perfekt genähte Rahmennaht

Das Kundengespräch hat oberste Priorität bei der Entwicklung eines Produkts,
das nicht nur in der Passform, sondern auch in der Wahl des Materials, der Farbe
und des Schnitts immer einzigartig ist. Auch der Kleidungsstil des Kunden ist zu
berücksichtigen, denn der perfekte Schuh vollendet das gesamte Erscheinungsbild seines Trägers. Bevor es an die eigentliche Fertigung geht, muss erst einmal
ein Leisten aus Buchenholz hergestellt werden, als getreues Abbild des individuellen Fußes. Der Leisten ist das Geheimnis der perfekten Passform – wenn hier
etwas nicht stimmt, kann der Schuh seinem Träger kein Vergnügen bereiten. Daher erklärt sich auch der stolze Preis von ca. 2.000 Euro, bei einer Erstbestellung
kommen noch 500 Euro für die Leistenanfertigung hinzu.

Die Regale in der Werkstatt sind bis zur Decke mit Leistenpaaren gefüllt; für
jeden Kunden ein eigener Leisten. Inzwischen sind es weit
über 1.000 Paare, alle von Benjamin Klemann eigenhän-
dig nach genauem Maßnehmen angefertigt. Jährlich finden
etwa 150 bis 200 Paar Maßschuhe von hier aus ihren Weg
zu Auftraggebern in insgesamt 19 Ländern: Herren- und
Damenschuhe vom klassischen Oxford bis zur feinen Stie-
felette, vom robusten Golfschuh bis zum bequemen Wan-
derstiefel. Für jugendliche Sneaker ist Vincent Klemann
zuständig, sein älterer Bruder Lennert hat sich auf Bowling-,
Rad- und Bootsschuhe spezialisiert. Je nach Modell muss
man mit einer Fertigungszeit von bis zu sechs, bei Erstlie-
ferungen auch bis zu acht Monaten rechnen. Gut Ding will
eben Weile haben. Das gilt ganz besonders für Schuhe, bei
denen jedes einzelne Paar ein Unikat ist, das nur diesem
einen Kunden und sonst niemandem passt. Man fühlt sich
an Cinderella erinnert: Offenbar trug sie in der Ballnacht
mit dem Prinzen Maßschuhe, von einem Meister wie Benjamin Klemann gefertigt.

97 holes punched individually by hand
into the cap of a half brogue.
97 einzeln von Hand gestanzte Löcher für
die Kappe eines Half Brogue.

LACO

"Laco – the joy of silk"
Jessica Bartling

TIES WHICH BREATHE …

With the utmost precision and loving attention to detail, seamstresses transform the silk fabrics into Laco ties in twelve individual steps. The silk is cut out by means of a steady hand instead of punching out several layers at once as is customary in other factories. Their whirring sewing machines sew unerringly straight seams in fabrics which are supplied to this traditional company's Hamburg headquarters from Italy's top weaving mills. With a practised hand, they insert the interfacing which, in Laco ties, is made of new wool. Why? "So that the tie can 'breathe' and the fibres can recover once the tie has been undone", explains Jessica Bartling, the firm's CEO, who, after training as a fashion designer, gathered professional experience in Italian and Swiss weaving mills. In this way, the creases will automatically disappear all by themselves before it is worn again. The interfacing therefore represents the "soul" of the tie and its quality is still evident even if it is invisible. "Pressing the ties is also an extremely important procedure", adds

Rüdiger Thumann, who handed over the running of the company to his daughter in 1995. "We stroke our ties with steam. This adds volume to the point of the tie instead of squashing it flat in an automated ironing press." Following a meticulous final check, one can literally feel the quality of a finished Laco tie. The colour of the distinctive logo, which was developed in the 1920s and inspired by the Bauhaus tradition, is coordinated to match the respective fabric design.

The seamstresses at this high-quality firm produce around 195,000 ties each year. In addition, the company also makes pochettes, i.e. pocket handkerchiefs, ascot ties to wear with morning coats, bow ties, reversible scarves and cummerbunds. The seamstresses have learnt their sewing skills within the company – 18 months' training to make a tie and 24 months to make bow ties.

Jessica Bartling & Rüdiger Thumann

HIGHEST STANDARDS STAND THE TEST OF TIME AND CHANGING FASHIONS

The Thumanns and their daughter Jessica Bartling are the sixth set of proprietors to own the firm since Charles Lavy. Lavy, a British businessman, established the factory in 1838: on the last day of the year, he entered the industrial court in Hamburg, which was then the largest commercial centre in northern Europe, and registered his firm. He began trading the very next day on New Year's Day. His suits, car coats, capes, walking canes and bed linen sets were soon being exported to clients in Egypt, Syria and Japan. He personally opened branches in Paris and London. And when ties became fashionable in the 1870s, his firm, with its 500 employees, quickly grew into Germany's largest tie manufacturer. Laco is now the world's oldest tie producer. "We want to offer more than just a product, we want to offer a lifestyle: sophistication", comments Rüdiger Thumann, pointing to the wooden, glass-fronted drawers behind the work tables. They are filled with striped and patterned ties, each carefully held together with a bow, and ready to be sent to Laco fans all over the world. "The Japanese prefer classic designs such as Paisley whilst red is not a popular colour in Moscow and Novosibirsk likes to keep up with the latest fashions", reveals Jessica Bartling.

HIGHEST QUALITY WITHOUT COMPROMISE

Convinced that attractive ties make men feel special, she is passionate about creating special silks. The company strategy which insists on the highest quality without compromise is rigidly adhered to. In order to respond promptly to any special requests, the company carries a large stock of fabrics. With an unerring professional instinct, Jessica Bartling picks out the season's trends twice a year from 1,000 different designs and develops some of her own – ranging from traditional regimental stripes, dots and micro-designs to wild duck and mille-fleurs themes. Coloured warp threads are used to produce the luminosity typical of Laco tie colours. Lively and modern, subtle and elegant, and always sporting the firm's distinctive signature, Laco ties have become serious trendsetters in recent years.

There is no shortage of famous Laco wearers. It is no exaggeration to say that the television is a veritable showcase for Laco products. In addition to a large number of politicians, generations of newsreaders have worn these handmade collector's items produced by this Hamburg manufacturer. However, at the end of the day, when the news broadcast, the meeting or evening engagement is over, the best way to ensure that the tie recovers from being knotted is to roll it up.

COMPANY Laco GmbH	UNTERNEHMEN Laco GmbH
FOUNDED IN 1838	GEGRÜNDET 1838
FOUNDER Charles Lavy	GRÜNDER Charles Lavy
HEADQUARTERS Hamburg, Germany	HAUPTFIRMENSITZ Hamburg, Deutschland
CEO Jessica Bartling	GESCHÄFTSFÜHRUNG Jessica Bartling
EMPLOYEES 22	MITARBEITER 22
PRODUCTS Ties, bow ties, pocket handkerchiefs, cravats, cummerbunds, scarves	PRODUKTE Krawatten, Schleifen, Einstecktücher, Krawattenschals, Kummerbunde, Schals
ANNUAL PRODUCTION Approx. 195,000 ties	JAHRESPRODUKTION Ca. 195.000 Krawatten
EXPORT COUNTRIES Australia, Austria, Azerbaijan, Belgium, Denmark, Iceland, Russia, Switzerland	EXPORTLÄNDER Aserbaidschan, Australien, Belgien, Dänemark, Island, Österreich, Russland, Schweiz

Precision work during production
Präzises Arbeiten in der Produktion

KRAWATTEN, DIE ATMEN...

Mit höchster Präzision und Liebe zum Detail behandeln die Näherinnen die Seidenstoffe, die sie in zwölf Arbeitsschritten in Laco-Krawatten verwandeln. Mit ruhiger Hand schneiden sie die Seiden in Form, statt sie, wie in anderen Betrieben üblich, in Lagen zu stanzen. Mit surrenden Nähmaschinen ziehen sie schnurgerade Linien über die Stoffe, die von den besten Webereien Italiens in den Hamburger Stammsitz der Traditionsfirma geliefert werden. Und sie bringen mit geübter Hand die Einlage ein, die bei Laco aus Schurwolle besteht. Warum? „Damit die Krawatte ,atmen' kann und sich die Fasern nach dem Aufknoten wieder entspannen", erklärt Jessica Bartling, die Chefin des Unternehmens, die nach ihrer Ausbildung zur Modedesignerin Berufserfahrung in italienischen und Schweizer Webereien gesammelt hat. Dann glättet sich die Krawatte bis zum nächsten Auftritt ganz von selbst. Die Einlage ist somit die „Seele" der Krawatte, deren Klasse sich auch dort manifestiert, wo man es nicht sieht. „Auch das Bügeln der Krawatten ist enorm wichtig", ergänzt Rüdiger Thumann, der seiner Tochter die Leitung der Firma 1995 übertrug. „Wir streicheln unsere Krawatten mit Dampf. So erhält die Krawattenspitze Volumen, anstatt im Bügelautomaten flachgequetscht zu werden." Nach einer genauen Endkontrolle kann man die Qualität der fertigen Laco-Krawatte sogar fühlen. Das prägnante Logo, das in den 1920er-Jahren, inspiriert von der Bauhaus-Formensprache, entwickelt wurde, wird farblich dem jeweiligen Stoffmuster angepasst.

Rund 195.000 Krawatten werden jährlich von den Näherinnen der Qualitätsmanufaktur hergestellt. Dazu kommen Pochettes, also Einstecktücher, Plastrons für den Cut, Schleifen, Doppel-Schals und Kummerbunde. Gelernt haben die Näherinnen die Fingerfertigkeit im Unternehmen selbst – 18 Monate lang, um eine Krawatte herzustellen, 24 Monate für die Fertigung von Schleifen.

MIT HÖCHSTEN WERTMASSSTÄBEN ZEITEN UND MODEN ÜBERDAUERN

Das Ehepaar Thumann und Tochter Jessica Bartling sind die sechsten Inhaber der Firma nach Charles Lavy. Der britische Geschäftsmann gründete die Manufaktur bereits 1838: Am letzten Tag des Jahres betrat er das Handelsgericht in Hamburg, damals der bedeutendste Waren-Umschlagplatz Nord-Europas, ließ seine Firma registrieren und begann schon am Neujahrstag Handel zu treiben. Seine Anzüge, Wagendecken, Capes, Spazierstöcke und Bettwäschesets erreichten schon bald Kunden in Ägypten, Syrien und Japan. Er selbst eröffnete Dependancen in Paris und London. Und als Krawatten in den 70er-Jahren des 19. Jahrhunderts in Mode kamen, avancierte seine Firma mit 500 Angestellten schnell zur größten Krawatten-Fabrikation Deutschlands. Heute ist Laco die älteste Krawattenmanufaktur weltweit. „Wir wollen nicht nur ein Produkt, sondern eine Lebenshaltung

Special silks ensure variety.
Besondere Seiden bestimmen die Vielfalt.

bieten: Kultiviertheit", sagt Rüdiger Thumann und zeigt auf die hölzernen Schubladen mit den Glasfenstern hinter den Arbeitstischen. Sorgfältig mit Schleifen umwickelt liegen hier gestreifte und gemusterte Krawatten zum Versand an Liebhaber in der ganzen Welt bereit. „Die Japaner schätzen klassische Muster wie Paisley, in Moskau wird wenig Rot getragen und Nowosibirsk kauft topmodisch", verrät Jessica Bartling.

BESTE QUALITÄT UND KEINE KOMPROMISSE

In der Überzeugung, dass schöne Krawatten den Männern ein besonderes Gefühl vermitteln, versucht sie mit ganzem Einsatz besondere Seiden entstehen zu lassen. Die Strategie des Unternehmens lässt keinen Interpretationsspielraum: Beste Qualität und keine Kompromisse. Um schnell auf spezielle Wünsche reagieren zu können, leistet sich das Unternehmen ein großes Stofflager. Die Saisontrends sucht Jessica Bartling mit professionellem Gespür zweimal im Jahr aus 1.000 verschiedenen Mustern aus und entwickelt eigene – von klassischen Regimentstreifen, über Tupfen und Microdessins bis hin zu Wildenten oder Millefleurs. Das leuchtende Farbenspiel erhalten Laco-Krawatten durch den Einsatz von farbigen Kettfäden. Spritzig und modern, ruhig und edel und immer mit erkennbarer Handschrift haben sie sich gerade in den letzten Jahren zu echten Trendsettern entwickelt.

An prominenten Laco-Trägern fehlt es nicht. Das Fernsehen lässt sich ohne Übertreibung als Schaufenster der Laco-Manufaktur beschreiben. Neben vielen Politikern tragen Generationen von Nachrichtensprechern die handgefertigten Liebhaberstücke aus der Hamburger Manufaktur. Doch ob nach den „Tagesthemen", einer Sitzung oder Einladung, am Ende des Tages sollte die Krawatte aufgerollt werden. So erholt sie sich am besten von dem Knoten.

Elegant ties from the house of Laco
Edelste Krawatten aus dem Hause Laco

Cutting out a reversible scarf
Zuschnitt eines Doppel-Schals

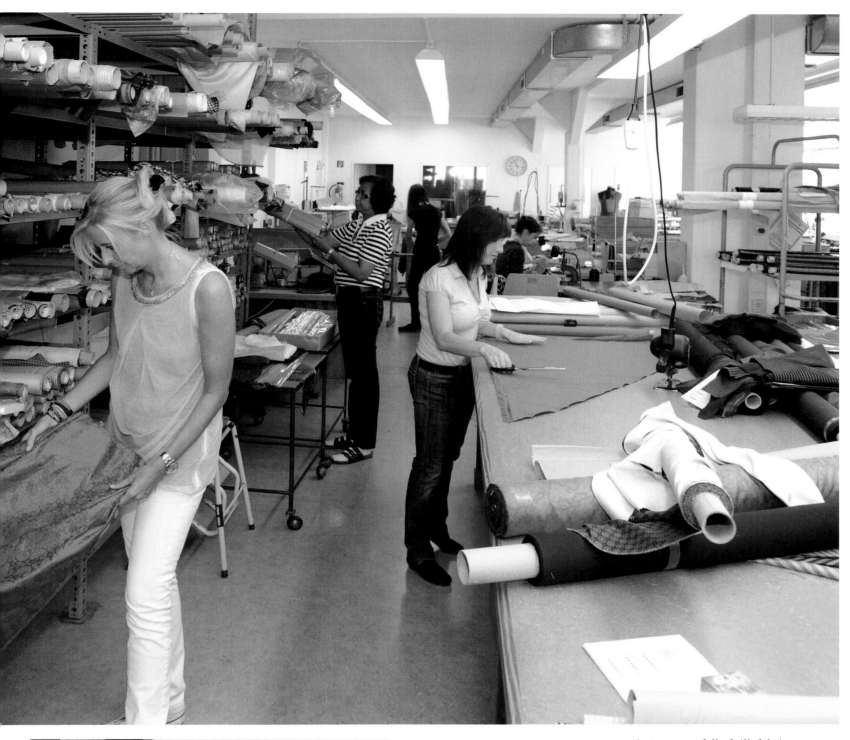

A storeroom full of silk fabrics
Ein Lager voller Seidenstoffe

Attaching the label
Annähen des Labels

Advertisement, "Herrenjournal" and "Elegante Welt", January 1956
Werbeanzeige, „Herrenjournal" und „Elegante Welt", Januar 1956

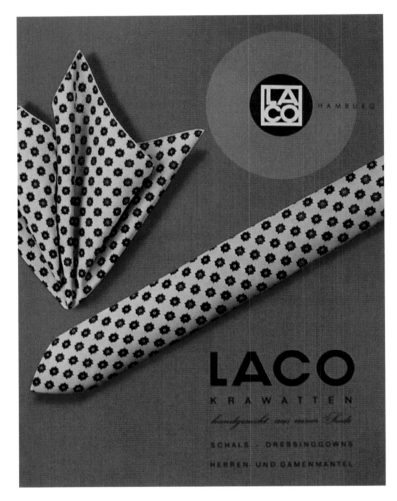

Advertisement, "Herrenjournal", March 1964
Werbeanzeige, „Herrenjournal", März 1964

Advertisement, "Herrenjournal", and "Elegante Welt", June 1957
Werbeanzeige, „Herrenjournal" und „Elegante Welt", Juni 1957

LUDWIG REITER

"One cannot afford to
buy cheap shoes."
Ludwig Reiter

SHOE MANUFACTURE BEHIND PALACE WALLS

The lawns surrounding the castle are coated with morning dew as the first employees arrive for work. Some of them enter through the gates of the former stables, others disappear into the old dovecote and dairy. In 2011, thanks to the traditional firm of Ludwig Reiter, the Renaissance palace of Schloss Süßenbrunn just outside Vienna was, like Sleeping Beauty, roused from a long sleep. Since then, the salons, storerooms and towers of this listed building, situated in 30,000 square metres of what is now productive arable land, are bustling with activity. It took family Reiter almost three years to complete the costly and delicate task of restoring the estate, add a few modern connecting buildings and convert the old workshops to meet the modern requirements of shoe manufacturing.

Meanwhile, the firm now employs around 100 workers who are involved in producing the approximately 30,000 pairs of shoes and other leather goods which are dispatched each year from Vienna to Germany, Sweden, Canada, Japan and many other countries throughout the world. The "Chelsea boot", for example, was invented by Joseph Sparkes Hall, Queen Victoria's shoemaker, in 1837. To make it easier to pull on this leather ankle-boot, he inserted elastic side pieces into the shoe. The "elastic-sided boot" became very popular in the mid-60s and was worn by celebrities such as John Lennon and Mick Jagger. Meanwhile, the "Chelsea boot", like many other classics by Ludwig Reiter, continues to fulfil customers' increased expectations in terms of comfortable fit and material quality. Richard Till Reiter describes the continued creative development of a best-selling style in response to new trends as "the future of tradition". As well as preserving Viennese shoemaking craftsmanship, tradition, in his view, also thrives on change.

Richard Till Reiter

EXPERIENCE AND A TALENT FOR MAKING MARONIBRATER AND DACHSTEIN BOOTS

Behind the palace walls, work continues much as it would in any other traditional workshop. Watching the craftsmen cutting, soling and stitching the shoes, you might almost think you had been transported back to 1885 when Ludwig Reiter produced his first pair of made-to-measure boots for the Imperial police station in his newly established shoe workshop in Vienna. Nowadays, this premium shoe manufacturer produces winter favourites such as the sporty "Dachstein" boots, which have a mountain profile sole which protects a walker from slipping on steep slopes. Or the legendary "Maronibrater" boots made from sturdy Russia leather, the upper part of which consists of felt and a lambskin lining – a rugged-looking classic, of which there have been many versions over the years. The summer range includes Docksider boots made of ultra-soft Nubuk leather with a boat-style crêpe sole. The ladies' collection includes the "Penny Loafer," a moccasin-style slip-on shoe with the distinctive slot in the shank strap to hold the spare penny. Despite the solid appearance of most of the shoes, the product descriptions reveal just how much effort and loving attention to detail has gone into their making. The popular "Traveller", for example, which Steve McQueen liked to wear, is an "ankle-high lace-up shoe with a plain tongue of smooth suede leather, flexibly stitched, with leather lining, oiled leather sole, and styled from English-style lasts with a flat instep and longer forefoot". The lasts are a genre in themselves. They are known as Salzburg, Viennese or Prague lasts. Their construction requires experience and skill. Anyone who wishes to commission his own personal combination of shoe model, last, upper leather and sole from Ludwig Reiter will, within a few weeks, be invited to a private fitting of a welt-stitched shoe. Although this is undoubtedly a more expensive option, it will last longer than a flexibly stitched shoe. The company has already maintained this level of quality for 125 years. There is a choice of around 10 different lasts for men's shoes in 2 to 4 widths and 16 lengths. New last models for made-to-measure shoes are rare nowadays. Even sophisticated mathematics does not always help in achieving the precise shape around the foot. Given the approximately 500 lasts available for Reiter customers to choose from, it is highly unlikely that a suitable one cannot be found. Shoes from the Schloss Süßenbrunn workshop are worth the extra money and will last a long time. And after that? – The firm's founder has an appropriate answer to the question: "One cannot afford to buy cheap shoes."

COMPANY	UNTERNEHMEN
Ludwig Reiter Schuhmanufaktur	Ludwig Reiter Schuhmanufaktur
FOUNDED IN	GEGRÜNDET
1885	1885
FOUNDER	GRÜNDER
Ludwig Reiter	Ludwig Reiter
HEADQUARTERS	HAUPTFIRMENSITZ
Schloss Süßenbrunn, Vienna, Austria	Schloss Süßenbrunn, Wien, Österreich
CEO	GESCHÄFTSFÜHRUNG
Richard Till Reiter	Richard Till Reiter
EMPLOYEES	MITARBEITER
Over 100	Über 100
PRODUCTS	PRODUKTE
Shoes, leather goods	Schuhe, Lederwaren
ANNUAL PRODUCTION	JAHRESPRODUKTION
30,000 pairs of shoes, leather goods, as required	30.000 Paar Schuhe, Lederwaren je nach Bedarf
EXPORT COUNTRIES	EXPORTLÄNDER
Belgium, Canada, China, France, Germany, Italy, Japan, Portugal, Russia, Spain, Sweden, Switzerland, The Netherlands, UK, Ukraine, USA	Belgien, China, Deutschland, Frankreich, Italien, Japan, Kanada, Niederlande, Portugal, Russland, Schweden, Schweiz, Spanien, UK, Ukraine, USA

LUDWIG REITER
WIEN 1885

Lukas, Richard Till & Uz Reiter

Hand-stitched shoes
Rahmengenähte Schuhe

DIE SCHUHMANUFAKTUR
HINTER SCHLOSSMAUERN

Rund um das Schloss liegt der Morgentau auf den Wiesen, als die ersten Mitarbeiter eintreffen. Einige von ihnen treten durch die Tore der ehemaligen Pferdestallungen, andere verschwinden im alten Taubenschlag und der Meierei. Seit die Traditionsfirma Ludwig Reiter das Renaissanceschloss Süßenbrunn vor den Toren Wiens 2011 aus dem Dornröschenschlaf geholt hat, herrscht wieder Betriebsamkeit in den Sälen, Speichern und Türmen der denkmalgeschützten Anlage, die sich über 30.000 Quadratmeter inmitten fruchtbaren Ackerlands erstreckt.

Fast drei Jahre nahm sich die Familie Reiter Zeit, um das Gutsgelände aufwendig und behutsam zu restaurieren, ein paar moderne Verbindungsbauten zu ergänzen und die alten Werkstätten für die modernen Arbeitsanforderungen der Schuhmanufaktur herzurichten.

Inzwischen sorgen etwa 100 Mitarbeiter dafür, dass jährlich rund 30.000 Paar Schuhe und andere Lederwaren von Wien aus Deutschland, Schweden, Kanada, Japan und viele andere Länder weltweit erreichen. Der „Chelsea Boot" zum Beispiel, den Joseph Sparkes Hall, der Schuhmacher Queen Victorias, im Jahr 1837 erdachte. Um das Anziehen der Lederstiefelette zu erleichtern, nähte er elastische Seitenteile in den Schuh. Zu den prominenten Trägern des „elastic-sided boot" gehörten Mitte der 1960er-Jahre auch John Lennon und Mick Jagger. Inzwischen erfüllen der „Chelsea Boot" ebenso wie andere Klassiker Ludwig Reiters längst die gestiegenen Ansprüche an Passform und Materialqualität. Die gestalterische Weiterentwicklung eines Bestsellers entsprechend neuesten Trends nennt Richard Till Reiter „die Zukunft der Tradition". Neben der Bewahrung des Wiener Schuhmacherhandwerks lebt Tradition für ihn auch von Veränderung.

The firm's founder Ludwig Reiter, Richard
Lauterbach and Ludwig Reiter Jr
Der Firmengründer Ludwig Reiter, Richard
Lauterbach und Ludwig Reiter junior

ERFAHRUNG UND GESCHICK FÜR MARONIBRATER UND DACHSTEIN-STIEFEL

Dennoch geht es hinter den Schlossmauern noch zu wie in einem traditionellen Handwerksbetrieb. Sieht man den Facharbeitern beim Schneiden, Besohlen und Nähen zu, fühlt man sich beinahe in das Jahr 1885 zurückversetzt, als Ludwig Reiter in Wien in seiner soeben gegründeten Schuhmacherwerkstatt das erste Paar Maßstiefel für die Wiener k. u. k. Polizeiwache fertigte. Heute entstehen bei dem Nobelschuhmacher für die Wintersaison Favoriten wie der sportliche „Dachstein-Stiefel", der mit seiner Bergprofilsohle Wanderer vor dem Abrutschen auf Steilhängen schützt. Oder der legendäre „Maronibrater" aus kräftigem Juchtenleder, einem Schaftoberteil aus Filz und Lammfellfutter – ein urtümlich anmutender Klassiker, der seit Jahren in vielen Varianten gefertigt wird. Im Sommer gehören „Docksider" aus samtweichem Nubuk mit boots-decktauglicher Crêpesohle ins Portfolio. Bei den Damen gehört der „Penny Loafer" zum Repertoire, ein Slipper im Mokassin-Look, mit dem charakteristischen Schlitz für den „letzten Penny" in der Schaftbrücke.

So zünftig die meisten Schuhe auch anmuten, die Produktbeschreibungen verraten, wie viel Aufwand und Liebe zum Detail in der Fertigung steckt: Der beliebte „Traveller" etwa, den Steve McQueen gerne trug, ist ein „knöchelhoher Schnürschuh mit unverziertem Vorderblatt aus geschmeidigem Velours, flex-genäht, mit Lederfutter, geölter Ledersohle sowie Engländer-Leisten mit flachem Rist und langem Vorfuß".

Die Leisten sind ein Genre für sich. „Salzburger" heißen sie, „Wiener" oder „Prager". Ihre Konstruktion erfordert Erfahrung und Geschick. Wer sich bei Ludwig Reiter seine eigene Kombination aus Schuhmodell, Leisten, Oberleder und Sohle zusammenstellen möchte, bekommt binnen weniger Wochen eine rahmengenähte Privatanfertigung, die zwar kostspieliger ist, aber länger hält als flexibel genähte Modelle. Für diese Qualität steht das Unternehmen schon seit 125 Jahren. Zur Auswahl stehen rund zehn verschiedene Leistentypen für Herren in je zwei bis vier Weiten und 16 Längen. Neue Leistenformen für Maß-schuhe, die individuell für Kunden angefertigt werden, sind heutzutage selten. Denn selbst ausgeklügelte Mathematik hilft nicht bei der exakten Abformung eines Fußes. Bei rund 500 Leistenmodellen, die für Reiter-Kunden zur Verfügung stehen, geht die Wahrscheinlichkeit gen Null, kein passendes zu finden. Schuhe aus der Manufaktur in Schloss Süßenbrunn sind ihren Preis wert und haben ein langes Leben. Die Investition lohnt sich, denn wie schon der Firmen-gründer befand: „Billige Schuhe kann man sich nicht leisten."

Maronibrater boots – a classic
Ein Klassiker: der Maronibrater

Sewing the shaft of the boot, "doubling", i.e. stitching together the frame and
outer sole and sewing together the inner sole and frame
Nähen des Stiefelschafts, Doppeln bzw. Vernähen von Rahmen und Laufsohle,
Einstechen bzw. Vernähen von Brandsohle und Rahmen

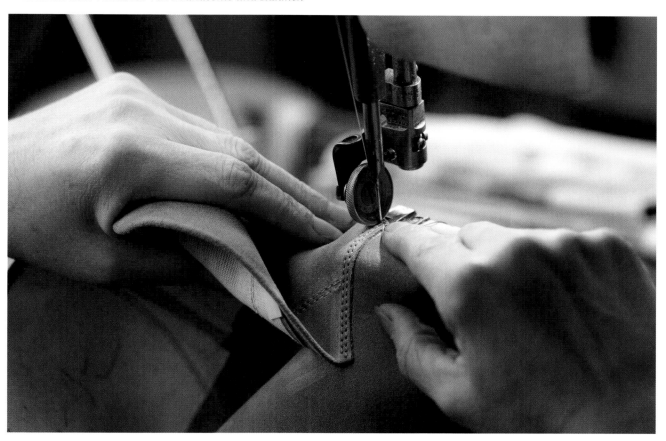

Left: The cutting-room in Schumanngasse,
Vienna, around 1960
Links: Die Zuschneiderei in der Schumanngasse,
Wien, um 1960

Pages/Seiten 212–213:
The production room at Schloss Süßenbrunn
Die Produktionshalle auf Schloss Süßenbrunn

REGENT

"We produce the most lightweight fabrics in the world."
Detlev Diehm

MADE BY HAND WITH LOVE AND SKILL

The main factory in the small, Bavarian town of Weißenburg in Altmühltal is filled with the hum of dozens of Pfaff sewing machines, whilst heavy shears cut through feather-light fabrics and pieces of material are constantly being steam-pressed by eight-kilogram irons. This is the Regent factory where the last of Germany's hand-finished suits are produced – around 50 of them a day. Each is unique and represents 15 hours of labour, innumerable, skilled steps which must be carried out by hand and 10,000 stitches. A seamstress takes 12 minutes to sew a single buttonhole. The fact that such hand-finishing even takes place in Germany is enough to endow the garment with luxury status. The tiny crown above the label, which reads "Handtailored by Regent", symbolises this. The name Regent is synonymous with a passion for tailoring craftsmanship.

Every check and stripe is aligned so perfectly that even the patterns along the sleeve seams and around the collar flow across the joins without interruption as if the jacket were cut from a single piece of fabric. A whole chapter could be devoted to the interfacing alone: it has to be as light as a feather and be placed under the outer fabric of the jacket's front panels. It turns the suit into a kind of modern-day armour for everyday wear – robust but sensual and flexible at the same time. The horse- or camel-hair interfacing and the wool fabric are sewn together using delicate, loose stitches. This is what makes these suits so different from ready-to-wear garments. In the latter case, the two materials are not basted together, i.e. the inlay and outer fabric are not loosely stitched, but are glued together. The hand-stitching of interfacings and the move away from heavy fabrics was revolutionary in its day as heavy materials were regarded as being particularly durable.

Fiorella Tombolini

A TURBULENT HISTORY

When Henryk Barig and Dr. Michael Aisenstadt founded Regent Handtailored in 1946 in Weißenburg, they began by concentrating production exclusively on high-quality shirts. One year after the end of the war, a gentleman should at least be able to meet his public wearing a smartly stiffened collar. The concept was a hit so much so that by the end of the 1950s, the firm's directors had set themselves a new target: they planned to produce the most lightweight suits in the world. In those days, a suit weighed 600 grams per metre of fabric. Regent halved the weight to 300 grams per metre. This, too, was a successful innovation as the international autographed cards now displayed along the corridors of the firm's headquarters testify.

Around ten years ago, the firm was taken over by the menswear specialist Tombolini, an Italian, family-run company. The fresh input helped to revive the somewhat flagging fortunes of this slightly old-fashioned firm and restore its reputation and prestige. The Italian managers shifted production back to Germany after it had previously been outsourced to Poland. They recruited a young chief designer, Detlev Diehm, and in 1999 gave him responsibility for all the different product groups: suits, sports jackets, trousers, coats, sportswear, shirts and ties. A new era had begun and Diehm exhibited a talent not only for design but also for marketing. By presenting so-called trunk shows of suits and casual wear in top international hotels, Regent attracted new clients.

Meanwhile, Regent Handtailored employs around one hundred workers, 95 of whom are involved in production. The reason for this high number of staff is that every suit, from cutting out the individual sections to the final pressing, is made in the original Weißenburg headquarters. And this will continue to be the case since the "owners have no plans whatsoever to abandon the Weißenburg site", according to Detlev Diehm. "On the contrary, they encourage us to seek ways of improving a jacket still further."

THE ULTIMATE LIGHTWEIGHT SUIT FABRIC

The firm's air-conditioned warehouses contain 30,000 metres of fabric supplied by the best weavers in England, Italy and Japan, ready to offer Regent's clients all over the world a large selection of elegant fabrics. Yet, the company is still not satisfied: research is constantly underway to find the ultimate fabric. Together with a Japanese scientist, the chief designer is also in charge of

COMPANY Regent Handtailored GmbH	UNTERNEHMEN Regent Handtailored GmbH
FOUNDED IN 1946	GEGRÜNDET 1946
FOUNDERS Henryk Barig, Michael Aisenstadt	GRÜNDER Henryk Barig, Michael Aisenstadt
HEADQUARTERS Weißenburg, Germany	HAUPTFIRMENSITZ Weißenburg, Deutschland
PROPRIETOR Fiorella Tombolini	EIGENTÜMERIN Fiorella Tombolini
CEO Teclio Ferranti	GESCHÄFTSFÜHRUNG Teclio Ferranti
EMPLOYEES 103	MITARBEITER 103
PRODUCTS Handmade suits and sports coats, upper casual	PRODUKTE Handgefertigte Anzüge und Sportjacken, gehobene Freizeitkleidung
EXPORT COUNTRIES Austria, CIS, Greece, Italy, Japan, Poland, Switzerland, UK, USA	EXPORTLÄNDER Griechenland, GUS, Italien, Japan, Österreich, Polen, Schweiz, UK, USA

the research and development department. His aim is to generate high-tech products by natural methods. "We produce the most lightweight fabrics in the world", he comments proudly. And the firm has also developed something called "silky powder", a kind of silk protein with wool fibres and Teflon properties. This innovative material is naturally stain resistant.

Whether innovative or traditional, anyone who wants to have a Regent suit tailored can bury himself in pattern books and choose anything from a light-weight sports jacket of Swiss cotton jersey with buffalo horn buttons to a downy cashmere suit in a wide range of textiles. Before the hand-finished garment leaves the factory en route to the client, the shape and fit must be critically checked by a member of staff in front of the old, three-piece mirror. Detlev Diehm's personal favourite is a black seersucker, which is so light that "you almost forget you are wearing it".

VON HAND, MIT HERZ UND GEIST GEFERTIGT

In der größten Produktionshalle des kleinen bayerischen Städtchens Weißen-burg im Altmühltal surren Dutzende schwarze Pfaff-Nähmaschinen, schwe-re Scheren schneiden durch federleichte Stoffe und unter dem Dampf von 8-kg-Bügeleisen werden Zuschnitte immer wieder in Form gebügelt. Hier bei Regent entstehen die letzten handgefertigten Anzüge Deutschlands. Rund 50 Stück täglich. Jeder von ihnen ist ein Unikat, in dem 15 Stunden Arbeit, unge-zählte routinierte Handgriffe und mehr als 10.000 Stiche stecken. 12 Minuten braucht eine Mitarbeiterin allein, um ein Knopfloch zu sticken. Schon die Tat-sache, dass diese handwerkliche Arbeit noch hierzulande passiert, macht das Knopfloch zum Luxusobjekt. Die kleine Krone über dem Etiketten-Schriftzug „Regent Handtailored" ist das Symbol dazu.

Regent ist Synonym für leidenschaftliches Schneiderhandwerk. Jedes Karo, jeder Streifen wird hier so deckungsgleich gelegt, dass die Musterverläufe an Ärmel und Kragen fließend ineinanderübergehen, als wäre das Sakko aus einem einzigen Stück Stoff geschnitten. Auch die Einlage ist ein Mode-Kapitel für sich: Federleicht soll sie sein und unter den vorderen Schnittteilen des Ober-stoffes die Brust formen. Sie macht den Anzug zu einer Art moderner Rüstung für den Alltag, stabil, aber zugleich sinnlich und wandlungsfähig. Das Ross-oder Kamelhaar der Einlage und der Wollstoff sind mit feinen, losen Stichen zusammengenäht. Hier liegt der Unterschied zur Konfektionsware. Dort wird nicht „pikiert", also Einlage und Oberstoff mit losen Stichen verbunden, son-dern geklebt. Handpikierte Einlagen und der Verzicht auf alles Schwere waren revolutionär, weil gerade schwere Stoffe als besonders langlebig galten.

EINE BEWEGTE GESCHICHTE

Als Henryk Barig und Dr. Michael Aisenstadt die Marke Regent Handtailored im Jahr 1946 in Weißenburg gründeten, produzierten sie zunächst ausschließlich qualitativ hochwertige Hemden. Ein Jahr nach Kriegsende sollte sich der Herr wenigstens mit adrett gestärktem Kragen zeigen können. Das Konzept kam an, sodass sich Ende der 1950er-Jahre die Geschäftsführer neue Ziele setzten: Sie wollten die leichtesten Anzüge weit und breit herstellen. 600 Gramm wog damals ein Anzug pro Meter Stoff. Regent halbierte das Gewicht auf 300 Gramm pro Meter. Auch dieses Konzept ging auf, wovon noch heute die internationalen Autogrammkarten in den Gängen des Firmensitzes erzählen.

Vor rund zehn Jahren übernahm der Herrenausstatter Tombolini, ein italienischer Familienbetrieb, das Unternehmen und verhalf dem in die Jahre gekommenen Betrieb erneut zu hohem Ansehen und Prestige. Die Italiener holten die Produktion, die zwischenzeitlich nach Polen verlagert worden war, zurück nach Deutschland. Sie übertrugen dem jungen Chefdesigner Detlev Diehm 1999 die Verantwortung für alle Produktgruppen: Anzüge, Sakkos, Hosen, Mäntel, Sportswear, Hemden und Krawatten. Eine neue Ära begann, und Diehm bewies nicht nur im Design Geschick, sondern auch im Marketing. Als er in sogenannten Trunkshows Anzüge und Casualwear in den besten Hotels der Welt vorführen ließ, gewann Regent Handtailored neue Kunden.

Heute beschäftigt Regent Handtailored rund 100 Mitarbeiter, davon 95 in der Produktion. Der Grund für diese hohe Zahl: Alle Anzüge werden vom Zuschnitt der Einzelteile bis zum Aufbügeln im Weißenburger Stammhaus gefertigt. Und das wird wohl auch so bleiben, denn die „Eigentümer denken überhaupt nicht daran, den Standort Weißenburg aufzugeben", sagt Detlev Diehm. „Sie bestärken uns hingegen, ein Jackett immer wieder zu optimieren."

VON DER LEICHTIGKEIT DES TRAGENS

30.000 Meter Stoff von den besten Webern in England, Italien und Japan liegen in klimatisierten Lagern bereit, um den Regent-Kunden weltweit eine große Auswahl edlen Tuches anbieten zu können. Und dennoch gibt sich das Unternehmen damit nicht zufrieden. Es wird immer weiter nach dem ultimativen Stoff geforscht. Zusammen mit einem japanischen Wissenschaftler leitet Chefdesigner Diehm auch die Forschungs- und Entwicklungsabteilung. Ihm geht es darum, Hightech-Produkte auf natürlichem Weg zu generieren. „Wir haben die leichtesten Stoffe der Welt im Programm", sagt er stolz. Und mit „silky powder" hat das Unternehmen eine Art Seidenprotein mit Wollfasern und Teflon-Eigenschaften entwickelt: Dieser innovative Stoff ist auf natürliche Weise fleckenabweisend.

Ob innovativ oder traditionell: Wer sich einen Regent-Anzug schneidern lassen möchte, kann in die Musterbücher eintauchen und vom legeren Sakko aus Schweizer Baumwolljersey mit Büffelhornknöpfen bis hin zum flauschigen Kaschmir-Anzug unter einer Vielzahl von Textilien wählen. Bevor das handgefertigte Stück dann die Manufaktur in Richtung Kunden verlässt, prüft ein Mitarbeiter vor dem alten dreiteiligen Spiegel kritisch Sitz und Passform. Detlev Diehms Lieblingsstück ist übrigens ein schwarzer Seersucker-Anzug aus reiner Seide, der so leicht ist, „dass man ihn beim Tragen fast vergisst".

Even the lining is cut out by hand.
Auch das Futter wird von Hand zugeschnitten.

The jacket in its unfinished state with the horsehair
padding tacked in.
Das Sakko im Rohzustand mit untergehefteter
Rosshaar-Wattierung

The basting stitches are removed.
Die Heftfäden werden entfernt.

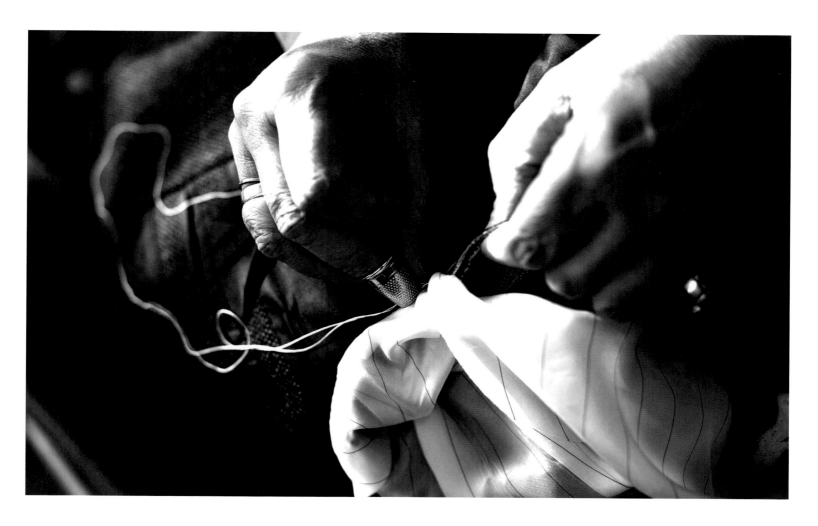

Entegrating a sleeve lining allows more freedom of movement.
Das Einstaffieren des Ärmelfutters führt zu mehr Bewegungsfreiheit.

ROECKL

"Gloves can do more
than warm our fingers,
they can spark fires."
Annette Roeckl

LIKE A SECOND SKIN

Once you have worn a pair of exclusive gloves made by the traditional Munich firm
of Roeckl, you will never want to be without them. They fit beautifully, protecting
and adorning your hands like a second skin. Be it long satin gloves for an evening
at the opera, the studded cut-off finger model "Glam Driver" for driving, finger-
less gloves lined with super-soft lambswool or cashmere for winter, or the "Karls-
bad" glove, with its airy cotton upper and side press-stud fastening for strolling
the pavements of the world's capital cities: Roeckl leather gloves are a reliable
accessory for all occasions. Annette Roeckl wears her own products, selecting
an appropriate model to match her mood and the occasion. In six generations
of the firm's history, she is the first woman to head the company. Annette Roeckl
has been at the helm of this internationally successful glove and accessories label
since 2003 and has introduced new product lines, including a junior collection
and a bag collection. She has proved herself very adept at combining her instinct
for fashion and trends with the traditional philosophy of the company.

LIVING CRAFTSMANSHIP TRADITION AND TIMELESS DESIGNS

The early beginnings of this family firm go back 170 years. Jakob Roeckl set up a small workshop next to his own Munich store in 1839 with the aim of creating fine-quality gloves. He began production of delicate glacé gloves fashioned from soft kid leather. Increasing national and international success led to the expansion of the Roeckl firm and the building of a large factory on the southern outskirts of Munich in 1870. The firm's unique reputation reached the ears of the royal court and in 1873 Roeckl was appointed "Supplier to the Royal Court of Bavaria". Roeckl gloves adorned not only the hands of King Ludwig II but also those of his cousin, the Austrian Empress Elisabeth II, better known as "Sissi". Roeckl, now a European market leader with an annual turnover of more than 25 million Euros, employs 330 employees in Germany and other European countries. In addition to the classic range of colours, the company also features seasonal highlights such as red and orange, combining them with other colours. Roeckl scarves also feature imaginative colours and designs which are reminiscent of tales from 1001 nights, African safaris or Mediterranean flower meadows. A wide diversity of patterns and ornamental designs are created by the continuous repetition of a motif. A design can incorporate up to 17 different colours which have to be drawn by hand to make the printing templates and are applied manually using screen printing techniques.

QUALITY AND SUSTAINABILITY BASED ON TRADITION

In strict accordance with the Washington Agreement on the Protection of Endangered Species, the Roeckl company only uses leather and hides from wild animals which also serve as a food source for the population. In addition to the luxurious peccary leather from the South American piglike mammal, these also include nappa leather from hairsheep, lambskin, deerskin and suede leather which Roeckl imports from Ethiopia, Spain and Portugal. "Peccary" is processed in Roeckl's own workshops in Romania in an elaborate sequence of steps. The glove is cut from the leather The glove-maker cuts the so-called French "table panels" out of the leather, the final form being punched out afterwards. Two thousand stitches are needed to sew up to 24 individual pieces together by hand.

WITH VISION TOWARDS THE FUTURE

Although the firm's headquarters continue to be based in Munich and the tradition of craftsmanship is still paramount, Annette Roeckl, who runs the firm, is guided by the motto: "tradition does not mean worshipping the ashes but passing on the fire" towards the future. Meanwhile, in addition to glove production, Roeckl not only offers a parallel line in scarves, bags, hats and small leather goods but, thanks to "Roeckl Intelligence", a fresh firework in terms of innovative ideas has been lit, which is both clever and elegant at the same time. In the current age of tablets and iPads, Roeckl's intelligent gloves are right on target. The secret lies in the patent-pending design, whereby a conductive material on the thumb and forefinger makes operating a touch display screen as easy as can be. This is where technology meets fashion expertise.

Annette Roeckl

COMPANY Roeckl Handschuhe & Accessoires GmbH & Co. KG	UNTERNEHMEN Roeckl Handschuhe & Accessoires GmbH & Co. KG
FOUNDED IN 1839	GEGRÜNDET 1839
FOUNDER Jakob Roeckl	GRÜNDER Jakob Roeckl
HEADQUARTERS Munich, Germany	HAUPTFIRMENSITZ München, Deutschland
CEO Annette Roeckl	GESCHÄFTSFÜHRUNG Annette Roeckl
EMPLOYEES 330	MITARBEITER 330
PRODUCTS High-quality leather gloves, leather bags, small leather goods and knitted accessories, silk scarves, shawls, junior collection, Roeckl Intelligence	PRODUKTE Hochwertige Lederhandschuhe, Ledertaschen, Kleinleder- und Strick-Accessoires, Seidentücher, Schals, Junior-Kollektion, Roeckl Intelligence
ANNUAL TURNOVER Over 25 million Euros	JAHRESUMSATZ Über 25 Millionen Euro
EXPORT COUNTRIES Austria, Belgium, Kazakhstan, Poland, Russia, Switzerland, The Netherlands and other core markets	EXPORTLÄNDER Belgien, Kasachstan, Niederlande, Österreich, Polen, Russland, Schweiz, und weitere Kernmärkte

View of the workshop
Blick in die Werkstatt

Gloves studded with Swarovski stones
Handschuhe, mit Swarovski-Steinen besetzt

WIE EINE ZWEITE HAUT

Hat man sie einmal übergestreift, möchte man die exklusiven Handschuh-kreationen der Münchner Traditionsfirma Roeckl nicht mehr missen. Sie passen sich an, schützen und zieren, sie sind wie eine zweite Haut. Ob nun die langen Satin-Handschuhe beim Opernbesuch, das nietenverzierte Halbfingermodell „Glam Driver" am Steuer, die Fingerlinge mit kuschelweichem Lammfell- oder Kaschmirfutter im Winter und der mit einer luftigen Baumwolloberhand und seitlichem Druckknopf versehene „Karlsbader"-Handschuh beim Flanieren über die Trottoirs der Weltmetropolen: Ein Roeckl-Lederhandschuh ist ein zu-verlässiger Begleiter in allen Lebenslagen.

Auch Annette Roeckl selbst trägt die Produkte ihres Hauses und wählt das jewei-lige Modell nach Stimmung und Anlass aus. Innerhalb der sechs Generationen überspannenden Firmengeschichte ist sie die erste Frau, die dem Unternehmen vorsteht. Annette Roeckl leitet das international erfolgreiche Handschuh- und Accessoire-Label seit 2003 und führte neue Produktlinien, wie die Junior- und Taschenkollektion ein. Der Unternehmerin gelingt es überzeugend, das Ge-spür für Mode und Trends mit der traditionsreichen Unternehmensphilosophie in Einklang zu bringen.

GELEBTE HANDWERKSTRADITION UND ZEITLOSES DESIGN

Die Anfänge des Familienunternehmens liegen über 170 Jahre zurück. Mit dem Anspruch, die besten Handschuhe herstellen zu wollen, gründete Jakob Roeckl 1839 einen kleinen Handwerksbetrieb nebst eigenem Verkaufsladen in München und begann mit der Produktion filigraner Glacéhandschuhe, die aus weichem Jungziegenleder hergestellt wurden. Mit zunehmendem nationalem und internationalem Erfolg expandierte die Firma Roeckl und baute 1870 am damaligen südlichen Stadtrand Münchens eine große Fabrik. Der einzigartige unternehmerische Ruf erreichte auch den Königlichen Hof und Roeckl avancierte 1873 zum „Königlich Bayrischen Hoflieferanten". Roeckl-Lederhandschuhe schmückten nicht nur die Hände König Ludwigs II., sondern auch die seiner Cousine, der österreichischen Kaiserin Elisabeth II., besser bekannt als Sissi. Heute, als europäischer Marktführer mit einem Jahresumsatz von über 25 Millionen Euro, beschäftigt Roeckl 330 Mitarbeiter in Deutschland und im europäischen Ausland. Das Unternehmen setzt neben der klassischen Farbauswahl auf saisonale Highlights wie effektvolles Rot und Orange, die mit anderen Farben kombiniert werden. Mit fantasievollen Farben und Mustern gestaltet sind auch die Tücher, die mal an ein Märchen aus 1001 Nacht, mal an eine afrikanische Safari oder an eine südländische Blumenwiese erinnern. Durch die „Rapportierung", die ständige Wiederholung eines Motivs, entstehen unterschiedlichste Musterungen oder Ornamente. Ein Design kann bis zu 17 verschiedene Farben aufweisen, die für die Druckvorlagen-Erstellung von Hand gezeichnet und via Siebdruckverfahren manuell aufgetragen werden.

QUALITÄT UND NACHHALTIGKEIT AUS TRADITION

Bei der Firma Roeckl werden ausschließlich Leder und Felle von freilebenden Tieren verarbeitet, die auch zur Ernährung der Bevölkerung dienen; streng nach den Vorschriften des Washingtoner Artenschutzabkommens. Dazu zählen neben dem edlen Peccary-Leder von südamerikanischen Nabelschweinen, das Haarschaf-Nappaleder, Lammfell, Hirschleder oder Veloursleder, die Roeckl aus Äthiopien, Spanien und Portugal bezieht. Das sogenannte Peccary wird in aufwendigen Handarbeitsschritten in hauseigenen Produktionsstätten in Rumänien verarbeitet. Mit dem französischen „Tafelschnitt" wird der Handschuh aus dem Leder geschnitten, die endgültige Form anschließend herausgestanzt. Die bis zu 24 Einzelteile werden mit über 2.000 Stichen von Hand zusammengenäht.

MIT VISIONEN IN DIE ZUKUNFT

Obwohl sich der Firmensitz nach wie vor in München befindet und die handwerkliche Tradition Bestand hat, orientiert sich die Firmenchefin Annette Roeckl gemäß dem Motto: „Tradition ist nicht die Anbetung der Asche, sondern das Weitertragen der Glut" in Richtung Zukunft. Nicht nur, dass es neben der Handschuh- auch eine Tuch-, Taschen-, Hut- und Kleinlederproduktion gibt, mit „Roeckl Intelligence" wurde ein weiteres Feuerwerk innovativer Ideen entfacht, das klug und elegant zugleich ist. Im Zeitalter von Tablets kommt Roeckls intelligenter Handschuh zur rechten Zeit. Das Geheimnis liegt in der zum Patent angemeldeten Schnittführung: In Kombination mit einem leitfähigen Material an Daumen und Zeigefinger ermöglicht diese das spielend leichte Bedienen der Touchdisplays . Hier trifft Technologie auf Fashionexpertise.

Spring/Summer Collection 2013
Kollektion Frühling/Sommer 2013

Coloured leather store 1913
Farblederlager 1913

The Roeckl factory,
late 19th century
Das Roeckl-Fabrikgelände,
Ende des 19. Jahrhunderts

223

SCABAL

"Our passion is to produce top-quality fabrics and turn them into distinctive, personalised clothing."
Peter Thissen

TOP-QUALITY FABRICS

They are called "Diamond Chip", "Gold Treasure" and "Lapis Lazuli": these extravagant sounding names do not belong to prize-winning racehorses but describe textile innovations developed by Scabal. This Belgian producer of luxury fabrics produced one fabric by incorporating tiny diamond splinters into finest-quality wool to give it its silky sheen and wove 22-carat gold threads into ultra-light merino wool to create another. Scabal made the fabric known as "Lapis Lazuli" by integrating microscopically tiny particles of this semi-precious stone into an Australian ultrafine wool-and-cashmere mix. The particles are captured by straightened fibres and evenly integrated in the cloth. This gemstone dust produces an intense shade of ultramarine blue in men's suits and is also said to have beneficial properties which strengthen the immune system. Small wonder that the producer of these luxury fabrics numbers numerous international premium labels among its clients: Brioni, Smalto, Tom Brown, Prada,

Gucci and Armani, all of whom have their suits made from Scabal fabrics – suits, which grace the wardrobes or costume departments of business tycoons, leading politicians as well as Hollywood stars. Daniel Craig, for example, appeared in his first James Bond film in an elegant suit which was "Made by Scabal". Pop star Justin Timberlake is insistent that his wax double at Madame Tussauds in London is dressed in a casually elegant outfit by Scabal. US President Barack Obama has also recently taken to wearing a made-to-measure Scabal suit. It is typical of the brand's image that Scabal operates his flagship store on the world's most famous menswear street – at No. 12, Savile Row in London. The label's most exclusive collection, a range of hand-sewn, Italian suits with distinctive shoulders and narrow waist, is named "N° 12" after the famous address.

Gregor & Peter Thissen

DESIRE FOR INDIVIDUALITY AND PERFECTION

A bespoke Scabal suit is based on exact measurements taken from the contours of the respective client's body. The essential qualities are simple elegance and top-quality material in blue, black or grey, sometimes with fine stripes or subtle checks. "Clients can choose in this respect from around 5,000 fabric qualities and designs", explains Matthias Rollmann, the managing director for the German market. A suit can, if desired, be made to measure within three weeks. With Scabal, almost anything is possible in terms of fit and detail: the tailors, all of whom have served a six-year apprenticeship, can, if the client so wishes, incorporate a perfectly fitting inside pocket for an iPod or airline tickets, genuine horn buttons with the customer's initials or "kissing buttons", which overlap slightly on the jacket sleeves. "Our clients want individuality, the trend is to personalise clothing." They also want perfection in the attention to detail: buttonholes are double-stitched, first using cotton, then with silk thread. These elegant and sophisticated touches are supervised by Gregor Thissen, the third generation to be at the helm of the firm.

Scabal – whose name is not the result of a marketing idea but an acronym of Société Commerciale Anglo, Belgo, Allemande and Luxembourgeoise – was established in Brussels in 1938 with six employees. The firm started out processing materials. Later on, it progressed to manufacturing fabrics and made-to-measure tailoring. Nowadays, the Scabal label also offers its own off-the-peg collections. All the sewing at the Brussels headquarters goes on behind an anonymous-looking façade on the Boulevard d'Anvers. What is hidden behind those old walls is all the more fascinating: there are almost a million metres of fabric on 10,000 bales. Next door to this huge selection of materials, the creative team is busy designing the "ready-to-wear" lines and accessories, including pullovers, Egyptian cotton shirts, silk ties and pocket handkerchiefs, all of them, needless to say, hand-stitched. Every year, Scabal's designers also produce 20 to 30 new fabric qualities, including cloth made from cashmere, silk, linen, mohair and the supersoft hair of the Vicuña lama from Peru. And it is probably not going to be long before these inventive textile designers come up with yet another, ultra-elegant fabric innovation – perhaps one with integrated platinum dust.

COMPANY	UNTERNEHMEN
Scabal S.A. / N.V.	Scabal S.A. / N.V.
FOUNDED IN	GEGRÜNDET
1938	1938
FOUNDER	GRÜNDER
Otto Hertz	Otto Hertz
HEADQUARTERS	HAUPTSITZ
Brussels, Belgium	Brüssel, Belgien
CEO	GESCHÄFTSFÜHRUNG
Peter Thissen	Peter Thissen
(President Scabal	(Vorstandsvorsitzender
Group)	Scabal Gruppe),
Gregor Thissen	Gregor Thissen
(CEO Scabal	(Geschäftsführer Scabal
Group)	Gruppe)
EMPLOYEES	MITARBEITER
600 worldwide	600 weltweit
PRODUCTS	PRODUKTE
Fabrics, ready-to-wear	Stoffe, Maßkleidung,
and made-to-measure	Ready-to-wear-Linien und
garments and accessories	Accessoires
ANNUAL PRODUCTION	JAHRESPRODUKTION
Own fabric production:	Eigene Stoffproduktion:
350,000 metres	350.000 Meter
Suit production:	Anzugproduktion:
80,000 garments	80.000 Kleidungsstücke
EXPORT COUNTRIES	EXPORTLÄNDER
Fabrics: worldwide	Stoffe: weltweit
Finished products:	Kleidungsstücke:
Asia, Europe, Russia	Asien, Europa, Russland

SCABAL
A PASSION FOR CLOTH

"Diamond Chip", a fabric collection with
diamond particles
„Diamond Chip", eine Stoff-Kollektion
mit Diamant-Partikeln

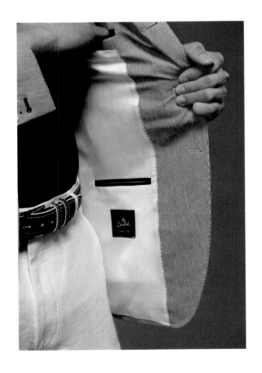

HOCHKARÄTIGE STOFFE

Sie heißen „Diamond Chip", „Gold Treasure" und „Lapis Lazuli": Die extravagant klingenden Namen gehören nicht etwa zu preisgekrönten Rennpferden, sondern bezeichnen Textil-Innovationen von Scabal. Der belgische Anbieter von Luxusstoffen vermischte für den einen Stoff feinste Wolle mit winzigen Diamantsplittern, die für seidigen Glanz sorgen, und webte für den anderen 22-karätige Goldfäden in ultraleichte Merinowolle. Für den Stoff namens „Lapis Lazuli" gelang es Scabal, mikroskopisch kleine Partikel des Halbedelsteins in einem australischen Wolle-Kaschmir-Mix zu verarbeiten. Die Teilchen werden durch die aufgespannten Fasern festgehalten und gleichmäßig integriert. Der Edelsteinstaub verleiht Herrenanzügen ein intensives Ultramarinblau und stärkt – so die Eigenschaft des Steins – auch gleich noch das Immunsystem.

Kein Wunder, dass der Anbieter dieser hochwertigen Stoffe zahlreiche internationale Premium-Marken zu seinen Kunden zählt: Brioni, Smalto, Tom Brown, Prada, Gucci und Armani, sie alle lassen ihre Anzüge aus Scabal-Stoffen schneidern – Anzüge, die bei Wirtschaftsbossen und Politgrößen ebenso wie bei Hollywood-Stars im Schrank oder in der Filmgarderobe hängen. So zeigte sich etwa Daniel Craig in seinem ersten Film als James Bond im eleganten Tuch „Made by Scabal". Popstar Justin Timberlake legt Wert darauf, dass sein Wachs-Double bei Madame Tussauds in London in ein lässig-schickes Outfit von Scabal gehüllt ist. Auch US-Präsident Barack Obama trägt neuerdings einen maßgefertigten Scabal-Anzug. Da passt es zum Image der Marke, dass Scabal seinen Flagship-Store an der berühmtesten Schneidermeile der Welt, der Savile Row N° 12 in London betreibt. Nach der exklusiven Adresse ist auch die Nobel-Kollektion der Marke benannt, eine in Italien von Hand genähte Anzuglinie mit markanten Schultern und schmaler Taille, namens „N° 12".

LUST AUF INDIVIDUALITÄT UND PERFEKTION

Ein maßgeschneiderter Scabal-Anzug orientiert sich exakt an den Konturen des männlichen Körpers. Gefragt sind schlichte Eleganz und hierzulande erstklassiges Tuch in Blau, Schwarz und Grau, mal mit feinen Streifen, mal mit dezenten Karos. „Dabei haben Kunden die Wahl zwischen rund 5.000 Stoffqualitäten und -designs", so Deutschand-Geschäftsführer Matthias Rollmann. Auf Wunsch wird ein Anzug auch innerhalb von drei Wochen maßgeschneidert.

Bei Scabal ist in puncto Passform und Ausstattungsdetails nahezu alles möglich: Die Schneider, die alle eine sechsjährige Lehrzeit hinter sich haben, integrieren auf Wunsch eine passgenaue Innentasche für den I-Pod oder für die Flugtickets, echte Hornknöpfe mit den Initialen des Kunden oder die „Kissing Buttons", die leicht übereinander liegenden Knöpfe an den Jackettärmeln. „Die Käufer haben Lust auf Individualität, der Trend geht zur Personalisierung der Kleidung." Und zu detailverliebter Perfektion: Knopflöcher sind doppelt genäht, erst mit Baum-

30,000 bundles of fabric patterns are assembled by hand every year.
Von Hand werden pro Jahr 30.000 Stoffmuster-Bündel zusammengestellt.

wolle, dann mit einem Seidenfaden. Über diese Feinheiten und Raffinessen wacht Gregor Thissen, Kopf des Unternehmens in dritter Generation.

Die Firma Scabal – deren Name übrigens keiner Marketing-Idee entsprungen ist, sondern ein Kürzel ist für Société Commerciale Anglo, Belgo, Allemande et Luxembourgeoise – wurde 1938 mit sechs Mitarbeitern in Brüssel gegründet. Ursprünglich wurde nur mit Tuch gehandelt, später kamen Stoffherstellung und Maßschneiderei dazu. Heute bietet die Marke Scabal auch eigene Kollektionen von der Stange. Mittlerweile laufen die Fäden aller Fertigungsschritte in der Brüsseler Firmenzentrale hinter einer unscheinbaren Fassade am Boulevard d'Anvers zusammen. Was sich hinter den alten Mauern verbirgt, ist dafür umso faszinierender: Auf über 10.000 Ballen lagern hier rund eine Million Meter Stoff. In unmittelbarer Nähe zu dieser vielfältigen Auswahl entwirft das Kreativteam die „Ready-to-wear"-Linien und Accessoires: Pullover, Oberhemden aus ägyptischer Baumwolle, Seidenkrawatten und Einstecktücher, alles selbstverständlich handgenäht. Außerdem fertigen die Scabal-Designer jedes Jahr 20 bis 30 neue Stoffqualitäten, darunter Tuche aus Kaschmir, Seide, Leinen, Mohair und aus dem flaumweichen Fell des Vicuna-Lamas aus Peru. Und sicher dauert es auch nicht mehr lange, bis die erfinderischen Textildesigner eine weitere, superedle Stoffinnovation entwerfen – vielleicht eine mit integriertem Platinstaub.

Handmade production of a "N°12" suit
Handfertigung eines Scabal-Anzuges „N°12"

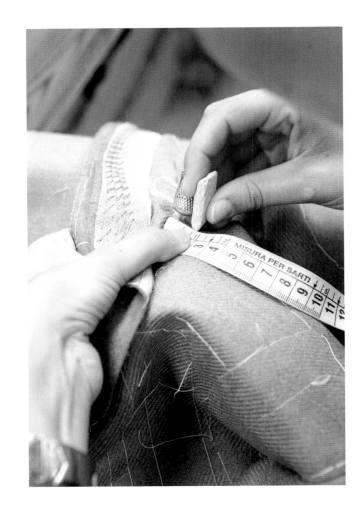

Atelier N° 12: Production site of
handmade "N°12" suits
Atelier N° 12: Produktionsstätte für
die handgefertigten Anzüge „N°12"

SEIDENSTICKER

"Everything I touched
turned to shirts."
Walter Seidensticker Sr.

A LABEL BECOMES
THE EPITOME OF A SHIRT

Seidensticker is practically a household name in Germany to anyone who has
a shirt hanging in their wardrobe. This is partly thanks to the Black Rose logo,
an image which became engraved on people's collective minds as many as fifty
years ago. Fans of top quality and distinctive style know, however, that Seidensticker is also right at home at the premium end of the market. The clients of
this family firm include the exclusive menswear firm of SØR and it also found a
niche for its own top brand with the Jacques Britt label. Decades of experience,
a long manufacturing tradition and a sure instinct for excellence have resulted
in top-quality shirt and blouse collections.

It all began in a room, four metres square, in Bielefeld, where, in 1919, Walter Seidensticker set up a business in his name in his parents' house. His sons,

Walter and Gerd Seidensticker, later established the brand, expanded the business into a consortium of firms and moved into an impressive 1930s building, which remains the firm's headquarters to this day. The firm is meanwhile run by the third generation and it is now cousins Gerd Oliver and Frank Seidensticker who are in charge of the continued development of the brand, which exports to 78 different countries across the world. To this day, this family-run firm, with its long history of tradition, remains committed to uncompromising quality. No member of the family would ever dream of changing the number of tiny stitches which go into the making of an excellent shirt. Nor would they question the elaborate production process which involves a shirt going through over 142 checks. Instead, they stick rigidly to their high standards. Quality and innovation go firmly hand in hand at Seidensticker's: in 1957, the company introduced "Toplin", the first shirt made from non-iron cotton to be launched on the German market – and, consequently, the first branded shirt of the Federal Republic. Another "invention" was the London Collar, the firm's own creation, which was bigger and sharper in appearance than the smaller cutaway collar, fashionable at that time. Seidensticker likewise introduced its high-tech "Splendesto Comfort" range of shirts with a non-iron and, thanks to nano technology, breathable finish. Double seams in the sleeves also guarantee additional durability.

Gerd Oliver Seidensticker, Detlef Adler, Frank Seidensticker

THE EXCLUSIVITY OFFENSIVE

In 1969, Gerd Seidensticker joined with Jacques Britt in developing this exclusive label, the very name of which suggests a combination of French elegance and British gentleman. Thanks to high-quality fabrics, excellent finishing and a combination of both classic and modern styling, Jacques Britt shirts continue to be popular with customers who appreciate perfection. Among the label's demanding clientele, the "Brown Label", with its choice of collars and easy-care fabric quality, is regarded as the business classic with its elegant, waisted styling. Stylish, younger clients prefer the new, slim-fit shirts in the "Blue Label" range. For special, social occasions, Seidensticker developed the Jacques Britt "Gala" range of dress shirts with wing collars. These Bielefeld shirt manufacturers think of every last detail – even down to the individually adjustable depth of the turn-back cuffs which must project at least two centimetres beyond the edge of the jacket sleeve since these, decorated with a pair of elegant cuff-links, are an indicator of a man with style. Seidensticker's high standards are similarly in tune with the company philosophy of SØR, Germany's leading menswear specialist in the exclusive fashion sector. Seidensticker manufactures the shirt and blouse collections for this label in a wide variety of styles. The textile designers are adept at providing SØR with an incomparable combination of elegant, sophisticated styles, first-rate finishing and a range of timeless, classic designs, which manage to cover the entire design spectrum from business chic, classic styles to leisurewear shirts. In order to keep the colours vibrant and create the maximum impact, Seidensticker not only uses top-quality cotton from Italian weaving companies but also favours featherlight fabrics such as satin and voiles. The style repertoire of familiar types of collar, such as the cutaway, Eton, Boston, Kent, Charles, tab and York collars, is further augmented by some larger versions whilst the small collar remains the preserve of self-coloured shirts. The Seidensticker name is just as intrinsically linked with a sense of style, an appreciation of values and innovation as it is with a special passion for shirts. This seems to be something inherent in the family's genes as even the company's founder Walter Seidensticker once remarked: "Everything I touched turned to shirts."

COMPANY Textilkontor Walter Seidensticker GmbH & Co. KG	**UNTERNEHMEN** Textilkontor Walter Seidensticker GmbH & Co. KG
FOUNDED IN 1919	**GEGRÜNDET** 1919
FOUNDER Walter Seidensticker Sr.	**GRÜNDER** Walter Seidensticker sen.
HEADQUARTERS Bielefeld, Germany	**HAUPTFIRMENSITZ** Bielefeld, Deutschland
CEO Frank Seidensticker, Gerd Oliver Seidensticker, Detlef Adler	**GESCHÄFTSFÜHRUNG** Frank Seidensticker, Gerd Oliver Seidensticker, Detlef Adler
EMPLOYEES 1,800	**MITARBEITER** 1.800
PRODUCTS Core products: shirts and blouses	**PRODUKTE** Kernprodukte: Hemden und Blusen
ANNUAL PRODUCTION Approx. 16 million shirts and blouses, more than 800 million shirts since its founding	**JAHRESPRODUKTION** Ca. 16 Millionen Hemden und Blusen, seit der Gründung mehr als 800 Millionen Hemden
EXPORT COUNTRIES Worlwide, 78 countries	**EXPORTLÄNDER** Weltweit, 78 Länder

seidensticker

The headquarters in Bielefeld
Die Bielefelder Unternehmenszentrale

EINE MARKE WIRD ZUM INBEGRIFF DES HEMDES

Der Name Seidensticker ist fast jedem ein Begriff, der ein Hemd in seinem Schrank hängen hat. Dies ist auch ein Verdienst der schwarzen Rose, die sich schon vor einem halben Jahrhundert ins kollektive Gedächtnis eingraviert hat. Liebhaber von höchster Qualität und besonderem Stil aber wissen, dass Seidensticker auch im Premium-Segment zu Hause ist. Produziert werden zum Beispiel Hemden für den exklusiven Herrenausstatter SØR, und mit dem Label Jacques Britt hat das Familienunternehmen seine eigene Top-Marke gut platziert. Hier münden jahrzehntelange Erfahrung, gewachsene Herstellertradition und ein sicheres Gespür für Erlesenes in feinste Hemden- und Blusenkollektionen. Angefangen hat alles in einem vier Quadratmeter großen Zimmer in Bielefeld. Dort, im Haus seiner Eltern, gründete Walter Seidensticker senior 1919 die gleichnamige Firma. Seine Söhne Walter und Gerd Seidensticker etablierten später die Marke, bauten das Unternehmen zu einem Firmenkonsortium aus und zogen in einen eindrucksvollen 1930er-Jahre-Bau, noch heute Firmensitz von Seidensticker. Mittlerweile kümmert sich bereits die dritte Generation, die Cousins Gerd Oliver und Frank Seidensticker, um die Weiterentwicklung des Labels, das weltweit in 78 Länder exportiert.

Bis heute steht das traditionsreiche Familienunternehmen für kompromisslose Qualität. Kein Mitglied der Familie würde je daran denken, die Anzahl der vielen dicht gesetzten Stiche zu ändern, die ein exzellentes Hemd ausmachen. Ebenso wenig würden sie die aufwendigen Fertigungsmethoden eines Hemdes infrage stellen, das über 142 Kontrollen durchläuft. Stattdessen halten sie an den hohen Standards fest. Qualität und Innovation sind bei Seidensticker untrennbar miteinander verbunden: 1957 präsentierte das Unternehmen mit „Toplin" das erste Hemd aus bügelfreier Baumwolle auf dem deutschen Markt – und damit das erste Markenhemd der Republik. Eine andere „Erfindung" war der Londoner Kragen, eine eigene Kreation, die größer und akkurater aussah als der damals modische, kleine Hai-Kragen. Von Seidensticker stammt ebenfalls das High-tech-Hemd „Splendesto Comfort", das bügelfrei und dank Nano-Technologie atmungsaktiv ist. Außerdem stabilisieren Doppelnähte, sogenannte Handkapp-nähte, die Ärmel.

DIE PREMIUM-OFFENSIVE

Mit Jacques Britt entwickelte Gerd Seidensticker 1969 die Premium-Marke, die bereits im Namen französische Noblesse mit britischem Gentleman-Bewusstsein verbindet: Bis heute überzeugt sie Kunden, die sich für Perfektion begeistern können, durch wertvollste Materialien, beste Verarbeitung und klassische wie modische Schnitte. Das „Brown Label" gilt bei seiner anspruchsvollen Klientel mit seinen Kragenvarianten und der pflegeleichten Stoffqualität als Business-Klassiker. Es besticht durch elegante, taillierte Schnitte. Junge, stilbewusste Kunden begeistern die neuen Slim-fit-Hemden des „Blue Label". Für die besonderen gesellschaftlichen Anlässe entwickelte Seidensticker die Jacques Britt Gala- und Smokinghemden mit Kläppchenkragen. Die Hemdenmacher aus Bielefeld denken an alle Details – sogar an die individuell anpassbare Weite der Umschlagmanschette, die unter einem Sakko mindestens zwei Zentimeter sichtbar sein sollte, denn, dekoriert mit einem Paar eleganter Manschettenknöpfe, verrät das Hemd einen Mann mit Stil.

Die hohen Ansprüche von Seidensticker passen auch zur Firmenphilosophie von SØR. Deutschlands führender Herrenausstatter im Premium-Segment lässt bei Seidensticker die Hemden- und Blusenkollektion des Labels in allen Stilrichtungen fertigen. Den Textildesignern gelingt für SØR eine unvergleichliche Kombination aus eleganten, raffinierten Schnitten, erstklassiger Verarbeitung und zeitlos-klassischen Dessins – und zwar für die gesamte Entwurfspalette, von Business-Chic über klassische Looks bis hin zu Freizeithemden, von Uni über Multicolorstreifen bis hin zu würfelgroßen Karos. Damit die Farbtöne lebendig erscheinen und sich ihre Wirkung optimal entfalten kann, setzt das Unternehmen neben feinster Baumwolle von italienischen Webern auch auf andere federleichte Stoffe wie Satin und Voile. Das Stilrepertoire der bekannten Kragentypen wie etwa Hai, Eton, Boston, Kent, Charles, Tab und York wird ergänzt durch voluminösere Varianten, während der kleine Kragen den Hemden in Uni vorbehalten bleibt.

Stilbewusstsein, Werteverständnis und Innovation sind mit dem Namen Seidensticker ebenso untrennbar verbunden wie die besondere Leidenschaft für Hemden. Sie scheint in den Genen der Familie zu liegen, denn schon Firmengründer Walter Seidensticker konnte feststellen: „Alles, was ich anfasste, wurde zu Hemden."

A trainee with her teacher, around 1950
Auszubildende mit ihrer Lehrmeisterin, um 1950

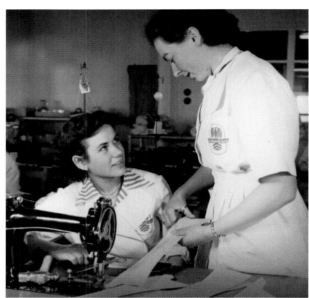

View of the Bielefeld sewing room, around 1950
Blick in den Bielefelder Nähsaal, um 1950

Seidensticker's present-day production hall at its Vietnam factory
Heutige Produktion: Der Nähsaal von Seidensticker in Vietnam

SØR
— SINCE 1956

"We dress Germany better!"
Thomas Rusche

THE OBLIGATIONS OF GOOD STYLE

Inspired by a desire to inject some international chic without all the chichi into Germany's economic miracle, Egon and Doris Rusche opened their first branch of SIR in Bielefeld, an old linen weaving town in eastern Westphalia, in 1956. This traditional family firm, which dates back to 1897, quickly extended its reputation beyond the borders of North Rhine Westphalia and grew with impressive speed to become Germany's premier menswear company. The range of international premium brands, as well as the SØR label itself, bore testimony to its owner's unerring fashion sense and met with considerable interest in cities like Hanover, Hamburg and Munich. Not only did he have an appreciation of aesthetic style and quality but Egon Rusche was also blessed with the attributes of discretion and modesty. He never sought out the rich and famous but they nonetheless liked coming to him. Regular customers included Axel Springer, the Prince of Thurn and Taxis, Heinz Rühmann and Herbert von Karajan, whose white SØR cashmere turtle-neck pullovers – in breach of all the usual etiquette – became an indispensable feature of his conductor's outfit. They all enjoyed wearing clothes picked from the timeless, elegant collections, which Egon and Doris Rusche assembled with an unerring instinct for quality and style and were suitable for every situation. In 1967, a dilemma regarding the label name SIR gave rise to an amusing and significant anecdote. One morning, as Egon Rusche was enjoying his usual breakfast of crispbread, he noticed with great excitement the Scandinavian letter "ø" on the Smørrebrød packet, thereby bringing weeks of agonising over a new name for Sir to a happy conclusion. The pronunciation was preserved whilst a new, memorable logo was coined which remains unique to this day.

Dr. Dr. Thomas Rusche

CLOTHING CULTURE IS A MATTER CLOSE TO THE HEART

In 1984, young Thomas Rusche acceded to his parents' wishes and joined them in the family firm. Encouraged by the changing times, this ambitious son introduced computer technology to the firm and developed his father's plans to build up a catalogue trade. Despite his open-minded approach to progress, Thomas Rusche, a qualified Doctor of Economics and Philosophy, remained committed to style and maintained his unique relationship with the culture of clothing. Consequently, in 1991, Rusche, long-standing president of the International Menswear Group (IMG) and passionate art collector, published "The little SØR guide to clothing culture". The book became the ultimate encyclopaedia for the well-dressed gentleman of the world, who recognised the cultural dimensions of clothing and was keen to dress with impeccable taste in every situation. It was one of the few works on the subject to be translated into English. To this day, the SØR guide is still regarded as the bible of clothes culture even in the country that invented the suit.

ARTFULLY LIMITING THE CHOICE TO JUST THE VERY BEST

SØR is a symbol for sheer pleasure in good style. Thanks to its diversity, the label can offer clothes which are in harmony with the wearer's personal dress style, providing a wide choice of men's and women's clothes suitable for all occasions; finest Italian cashmere knitted collections, shirts and blouses from the best Italian and German weaving mills, suits bearing the hallmark of top-class tailoring craftsmanship, beautifully made chinos, accessories, including ties and scarves from German silk weaving companies, shoe collections of the finest Italian calfskin – the selection is enormous. In this way, the SØR approach combines clothing culture and luxury: mind you, as far as SØR is concerned, luxury simply means artfully limiting the choice to just the very best. "We just dress Germany better!" – SØR has successfully and confidently upheld this guiding principle for many years.

In 58 SØR branches, situated in locations from Sylt to Rottach Egern, customers receive competent style advice in the classic ambience of a fashion salon. The distinctive chequered marble floor and original English antiques, which adorn every SØR store, allow the customer to escape for a moment from the hectic atmosphere and unpredictability of normal shopping centres. Here, you will find a mix of tradition and fashion, a place which brings together culture and the spirit of the times, as demonstrated by the large number of top-quality brands, some of which have been collaborating with the family firm for over 75 years. The soul of SØR is all about timeless beauty and what is elegantly good; Redi ad pulchrum – return to beauty (Augustinus).

COMPANY	UNTERNEHMEN
SØR Rusche GmbH	SØR Rusche GmbH
FOUNDED IN	GEGRÜNDET
1956	1956
FOUNDER	GRÜNDER
Egon Rusche	Egon Rusche
HEADQUARTERS	HAUPTFIRMENSITZ
Oelde, Germany	Oelde, Deutschland
CEO	GESCHÄFTSFÜHRUNG
Dr. Dr. Thomas Rusche	Dr. Dr. Thomas Rusche
EMPLOYEES	MITARBEITER
280	280
PRODUCTS	PRODUKTE
High-quality clothing for men and women	Hochwertige Bekleidung für Herren und Damen

Stylish clothes culture
Stilvolle Kleidungskultur

GUTER STIL VERPFLICHTET

Internationalen Chic ohne Chichi ins deutsche Wirtschaftswunderland zu tragen, von diesem Credo beflügelt, eröffneten Egon und Doris Rusche im Jahr 1956 die erste SIR-Filiale in der ostwestfälischen Leineweberstadt Bielefeld. Das traditionsreiche Familienunternehmen, dessen Wurzeln bis ins Jahr 1897 zurückreichen, überschritt schon bald zielsicher die Landesgrenzen Nordrhein-Westfalens und avancierte in beachtlicher Geschwindigkeit zu *dem* deutschen Herrenausstatter. Das Sortiment aus internationalen Premium-Brands sowie der Marke SØR war stilsicher zusammengestellt und stieß in Städten wie Hannover, Hamburg und München auf großes Interesse. Neben dem Sinn für Ästhetik und Qualität waren Diskretion und Bescheidenheit die Attribute von Egon Rusche. Die Nähe zu den Schönen und Reichen hat er nie gesucht; aber sie kamen gerne zu ihm. Zu den Stammkunden gehörten Axel Springer, der Fürst von Thurn und Taxis, Heinz Rühmann oder Herbert von Karajan, für den die weißen SØR Kaschmir-Rollis, aller Etikette zum Trotz, zum unverzichtbaren Detail seiner Dirigenten-Garderobe wurden. Sie alle genossen es, sich mit den zeitlos eleganten und anlassgerechten Kollektionen zu kleiden, die Egon und Doris Rusche mit ihrem Gespür für Qualität und Stil auswählten. 1967 kam es aufgrund einer markenrechtlichen Auseinandersetzung um den Namen SIR zu einer amüsanten und prägenden Anekdote. Als Egon Rusche morgens sein typisches Knäckebrot-Frühstück zu sich nahm, entdeckte er hellauf begeistert das skandinavische „ø" auf der Smørrebrød-Packung. Damit hatte das wochenlange Grübeln über einen neuen Namen für SIR ein gutes Ende gefunden. Die Aussprache blieb, und ein bis heute einzigartig einprägsames Schriftbild manifestierte sich.

KLEIDUNGSKULTUR IST HERZENSANGELEGENHEIT

1984 stieg der junge Thomas Rusche auf Wunsch der Eltern mit ins Unternehmen ein. Begleitet vom Wind des Zeitgeistes installierte der ambitionierte Sohn die Computertechnologie in der Firma und realisierte die Idee seines Vaters, einen Versandhandel aufzubauen. Ebenso wie er dem Fortschritt aufgeschlossen gegenüberstand, fühlte sich Thomas Rusche dem Stil verpflichtet. Der promovierte Wirtschaftswissenschaftler und Philosoph pflegt eine unverwechselbare Verbundenheit zu der Kultur des Kleidens. Und so veröffentlichte der langjährige Präsident der IMG International Menswear Group und passionierte Kunstsammler 1991 „Das kleine SØR-Brevier der Kleidungskultur". Der Titel wurde die ultimative Enzyklopädie für den gut gekleideten Herrn von Welt, der die kulturelle Dimension der Kleidung erkennt und sich dem Anlass entsprechend tadellos kleiden möchte. Als eines von wenigen Werken aus diesem Segment wurde es ins Englische übersetzt. Bis heute gilt das SØR-Brevier auch im Heimatland des Anzuges als Standardwerk der Kleidungskultur.

DIE RAFFINIERTE BESCHRÄNKUNG AUF DAS BESTE

SØR ist reine Freude am guten Stil. Das Label ermöglicht angesichts der Pluralität der Mode, die Einheit des persönlichen Kleidungsstils in anlassgerechter Vielfalt für Damen und Herren; feinste italienische Kaschmir-Strickkollektionen, Hemden und Blusen aus erstklassigen italienischen und deutschen Webereien, Anzüge, die von bestem Schneiderhandwerk zeugen, aufwendig gearbeitete Chinos, Accessoires wie Krawatten und Schals aus deutschen Seiden-Webereien, Schuh-Kollektionen aus feinstem italienischen Kalbsleder – das Sortiment ist immens. So vereint die Welt von SØR Kleidungskultur und Luxus. Wohlgemerkt Luxus bedeutet bei SØR schlicht die raffinierte Beschränkung auf das Beste: „Wir ziehen Deutschland besser an!" – diesen Leitspruch verfolgt SØR selbstbewusst und seit vielen Jahren mit Erfolg.

In den 58 SØR-Filialen, von Sylt bis Rottach-Egern, werden die Kunden im klassischen Ambiente eines Modesalons stilvoll und kompetent beraten. Der typische Marmor-Schachbrettboden und die original englischen Antiquitäten, die jedes SØR-Geschäft schmücken, ermöglichen den Kunden, für einen Augenblick der Hektik und Beliebigkeit gewöhnlicher Einkaufsmeilen zu entfliehen. Hier trifft Tradition auf Mode, verbindet sich Kultur mit Zeitgeist, verkörpert in den vielen Premium-Marken, mit denen das Familienunternehmen teilweise schon eine über 75-jährige Partnerschaft verbindet. Die Seele von SØR ist das zeitlos Schöne und das vornehme Gute; Redi ad pulchrum – Kehre ein zum Schönen (Augustinus).

Modern elegance
Moderne Eleganz

Top-quality materials and finishing
Erstklassige Materialien und Verarbeitung

243

STEFFEN SCHRAUT

— SINCE 2002

"I would like women of all ages and figures to feel good in my styles."
Steffen Schraut

RATED: VERY STYLISH

Steffen Schraut knows how to start trends. Within ten years, his fashion label has become firmly established in the fashion world – offering luxury feminine fashion with a feel-good factor and a hint of sexiness. The Steffen Schraut label is now available worldwide in the top stores. He has managed to turn his label into a high-end brand and is rightfully rated as "very stylish".

This Düsseldorf designer creates fashion which he describes as minimalist but full of detail. It emphasises the personality of the wearer. His many years of experience as a fashion scout for major firms are a great help in thinking up ideas and in his creative work.

Steffen Schraut is modest, sensitive but very ambitious. His first collection of blouses and T-shirts was a relatively small scale affair. In the meantime, the scale of his business has expanded. His showroom and headquarters in Düsseldorf send out a clear message in this respect. His large, white loft, which is 600 square metres in size, has the cool look of a New York or Berlin gallery. Steffen Schraut's main concern in this respect is that nothing should distract and that his rooms should provide the perfect ambience for any creation without the room itself dictating parameters. It is a room in which any new models can make the maximum impact when they are first presented. The uncomplicated but elegant, trendy and wearable clothes should command the centre of attention.

Steffen Schraut

MODERN, BUT NOT TRENDY – LUXURIOUS BUT NOT EXPENSIVE

Steffen Schraut, who comes from Reutlingen in Swabia, is a whizz kid, who has achieved his success through discipline, consistency and analytical intellect, coupled with passion, perfectionism and an instinct for trends – in other words, all the qualities needed by a successful designer. Steffen Schraut is primarily inspired by art and architecture. He positively absorbs culture, particularly when he's visiting fashionable areas of big cities.

Steffen Schraut is passionate about producing clothes for his target group: middle-aged women who still want to be chic. He has the knack of being able to design exactly the kind of garment that adult women (and their daughters) are seeking: modern, but not trendy, luxurious but not too expensive, elegantly cut but at the same time delightfully comfortable. Albert Eickhoff formulates this approach to the fashion industry as follows: "Steffen Schraut creates, produces, discovers what women really want and not what the fashion world thinks they want."

AN HOMAGE TO FEMININITY

Perfect fashion is fashion which skilfully achieves a balance between proportions, contours and high-quality materials. It is extremely important to Steffen Schraut that the wearer feels good in her clothes, that they give her self-confidence and make her feel well-dressed in every situation. "I would like to create favourite clothes which women will wear for many years because they feel good about themselves in them."

When it is finished, each garment is sent to be tried on in the showroom. Whether a design is finally accepted by the designer depends first and foremost on whether the fit is perfect, on the grading of the styles and the luxurious materials. Each year, Steffen Schraut and his team design about 500 models which appeal to different generations of women in 22 countries of the world. His collections are available at Bergdorf Goodman in New York, Harrods in London, Luisa-ViaRoma in Florence, Unger in Hamburg and at Eickhoff on the Königsallee in Düsseldorf where – it goes without saying – they are displayed alongside all the famous, international designers.

COMPANY Steffen Schraut GmbH	UNTERNEHMEN Steffen Schraut GmbH
FOUNDED IN 2002	GEGRÜNDET 2002
FOUNDER Steffen Schraut	GRÜNDER Steffen Schraut
HEADQUARTERS Düsseldorf, Germany	HAUPTFIRMENSITZ Düsseldorf, Deutschland
CEO Steffen Schraut	GESCHÄFTSFÜHRUNG Steffen Schraut
PRODUCTS Womenswear collection, accessories	PRODUKTE Damenkollektion, Accessoires
ANNUAL PRODUCTION 8 delivery dates	JAHRESPRODUKTION 8 Liefertermine
EXPORT COUNTRIES 22 countries	EXPORTLÄNDER 22 Länder

STEFFEN SCHRAUT

Fall/Winter campaign 2012/13
Kampagne Herbst/Winter 2012/13

PRÄDIKAT:
BESONDERS STILVOLL

Steffen Schraut versteht sich als Trendsetter. Innerhalb von zehn Jahren hat der Modemacher sein gleichnamiges Unternehmen in der Branche etabliert. Seine luxuriöse feminine Fashion vereint ihren Wohlfühlcharakter mit einem Hauch Sexiness. Heute ist Steffen Schraut international in den besten Stores vertreten – es ist ihm gelungen, aus seinem Label eine Top-Marke zu machen. Prädikat: besonders stilvoll.

Der Düsseldorfer entwirft Mode, die er als minimalistisch, aber detailverliebt bezeichnet. Sie unterstreicht die Persönlichkeit der Trägerin. Bei der Ideenfindung und der kreativen Arbeit hilft ihm seine jahrelange Erfahrung als Trendscout für große Unternehmen.

Steffen Schraut ist bescheiden, feinsinnig, leise, aber sehr zielstrebig. Seine erste Blusen- und T-Shirt-Kollektion entstand noch im kleinen Rahmen – heute haben sich die Dimensionen erweitert. Mit seinem Showroom und Firmensitz in Düsseldorf setzt er ein deutliches Zeichen: Das 600 Quadratmeter große, schneeweiße Loft vermittelt den coolen Look einer Galerie in New York oder Berlin. Für Schraut ist dabei das Wichtigste, dass nichts ablenkt, dass er in seinen Räumen eine Atmosphäre schafft, in der alles entstehen kann, weil der Raum selbst keine Vorgaben macht. Hier finden seine neuen Modelle bei ihrem ersten Auftritt die größtmögliche Präsenz. Die gleichermaßen unkomplizierte wie elegante, trendige wie tragbare Mode steht im Mittelpunkt.

MODERN, ABER NICHT MODISCH – LUXURIÖS, ABER NICHT TEUER

Der aus dem schwäbischen Reutlingen stammende Steffen Schraut ist ein Senkrechtstarter, der sich seinen Erfolg mit Disziplin, Beständigkeit und analytischem Verstand erarbeitet hat. Gepaart mit Leidenschaft, Perfektion und einem Gespür für Trends. Alles Eigenschaften, die ein erfolgreicher Designer haben muss. Inspirieren lässt sich Steffen Schraut in erster Linie von Kunst und Architektur. Er saugt die Kultur förmlich auf, insbesondere auf seinen Reisen in die angesagten Viertel der Mega-Cities.
Mit Leidenschaft bedient Steffen Schraut auch seine Zielgruppe: Die Frau mitten im Leben, die unaufgeregt chic sein will. Er entwirft exakt die Mode, die erwachsene Frauen (und ihre Töchter) immer suchen: modern, aber nicht modisch, luxuriös, aber nicht teuer, fein geschnitten, aber gleichzeitig herrlich bequem. Albert Eickhoff formuliert dieses Anliegen im Hinblick auf die Modebranche folgendermaßen: „Steffen Schraut macht das, produziert das, erfindet das, was die Frau wirklich will, und nicht, was Modeleute glauben, was Mode wird."

EINE HOMMAGE AN DIE WEIBLICHKEIT

Perfekte Mode ist Mode, die das Zusammenspiel von Proportionen, Konturen und edlen Materialien gekonnt vereint. Steffen Schraut liegt viel daran, dass sich die Trägerin in einem Kleidungsstück wohlfühlt, dass es ihr Selbstsicherheit gibt und dass sie sich damit überall gut angezogen fühlt. „Ich möchte Lieblingsteile entwerfen, die Frauen viele Jahre lang gerne tragen, weil sie sich darin mögen." Jedes Teil wird nach der Fertigung zur Anprobe in den Showroom geschickt. Ob ein Entwurf vor dem Designer bestehen kann, hängt in erster Linie von der perfekten Passform, der Gradierung der Schnitte und den luxuriösen Materialien ab.
Jedes Jahr entwirft Steffen Schraut mit seinem Team rund 500 Modelle, die Frauen unterschiedlicher Generationen in 22 Ländern der Welt anziehend finden. Seine Kollektionen hängen an den Kleiderstangen bei Bergdorf Goodman in New York, Harrods in London, LuisaViaRoma in Florenz, Unger in Hamburg oder bei Eickhoff auf der Düsseldorfer Kö – und überall ganz selbstverständlich neben allen namhaften internationalen Designern.

Poncho from the Fall/Winter
2012/13 collection
Poncho aus der Kollektion
Herbst/Winter 2012/13

VALSTAR
— SINCE 1911

"A Valstar garment is
always worth much more
than the money it costs."
Sai Vita

ICONS WEAR VALSTAR

For almost 100 years, Valstar – with its unfailing instinct for the latest trends
and its customers' needs – has displayed an apparently intuitive flair for con-
verting outerwear into high-end fashion with an individual touch. This is especially true of the leather blouson jacket, originally designed in 1935 and
registered under the "Valstarino" trademark in 2009. This style of jacket has,
right from the start, exuded a uniquely individual air of sophistication and
casual chic.

It was the first blouson-style jacket to be made of unlined suede leather. Typical
features of a Valstarino jacket include its sporty, high, soft, knitted collar with
embroidery, its front double-entry patch pockets, the hand-stitched seams, its
eleven buttons with hand-finished, double-stitched buttonhole detail as well
as a ribbed waistband which emphasises the waist. To this day, the Valstarino
jacket is still made from a single piece of leather, both for nappa and suede,
thanks to a meticulous selection of the raw material.

But the first masterpiece of Valstar was the trench coat: with its raglan sleeves, belt, in light coloured waterproof gabardine, the trench coat has not changed ever since its first appearance, becoming a basic garment of a man's wardrobe. In the 40s Valstar was officially affirmed as royal supplier, dressing meanwhile many famous actor and actresses that due to the movie industry of the 20s and 30s felt in love with this style.

CASUAL CHIC MADE FROM THE BEST MATERIALS

The cornerstone of the Valstar enterprise was laid by "English Fashion Waterproof", a branch of the British firm Mandleberg Ltd, which established itself in Milan in 1911 and had succeeded in industrially manufacturing a raincoat in waterproof yarn. When the English element withdrew from the business a few years later, Chinese-born Sai Vita, who had Milanese origins, took over the running of the firm and adopted the attractive new name of Valstar. Sai Vita's great passion was travelling. From the very beginning, the philosophy of the company was influenced by this cosmopolitan entrepreneur with his strong instinct for quality, his sensitive flair for elegance and comprehensive knowledge of fine materials. And he did indeed succeed in making history. Valstar is a made-up name with no specific meaning and yet for decades it has been symbolic of so much. Having withstood the test of time, Valstar's internationally bestselling lines epitomise the cachet of a "Made in Italy" tag in the world of fashion and ensure that people's fascination with casual chic and enduring quality is passed on from one generation to the next.

In 1978 the company created a new icon: a little man, small, round-headed with white eyes. A new logo expressing the dynamism and the internationality of the brand. And this logo became the Italian football team sponsor for the world championship in Argentina. Today, with a touch of colour, it is the protagonist of the Valstarino brand label, especially dedicated to Italy and Japan.

QUALITY DOWN TO THE FINEST DETAIL

Valstar clothes, which are produced exclusively in Italy, and created by a team of designers, are still very popular on account of their soft, flowing lines, the harmony of the fabrics and the choice of attractive, natural colours. The materials are sourced from Japan, Italy, Germany and France and guarantee the durability of every Valstar product. Its inspired fashions are characterised by great attention to detail: coats and blousons, for example, are finished with top-quality horn or Corozo (known as vegetable ivory) buttons which, as well as the high level of craftsmanship involved, also adds an additional haptic element to every Valstar product.

This world leader in the domain of "casual chic" is still producing fashions for both men and women which are as sophisticated as they are weatherproof. Functionality is what determines the firm's design tradition and the philosophy that "form follows function" is evident in every collection: comfortable, breathable and waterproof fabrics keep out both London rain as well as autumn storms on the Champs-Elysées. Designs which effortlessly combine timeless elegance with an urban lifestyle are as much at home on the Corso Buenos Aires as on 5th Avenue in New York.

Stefano Massa

COMPANY	UNTERNEHMEN
Valstar S.p.A.	Valstar S.p.A.
FOUNDED IN	GEGRÜNDET
1911	1911
FOUNDER	GRÜNDER
Sai Vita	Sai Vita
HEADQUARTERS	HAUPTFIRMENSITZ
Milan, Italy	Mailand, Italien
CEO	GESCHÄFTSFÜHRUNG
Stefano Massa	Stefano Massa
EMPLOYEES	MITARBEITER
25	25
PRODUCTS	PRODUKTE
Outerwear for men	Outerwear für Damen
and women	und Herren
EXPORT COUNTRIES	EXPORTLÄNDER
Worldwide	Weltweit

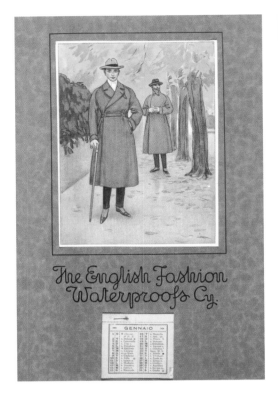

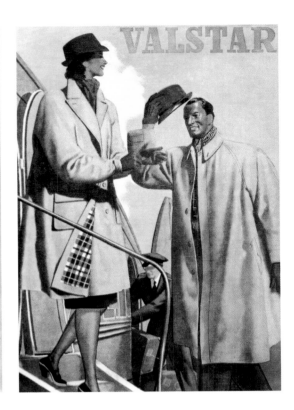

IKONEN TRAGEN VALSTAR

Above from left to right:
Company's calendar dated 1925 when
Valstar was still English Fashion Water-
proof, and advertising images of Valstar's
raincoats, 1940s–50s
Oben von links nach rechts:
Firmenkalender aus dem Jahr 1925, als
Valstar noch English Fashion Waterproof
hieß und Werbeplakate für Valstar-Regen-
mäntel, 1940er–50er-Jahre

Scheinbar intuitiv, mit einem sicheren Gespür für Trends und die Bedürfnisse seiner Kunden verwandelt Valstar seit fast 100 Jahren Outerwear in hochwertige Mode mit einem individuellen Touch. Das gilt insbesondere für den 1935 entworfenen Lederblouson, der 2009 auf den Namen „Valstarino" getauft und eingetragen wurde. Dieser Jacken-Entwurf war von Anfang an einzigartig, unverwechselbar im Stil und von einer überzeugend lässigen Coolness. Er war der erste Blouson, der aus ungefüttertem Wildleder bestand. Zu den charakteristischen Details eines Valstarino-Blousons zählen der sportliche, in anschmiegsamem Strick gearbeitete Stehkragen, die vorne aufgesetzten Taschen mit zusätzlichem Seiteneingriff, der sichtbare Steppstich, die insgesamt elf Knöpfe, die handgearbeiteten Knopflöcher mit Doppelbordierung sowie der abschließende Strickbund mit Stickereien, welcher die Taille betont. Der Valstarino-Blouson wird auch heute noch, dank der akribischen Auswahl des Rohmaterials aus Nappa- und Wildleder, aus einem einzigen Stück gefertigt.
Der erste Klassiker jedoch, den Valstar schuf, war der Trenchcoat: Hergestellt aus hellem, wasserfestem Gabardine mit Raglan-Ärmeln und Gürtel ist er seit seinem ersten Erscheinen im Prinzip unverändert geblieben. Dieser Mantel gehört zur Grundausstattung der Herrenbekleidung. Noch bevor Valstar in den 1940er-Jahren offiziell zum königlichen Hoflieferanten ernannt wurde, kleidete das Unternehmen viele berühmte Schauspielerinnen und Schauspieler ein. Die Filmindustrie der 1920er- und 1930er-Jahre hatte einen Modestil weitergetragen, in den sich viele der zeitgenössischen Leinwand-Ikonen verliebten.

SPORTLICHER CHIC AUS BESTEN MATERIALIEN

Den Grundstein des Unternehmens Valstar legte die „English Fashion Water-proof", eine Filiale der britischen Firma Mandleberg Ltd., die sich im Jahr 1911 in Mailand niedergelassen hatte. Ihr war es gelungen, einen Regenmantel aus wasserundurchlässigem Kammgarn in industrieller Produktion herzustellen. Als sich die Engländer einige Jahre später aus dem Geschäft zurückzogen, übernahm der in China geborene Sai Vita, der Mailander Wurzeln hatte, die Leitung des Unternehmens und verlieh ihm den wohlklingenden Namen Valstar. Sai Vitas Leidenschaft war das Reisen. So prägte der Kosmopolit mit hohem Qualitätsbewusstsein, einem sensiblen Gespür für Eleganz und umfassender Kenntnis feiner Stoffe von Anfang an die Philosophie des Unternehmens. Und es ist ihm gelungen, Geschichte zu schreiben. Der Name Valstar ist eine reine Wortschöpfung, trägt keine bestimmte Bedeutung und steht doch seit Jahrzehnten für so Vieles. Die Zeiten überdauernd, repräsentieren die weltweiten Bestseller das „Made in Italy" auf dem internationalen Bekleidungsmarkt und sorgen dafür, dass sich die Faszination für sportlichen Chic und langlebige Qualität von einer Generation auf die nächste überträgt.

1978 schuf das Unternehmen ein neues Piktogramm: eine kleine Figur mit rundem Kopf und weißen Augen, die als neues Logo die Dynamik und Internationalität der Marke verkörpern sollte. Sie wurde zum Symbol des Sponsors der italienischen Fußballmannschaft bei der Weltmeisterschaft in Argentinien im gleichen Jahr. Heute steht diese Figur, um etwas Farbe bereichert, für das Label Valstarino, insbesondere in Italien und Japan.

QUALITÄT BIS INS KLEINSTE DETAIL

Die ausschließlich in Italien hergestellten und von einem mehrköpfigen De-signteam entworfenen Produkte bestechen auch heute noch durch ihre weichen, fließenden Schnitte, die Harmonie der Materialien und die natürliche, ausgewogene Farbgebung. Die Materialien stammen aus Japan, Italien, Deutschland und Frankreich, und sie garantieren die Langlebigkeit eines jeden Valstar-Produktes. Mit großer Liebe zum Detail setzt Valstar seine modischen Inspirationen um: So sind zum Beispiel Mäntel und Blousons versehen mit hochwertigen Knöpfen aus Horn oder dem elfenbeinartigen, rein pflanzlichen Corozo. Sie verleihen, neben der guten handwerklichen Verarbeitung, jedem Valstar-Produkt eine besondere haptische Note.

Die international führende Marke im Bereich Casual Chic kleidet bis heute sowohl die Dame als auch den Herrn ebenso raffiniert wie witterungsunabhängig. Funktionalität bestimmt diese Designtradition und das Credo „Form follows function" ist in allen Kollektionen spürbar: Bequeme, atmungsaktive und wasserdichte Stoffe halten dem Londoner Regen ebenso stand wie Herbststürmen auf den Champs-Elysées. Schnitte, die mühelos zeitlose Eleganz mit urbanem Lifestyle verbinden, kommen auf dem Corso Buenos Aires genauso gut an wie in der 5th Avenue in New York.

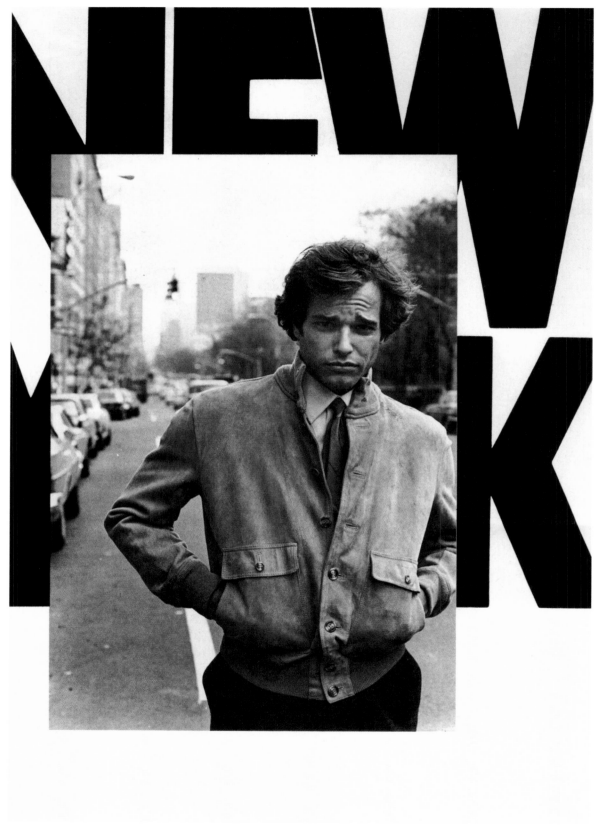

Advertising of the famous Valstar jacket, 1970s
Werbeanzeige für den berühmten Valstar-Blouson, 1970er-Jahre

l'ombrello
si può anche
dimenticare
se si ha
un impermeabile

Valstar

*Icon used for the Italian football team at
the World Cup 1978 in Argentina.
Logo, das für die italienische Fußballmannschaft bei der WM 1978 in Argentinien zum Einsatz kam.*

253

VAN BOMMEL
— SINCE 1734

"My shoes have been lying under a chair in our bedroom for a few months. I keep wanting to throw them away, but whenever I pick them up I just can't do it."
A customer

THE OLDEST SHOE MANUFACTURER IN EUROPE

Wooden shoe forms are piled high in dozens of wire baskets. Floris van Bommel, casually dressed in jeans and a T-shirt, makes his way along the aisles of the Dutch factory, checking the different shoe models. For this young entrepreneur, perfect shoes are symbolic and an indication of an attitude towards life. Van Bommel, who is Head of Design and Marketing, and his brothers Reynier and Pepijn are the ninth generation to run this 270-year-old family firm. Since 1734, around 25 million boxes of exclusive shoes – originally for men but later also for women – have been dispatched from the firm's Moergestel headquarters all over the world. Van Bommel's reputation as a manufacturer of top-quality, hand-stitched men's shoes has been consolidated over the course of several centuries. The combination of tradition and progress has always been an important element of Van Bommel's shoe manufacture. And the firm's current junior director is likewise very keen to preserve the unique character of the label whilst, at the same time, keeping abreast of fashion trends. The three most popular lines marketed by this master shoe manufacturer bear testimony to this. "Noble Blue" shoes, for example, which are made by hand in a series of over 300 stages, are the epitome of pure luxury. Van Bommel's Derby full brogues are similarly a great classic. Their elegant form developed from the golf shoe and they were made to such perfection by shoemakers in Budapest that they became popularly known as Budapests. Some of the firm's more recent models include ankle-high boots, sporty boat shoes, suede loafers and moccasins. The firm's young manager has established his own "Floris van Bommel" label, which ranks among the top international fashion brands, and features trendy crossover shoe creations, ranging from metallic shiny leather, crocodile finish and bold colours.

Pepijn, Reynier & Floris van Bommel

ROYAL FOOTWEAR IN 260 STAGES

The process of producing handmade shoes involves four separate stages: specialists in the design department develop lasts to suit specific types of feet, the individual pieces of leather are cut out in the cutting department and then sewn together in the stitching department. The assembly department is then responsible for constructing the shoe on the last. Shoes have been manufactured in much the same way – albeit in just a two-man operation – since 1734 when Adriaan and Christiaan van Bommel signed a document which described them as master shoemakers. Subsequent generations gradually earned the "Van Bommel" label a prestigious reputation. Two hundred years later in 1936, the royal court commissioned a pair of sandals in the colours of the royal house of Lippe-Detmold for Princess Juliana of the Netherlands on the occasion of her engagement to Prince Bernhard. In 1952, van Bommel was awarded the title of "official supplier to the royal court". These "royal shoes" made by Europe's oldest shoe manufacturer are the epitome of high quality. They are hand-stitched – which is the highest and finest accolade that can be attributed to a pair of shoes – and each shoe must undergo 260 manual operations and takes about eight weeks to complete. About 80 per cent of the shoes are manufactured using the Goodyear system, which is easily identifiable by the double seam in the leather sole. The less common Ago system uses special adhesives, which fix the uppers to the insole, thereby guaranteeing a high level of durability. An additional refinement is the feather, known as the "cambreur", which is situated between the insole and the outer sole in all shoe models and supports the arch of the foot.

SHOES FOR LIFE

It goes without saying that the most important elements in every collection are the selection of raw materials and elaborate production methods. Experts travel all over the world visiting the best leather factories in search of the perfect leather for uppers and soles. The inside of a "Full Brogue", for example, is lined exclusively with calf or goat leather since these are the best types for allowing the foot to breathe. A cork layer on its underside makes a shoe more comfortable to wear and the double-stitched seams are practically guaranteed to last. The point here is that however much heavy wear, the thread will not come loose from the sole because it has been impregnated with warm pitch. This reinforcing technique makes the seam virtually indestructible. If they are well looked after, custom-made shoes will last a lifetime.

COMPANY	UNTERNEHMEN
Schoenfabriek wed. J.P. van Bommel BV	Schoenfabriek wed. J.P. van Bommel BV

FOUNDED IN	GEGRÜNDET
1734	1734

FOUNDER	GRÜNDER
Reynier van Bommel	Reynier van Bommel

HEADQUARTERS	HAUPTFIRMENSITZ
Moergestel, The Netherlands	Moergestel, Niederlande

CEO	GESCHÄFTSFÜHRUNG
Floris (Creative Director), Reynier (CEO) and Pepijn (Commercial Director) van Bommel	Floris (Chef-Designer), Reynier (Geschäftsführer) und Pepijn (kaufmännischer Leiter) van Bommel

EMPLOYEES	MITARBEITER
140 in Moergestel	140 in Moergestel

PRODUCTS	PRODUKTE
Ladies' and men's shoes	Damen- und Herrenschuhe

ANNUAL PRODUCTION	JAHRESPRODUKTION
445,000 (sold shoes in 2011)	445.000 (verkaufte Paare 2011)

EXPORT COUNTRIES	EXPORTLÄNDER
Worldwide	Weltweit

The van Bommel family, 1887
Familie van Bommel, 1887

Production hall, 1955
Fabrikhalle, 1955

DIE ÄLTESTE
SCHUHMANUFAKTUR EUROPAS

In Dutzenden von Drahtkörben stapeln sich hölzerne Schuhmodelle. Floris van Bommel schlendert, lässig gekleidet in Jeans und T-Shirt, durch die Reihen der niederländischen Manufaktur und prüft die unterschiedlichen Passformen. Für den jungen Inhaber sind meisterliche Schuhe Ausdruck und Verwirklichung eines Lebensgefühls. Zusammen mit seinen Brüdern Reynier und Pepijn leitet er das über 270 Jahre bestehende Familienunternehmen als Head of Design and Marketing in neunter Generation. Seit 1734 wurden vom Firmensitz Moergestel aus rund 25 Millionen Kartons mit exklusiven Schuhen – zunächst für Herren, später auch für Damen – in alle Welt verschickt. Über die Jahrhunderte hinweg festigte van Bommel seinen Ruf als Hersteller rahmengenähter Herrenschuhe in Spitzenqualität.

Die Verbindung von Tradition und Fortschritt waren in der Schuhmanufaktur van Bommel schon immer feste Größen. Und auch dem heutigen Juniorchef liegt viel daran, die Einzigartigkeit der Marke zu wahren und gleichzeitig trendbewusst zu bleiben. Die drei Erfolgslinien des Meisterschuhmachers beweisen das: So sind zum Beispiel die „Noble Blue"-Schuhe, die in über 300 Arbeitsschritten per Hand gefertigt werden, Sinnbild für puren Luxus. Auch die „Derby-Full Brogues" gehören zu den Klassikern. Ihre elegante Form wurde aus dem Golfschuh entwickelt und ihre Herstellung von den Schuhmachern in Budapest so perfektioniert, dass sie im Volksmund zum „Budapester" wurden. Zu den jüngeren Schuhmodellen gehören knöchelhohe Boots, sportliche Segelschuhe, Wildleder-Loafer und Mokkassins. Unter dem Namen „Floris van Bommel" hat der Jungmanager mit hippen Crossover-Schuhkreationen, teils in metallisch glänzendem Leder, mit Krokoprägung und mutigen Farben, sein eigenes Label etabliert, das in der Top-Riege internationaler Modemarken mitspielt.

KÖNIGLICHES SCHUHWERK IN 260 ARBEITSSCHRITTEN

Der Produktionsprozess handgearbeiteter Schuhe erstreckt sich über vier Phasen: In der Modellabteilung entwickeln Spezialisten anhand spezifischer Fußtypen die Leisten, die Stanzerei stanzt die Lederformen aus und die Näherei fügt die Lederteile zum Schaft aneinander. Abschließend befestigt die Montageabteilung den Schaft auf den Leisten.

So ähnlich, nur im Zwei-Mann-Betrieb, funktionierte das Schuhmacher-Handwerk schon 1734, als Adriaan und Christiaan van Bommel ein Dokument unterschrieben, aus dem hervorgeht, dass sie Schuhmachermeister waren. Die folgenden Generationen verhalfen der Marke „van Bommel" nach und nach zu großem Ansehen. Zweihundert Jahre später, 1936, ließ sogar das niederländische Königshaus Sandaletten in den Farben des Fürstenhauses Lippe-Detmold für Prinzessin Juliana anlässlich ihrer Verlobung mit Prinz Bernhard anfertigen. Im Jahre 1952 erhielt van Bommel das Prädikat „Hoflieferant durch königlichen Erlass". Diese „königlichen Schuhe" der ältesten Schuhmanufaktur Europas sind in Sachen Qualität das Nonplusultra: Sie sind rahmengenäht – die hochwertigste und edelste Machart, die es für Schuhe gibt – und jeder Schuh wird in rund acht Wochen und 260 Arbeitsschritten gefertigt. Rund 80 Prozent der Schuhe werden in der Good-Year-Manier hergestellt, die leicht an der Doppelnaht in der Lederlaufsohle zu erkennen ist. Bei der selteneren Ago-Fertigung garantieren spezielle Kleber, die den Schaft auf der Brandsohle fixieren, eine hohe Haltbarkeit. Eine weitere Raffinesse ist die Gelenkfeder, genannt Cambreur, zwischen der Innensohle und der Laufsohle, die bei allen Modellen den Fußbogen stützt.

SCHUHE FÜR DAS GANZE LEBEN

Pepijn van Bommel

Natürlich spielen bei allen Kollektionen die Auswahl der Rohstoffe und die ausgefeilten Herstellungsmethoden die wichtigste Rolle. Nach Oberleder und Sohlenleder recherchieren Fachkräfte weltweit in den besten Lederfabriken. Das Schuhinnere eines Fullbrogue zum Beispiel wird ausschließlich mit Kalbs- oder Ziegenleder gefüttert, da diese Lederarten besonders atmungsaktiv sind. Eine Korkschicht an der Unterseite des Schuhs sorgt für Tragekomfort, und die doppelten Pechdrahtnähte sind praktisch verschleißfest. Der Clou: Bei hoher Beanspruchung lässt der Draht die Sohle nicht los, weil er vor der Verarbeitung mit warmem Pech durchtränkt wurde. Diese Befestigungstechnik hält die Verbindung unzerstörbar zusammen. Und wer seinen Maßschuh pfleglich behandelt, hat das ganze Leben etwas davon.

VAN LAACK
— SINCE 1881

"A person's inner disposition always influences his outward appearance."
The founders

THE ROYAL SHIRT

In 1881, when Heinrich van Laack and his partners Wilhelm Schmitz and Gustav Eltschig were considering the idea of establishing their first shirt-manufacturing company in Berlin, the type of clientele they had in mind included successful merchants, respected judges and prestigious doctors. Their aim was to tailor a luxury shirt for the elegant gentleman – a shirt which stood out from the crowd and distinguished itself from industrially produced factory garments. In those days, clothes were, after all, an indication of the wearer's social status. The three gentlemen were soon in accord regarding the qualities which were to distinguish the van Laack label: top-quality materials, outstanding workmanship and exclusive styles. The firm's maxim was that "a person's inner disposition always influences his outward appearance". Despite the ambitious goal, their vision paid off: sewing machines were soon clattering away in a factory on the Greifswalderstrasse where women with pinned-up hair and men wearing visor caps sewed collars, sleeves and shirt bodies together. The textiles were, even then, supplied by the finest Italian and Swiss weaving mills. When nimble-fingered seamstresses began embroidering a crown on each shirt above the Laack name – the world's first embroidered brand label – and coined the slogan "van Laack, the royal shirt", the label turned into a status symbol of the Golden Twenties.

It took a further 50 years before the first women's collection was produced in 1972. In those days, the vogue was mainly for figure-hugging styles with bow collars and tucks. Nowadays, the ladies' collection, likewise characterised by meticulous detail, comprises a selection of garments ranging from suits to tunics and shorts.

After more than 125 years of history, the van Laack name still stands for a sure instinct for style, for luxury fabrics and perfect finishing. Today, the company's headquarters in a new glass building in Mönchengladbach represent the heart of the firm. From here, Christian von Daniels directs and supervises the designs produced by the creative team and monitors the label's expansion course. These top-quality products are manufactured in van Laack's own factories in virtually all parts of the world, all of them equipped with a training centre and monitored by strict quality control.

Christian von Daniels

165 STITCHES FOR ONE BUTTON

The current collection includes blouses and blazers, cashmere and merino wool pullovers, piqué polo shirts, jersey rugby shirts, ties, night attire and beachwear, which are as popular with the sheikhs of Dubai as with members of the British aristocracy or German business clients. The precision work on such a shirt begins in the fine detail: precisely 165 stitches surround a buttonhole, which accommodates a distinctive, patented three-hole button, cut from a deep-sea mollusc known as Trochacea. Each button is sewn on by hand with a shank. All shirts have a choice of collars: regardless of whether the collar in question is an Italian cutaway, a button-down, a formal tab or small Kent collar, it consists of four parts, an inner and outer collar band as well as an upper and lower collar, to ensure a perfect fit around the neck. The same naturally applies in particular to a bespoke garment, which consists of 31 individual pieces and takes an average of 180 minutes for a seamstress to complete.

The shirt fabrics are made exclusively from the fibres of ripe cotton bolls since these produce the whitest colour and lend the finished product a silky feel. A further factor to be considered is: the longer the fibre, the finer the resulting weave. Once the cotton threads have been combed and cleaned, they are woven into different types of weave – Jacquard for floral patterns, zephyr batiste for stripes, diamond patterns and Paisley designs, herringbone, flannel, seersucker, ribbed poplin and transparent voile. The fabrics are selected from the best Italian fabric producers after being visually checked and felt by hand. Christian von Daniels encourages every shirt-buying customer to personally check the feel of the fabric and not miss out on this haptic experience when choosing a fabric. It is not uncommon for him to acquire the first, exclusive rights to a particular fabric. In this way, some van Laack products on the international market are unique – and will remain so.

The fact that despite all its new, trend-conscious creations, the brand still remains true to its origins and maintains its extremely high standards of quality, would have delighted the firm's founding fathers. Their black-and-white portrait, which hangs in the director's office, is a reminder of the company's long, successful history.

COMPANY	UNTERNEHMEN
van Laack GmbH	van Laack GmbH
FOUNDED IN	GEGRÜNDET
1881	1881
FOUNDER	GRÜNDER
Heinrich van Laack	Heinrich van Laack
HEADQUARTERS	HAUPTFIRMENSITZ
Mönchengladbach, Germany	Mönchengladbach, Deutschland
CEO	GESCHÄFTSFÜHRUNG
Christian von Daniels, Dr. Sebastian Potyka	Christian von Daniels, Dr. Sebastian Potyka
EMPLOYEES	MITARBEITER
1,668	1.668
PRODUCTS	PRODUKTE
Key products: shirts, blouses, ties and polo shirts	Kerngeschäft: Hemden, Blusen, Krawatten und Poloshirts
ANNUAL PRODUCTION	JAHRESPRODUKTION
1,550,000 items	1.550.000 Artikel
EXPORT COUNTRIES	EXPORTLÄNDER
Worldwide, 86 countries	Weltweit, 86 Länder

DAS KÖNIGLICHE HEMD

"Rigo Royal" shirt with a Kent collar
Hemd „Rigo Royal" mit Kentkragen

Erfolgreiche Kaufleute, angesehene Richter und renommierte Ärzte hatten Heinrich van Laack und seine Partner Wilhelm Schmitz und Gustav Eltschig vor Augen, als sie 1881 in Berlin an einem Konzept für ihre erste Hemdenmarke tüftelten. Ein feines Hemd für den eleganten Herrn wollten sie schneidern. Eines, das aus der Masse herausragt und sich abhebt von schnell angefertigter Fabrikware. Schließlich verriet damals die Kleidung die gesellschaftliche Position ihres Trägers. Über die Erkennungsmerkmale der Marke waren sich die Herren schnell einig: feinste Materialien, meisterliche Verarbeitung und exklusive Schnitte. Ihre Maxime: „Die innere Einstellung bestimmt immer auch die äußere Erscheinung." Das Ziel war hochgesteckt, doch die Vision hatte Erfolg: Schon bald ratterten die Nähmaschinen in einer Fabrik an der Greifswalderstraße. Frauen mit Hochsteckfrisur und Männer mit Schirmmützen nähten Kragen, Ärmel und Body zusammen. Die Textilien wurden schon damals aus den besten Webereien Italiens und der Schweiz geliefert. Als die Näherinnen zusätzlich mit flinken Händen auf jedes Hemd eine Krone über den van Laack-Namenszug stickten – das weltweit erste gestickte Markenzeichen – und es mit dem Slogan „Das königliche Hemd" kombinierten, avancierte die Marke in den goldenen 1920er-Jahren zum Statussymbol.

Es dauerte dann rund 50 Jahre, bis die erste Damenkollektion 1972 in die Läden kam. Damals waren besonders figurbetonte Modelle mit Schleifenkragen und eingenähten Biesen en vogue. Inzwischen umfasst die detailverliebte Damenlinie Kollektionsteile vom Anzug über die Tunika bis zur Shorts.

Nach über 130 Jahren Firmengeschichte steht van Laack immer noch für sicheres Stilempfinden, hochwertigste Stoffe und beste Verarbeitung. Das Herz des Unternehmens ist heute ein glasummantelter Kubus in Mönchengladbach. Von hier aus dirigiert und überwacht Christian von Daniels die Designs des Kreativteams und den Expansionskurs der Marke. Gefertigt werden die hochwertigen Produkte in van-Laack-eigenen Fabriken nahezu auf der ganzen Welt. Alle ausgestattet mit einem Trainingscenter und einem strengen Qualitätsmanagement.

165 STICHE FÜR EINEN KNOPF

Zur Kollektion gehören mittlerweile auch Blusen und Blazer, Pullis aus Kaschmir und Merinowolle, Poloshirts aus Piqué, Rugbyshirts aus Jersey, Krawatten, Nachtwäsche und Beachwear, die den Scheichs von Dubai ebenso gefallen wie der britischen Aristokratie oder deutschen Geschäftsleuten. Die Präzisionsarbeit für ein solches Hemd beginnt im Detail: Exakt 165 Stiche umrahmen ein Knopfloch. Hindurch passt ein patentierter Drei-Loch-Knopf, geschnitten aus der Tiefseeschnecke Trochacea, jeder einzelne auf Stiel genäht. Die Kür bei allen Hemden ist der Kragen: Ob italienischer Haifischkragen, Buttondown, formeller Tab-Kragen oder kleiner Kentkragen – damit er sich der Halsform optimal anschmiegt, wird er immer aus vier Teilen „aufgebaut": aus Innen-

und Außensteg sowie Ober- und Unterkragen. Das gilt natürlich besonders für eine Maßanfertigung, die immerhin aus 31 Einzelteilen besteht und für die eine Näherin im Schnitt 180 Minuten braucht.

Für die Stoffe werden nur Fasern aus reifen Baumwollblüten verwendet. Denn sie strahlen am weißesten und fühlen sich, fertig verarbeitet, griffig-seidig an. Außerdem gilt: je länger die Faser, desto feiner die Verarbeitung der Garne. Sobald die Baumwollgarne gekämmt und gesäubert sind, werden sie in verschiedensten Webungen verarbeitet. In Jacquard-Technik für florale Muster, in Zefir-Batist für Streifen-, Karo- und Paisley-Dessins, Fischgratgewebe, Flanell, Seersucker, gerippten Popeline und transparentem Voile. Ausgesucht werden die Stoffe bei den besten Tuchfabrikanten in Italien. Man sieht und fühlt es den Stoffen an. Christian von Daniels empfiehlt jedem Hemdenkunden in den Stoff hineinzugreifen und sich das haptische Erlebnis bei der Auswahl nicht entgehen zu lassen. Nicht selten erwirbt er die erste und einzige Option auf einen bestimmten Stoff. Auf diese Weise kommen van Laack-Produkte auf den weltweiten Markt, die unverwechselbar sind und bleiben.

Dass sich die Marke neben all ihren neuen, trendbewussten Kreationen jedoch immer wieder auf ihre Ursprünge und somit auf den hohen Qualitätsanspruch besinnt, hätte wohl auch den Gründungsvätern gefallen, deren Schwarz-Weiß-Porträt noch heute im Büro der Geschäftsführung an die lange, erfolgreiche Unternehmensgeschichte erinnert.

Cutting and pressing the collar and cuffs,
a van Laack bestseller – "Alice" blouse
with stand-up collar
Zuschnitt, Bügeln von Kragen und Manschetten,
van Laack-Bestseller Kelchkragenbluse „Alice"

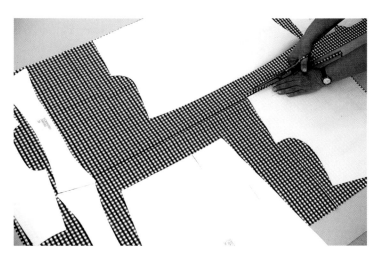

The first van Laack women's collection was launched in 1972.
1972 entsteht die erste van Laack-Damenkollektion.

Seamstresses in the
Mönchengladbach factory
in the mid-1950s
Näherinnen in der Produktions-
stätte in Mönchengladbach,
Mitte der 1950er-Jahre

267

WIGÉNS
— SINCE 1906

"Our label stands for high quality, the best fitting and timeless fashion."
Jan Gustafsson

A TRUE STORY FROM SMÅLAND

Astrid Lindgren has made Småland in southern Sweden famous through her stories. It is considered one of the country's most beautiful regions. One of the true stories from this region is that of Oscar Wigén from the small town of Tranås. In 1906, it occurred to the 26-year-old Wigén that although people used their heads for many different things with varying degrees of success, they did not pay them the attention they deserved. To correct this unsatisfactory state of affairs and provide this precious part of the body with both protection and adornment, he acquired a small factory manufacturing hats for men and women. This young, ambitious businessman was a past master at his craft and the firm quickly became extremely popular. It was not long before his high-quality caps and hats attracted the attention of the Swedish royal family and Oscar Wigén was appointed supplier to the royal court. Now, more than 100 years later,

Wigéns is a successful company with an international reputation and a substantial annual turnover of 42 million Swedish kronor.

Wigéns headquarters are still located in the idyllic little town of Tranås. 14 members of staff are in charge of design, buying and selling and administration. Production is carried out in a factory in Estland where 45 women work at their sewing machines and cutting tables, devoting great attention to detail and ensuring that 200,000 top-quality hats – a must-have, fashionable and functional accessory for Wigéns' customers – are produced each year.

PILOT'S CAPS AND STRAW HATS

Many of Wigéns designs incorporate a sense of timeless chic and have remained a core part of the company's repertoire for over 100 years: they include casual caps, straw hats, pilot's caps, felt hats and the traditional student caps worn by Swedish high-school graduates at their graduation party. However, not only do Swedish people have a strong sense of tradition but they are also known to be decidedly fashion conscious, which is why Wigéns' CEO, Jan Gustafsson, likes – in his own words – to keep his ear to the ground to keep up to date with the latest word on the fashion grapevine. Consequently, any new trends are always reflected in the latest Wigéns collection designs.

Quality is the top priority when it comes to choosing fabrics. Tweed is sourced in Ireland, herringbone is imported from Scotland and elk leather is obviously obtained from Sweden. Jan Gustafsson is always delighted at the prospect of a particularly cold and severe winter as winter caps and hats are Wigéns' biggest sellers. The firm's summer collections comprise a mere 20 per cent of the turnover. Most of Wigéns clients are from North America, Europe or similar places with long, extremely cold winters. Up until a few years ago, the typical customer was described as follows: "Men, aged 40 or more, who spend a lot of time outdoors either working or pursuing leisure activities".

The situation today is quite different as Wigéns products have now become popular accessories for trendy young men and women. A Wigéns fur-lined cap with earflaps is practically a compulsory, must-have winter accessory. Following in the tradition of the company's founder Oscar Wigén, the staff are all very proud of the fact that Tranås craftsmanship is gracing and protecting heads across the entire world. We will never know whether Oscar Wigén ever met Astrid Lindgren in beautiful Småland but it is more than likely that little Michel Lönneberga was wearing a classic Wigéns dark blue, peaked cap during his adventures.

Oscar Wigén

COMPANY	UNTERNEHMEN
AB Oscar Wigén	AB Oscar Wigén
FOUNDED IN	GEGRÜNDET
1906	1906
FOUNDER	GRÜNDER
Oscar Wigén	Oscar Wigén
HEADQUARTERS	HAUPTFIRMENSITZ
Tranås, Sweden	Tranås, Schweden
CEO	GESCHÄFTSFÜHRUNG
Jan Gustafsson	Jan Gustafsson
EMPLOYEES	MITARBEITER
14 in Sweden,	14 in Schweden,
45 in Estonia	45 in Estland
PRODUCTS	PRODUKTE
Caps, hats	Mützen, Hüte
and accessories	und Accessoires
ANNUAL PRODUCTION	JAHRESPRODUKTION
220,000 items	220.000 Artikel
EXPORT COUNTRIES	EXPORTLÄNDER
Europe, Japan,	Europa, Japan,
North America	Nordamerika

EINE WAHRE GESCHICHTE
AUS DEM SMÅLAND

Astrid Lindgren hat es mit ihren Erzählungen berühmt gemacht: das Småland in Süd-Schweden. Es gilt als eine der schönsten Regionen des Landes. Eine der wahren Geschichten, die sich dort zugetragen haben, ist die von Oscar Wigén aus dem kleinen Städtchen Tranås. 1906 fiel dem damals 26-Jährigen auf, dass die Menschen ihren Kopf zwar für so viele Dinge benutzen, mal mehr und manchmal weniger erfolgreich, ihm aber keineswegs genügend Aufmerksamkeit zollen. Um dieses Missverhältnis zu beenden und den wertvollen Kopf zu schützen und zu schmücken, erwarb er eine kleine Manufaktur zur Herstellung von Herren- und Damenhüten. Der junge geschäftstüchtige Unternehmer beherrschte das Handwerk wie kaum ein anderer und so erlangte seine Firma schnell große Popularität. Schon bald wurde auch das schwedische Königshaus auf die hochwertigen Mützen, Hüte und Kappen aufmerksam und ernannte Oscar Wigén zu seinem Hoflieferanten. Heute, mehr als ein Jahrhundert später, ist Wigéns ein international angesehenes und erfolgreiches Unternehmen, mit einem beachtlichen Jahresumsatz von 42 Millionen Schwedischen Kronen. Nach wie vor befindet sich der Hauptsitz des Unternehmens in dem idyllischen

Städtchen Tranås. 14 Mitarbeiter sind dort für Design, Ein- und Verkauf sowie für die Verwaltung zuständig. Die Produktion findet in einer Manufaktur in Estland statt. Dort sorgen 45 Damen an ihren Nähmaschinen und Zuschneidetischen mit viel Liebe zum Detail dafür, dass 220.000 hochwertige Kopfbedeckungen pro Jahr zum unverzichtbaren, modischen und funktionalen Accessoire der Wigéns-Kunden werden können.

VON SCHIEBERMÜTZEN UND MAUERSEGLERN

Viele der Wigéns-Modelle zeichnen sich durch zeitlosen Chic aus und gehören seit über 100 Jahren zum festen Repertoire des Unternehmens: Dazu gehören lässige Schiebermützen, Strohhüte, Mauersegler, Pilotenmützen, Wollfilzhüte und die traditionellen weißen Schirmmützen, welche die schwedischen Abiturienten bei ihrer festlichen Abschlussfeier tragen. Doch neben ihrem Sinn für Tradition sind die Schweden auch bekannt für ein ausgeprägtes Modefaible. Deswegen legt der Geschäftsführer Jan Gustafsson, nach eigenen Angaben, gerne mal sein Ohr auf den Boden und hört genau hin, was ihm die Buschtrommeln der Fashion-Szene berichten. Und so spiegeln sich die verschiedenen neuen Trends immer auch in den Dessins der Wigéns-Kollektionen wider.

Für die Wahl der Materialien steht die Qualität an oberster Stelle: Der Tweed kommt aus Irland, das Fischgrat aus Schottland und das Elchleder natürlich aus Schweden. Ist der Winter extrem kalt und hart, freut sich Jan Gustafsson. Denn den größten Absatz macht Wigéns mit seinen Wintermützen- und kappen. Die Sommerkollektionen machen gerade einmal 20 Prozent des Umsatzes aus. Die meisten Wigéns-Kunden findet man in Nordamerika, Europa und dort, wo die Winter lang und fürchterlich kalt sind. Bis vor einigen Jahren beschrieb man den typischen Kunden in etwa so: „Männer ab 40 aufwärts, die sich beruflich oder in der Freizeit häufig an der frischen Luft aufhalten."

Heute sieht das ganz anders aus, die Produkte sind in der Zwischenzeit beliebte Accessoires für junge modische Männer und Frauen geworden. Ein geradezu unverzichtbares Winter-Must-Have ist die Wigéns-Ohrenklappen-Mütze mit Fellbesatz. Die Mitarbeiter sind, ganz im Sinne des Gründervaters Oscar Wigén, sehr stolz darauf, dass die Handwerkskunst aus Tranås auf der ganzen Welt Köpfe schützt und schmückt. Ob Oscar Wigén Astrid Lindgren im schönen Småland über den Weg gelaufen ist, sei dahingestellt. Aber mit allergrößter Wahrscheinlichkeit war die typische, nachtblaue Schirmmütze, die der kleine Michel aus Lönneberga bei seinen Abenteuern trug, aus dem Hause Wigéns.

The hat bodies are pulled over the wooden blocks.
Über diese Holzformen werden die Hutstumpen gezogen.

Headquarters in Tranås, around 1960
Firmensitz in Tranås, um 1960

View into the sewing department, 1912
Blick in die Näherei, 1912

273

WINDSOR.
— SINCE 1889

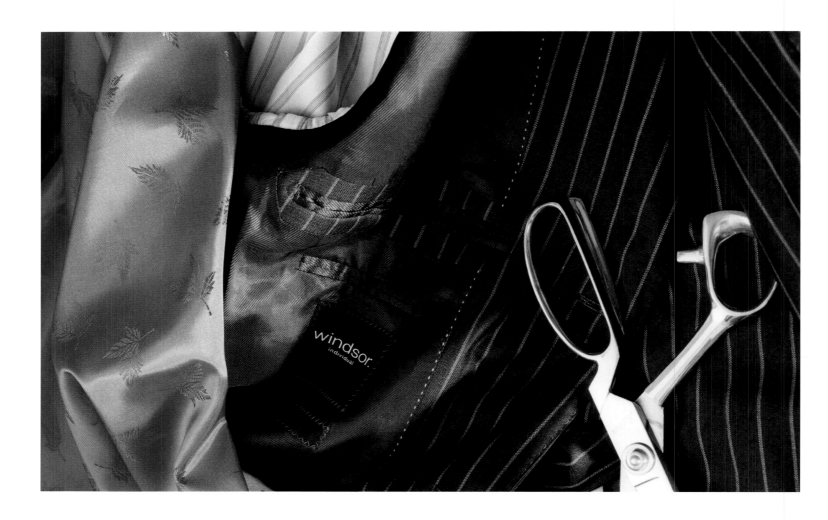

"We view fashion not as
a product but as a little
work of art."
Frank Wojczewski, Head of
Design windsor. women

SOPHISTICATED
UNDERSTATEMENT

Simplicity in fashion can be rather exciting as windsor. demonstrates. Accenting soft, minimalist lines with sophisticated details and introducing fresh proportions, authentic colours and cool accents to well-defined styles can turn classics into favourites. The task of the design teams of the windsor. women and windsor. men collections is to create many such garments with precisely this in mind.

The two chief designers, Frank Wojczewski and Tobias Harprecht, are aware that nothing is more difficult than creating a garment which stands out precisely because of its understatement. Consequently, every detail assumes the greatest importance: piqué lapels, collar and seam details hand-finished to the highest standard are as much an essential part of the repertoire as high-quality interlinings, the finest fabrics and stylish designs. "Our clients value the fact that we tailor high-quality fashions which fit straight away", remarks Matthias Mey,

Managing Brand Director of windsor. men. A perfectly fitting garment guarantees the wearer an unparalleled and natural experience in terms of comfort. No doubt the consistent success of windsor. in producing a harmonious balance between inner well-being and outer elegance is due to the fact that fashion is viewed not as a product but always as a little masterpiece.

THE WINDSOR. APPROACH UNITES PEOPLE

The windsor. company's philosophy is based on solid principles: style expertise, elegant effortlessness, use of the best Italian fabrics, well-defined styles and professional tailoring. These were also the cornerstones of the business established by Leo Roos and Isidor Kahn, two businessmen who founded the Roos & Kahn men's clothing factory in Bielefeld in 1889. In those days, the factory made clothes from linen, lustre fabrics and loden weaves. After 1902, in the wake of revolutionary inventions such as sewing machines and ironing presses, the firm began manufacturing suits and jackets. In 1960, managing director Günter Klasing was instrumental in developing a new approach to fashion: men's suits and coats were to be made from lightweight fabrics, with a soft finish and fashionable details. What is nowadays an integral feature of windsor. products was, at that time, an experiment. Klasing chose the firm's new name as a tribute to the fine English cloth which he so admired. It was not until 1977 that windsor. produced its first womenswear collection, which was strongly inspired by the menswear line.

HIGH-QUALITY, STYLISH AND COSMOPOLITAN

Since 2004, the firm has been run by the Swiss group of Strellson AG / Holy Fashion Group. Since then, windsor. has developed a cosmopolitan look, inspired by the pulsating lifestyle of the world's metropolises and designed for people with a taste for quality. People who wear windsor. clothes exude confidence, appreciate high-quality textiles and style. This premium label combines an appreciation of classic styles with an awareness of the times in which we live. A windsor. product, be it a man's or woman's suit, must undergo up to 225 steps before it is ready for sale. The knowledge and experience of the tailors and designers play a decisive role in this respect. Even if all-time favourites such as jackets and blazers are given a fresh interpretation, this never detracts from their sense of class. Quality remains the key at all times. Jacket chest pieces are interlaid with horsehair or goat hair, the buttons are made from buffalo horn or corozo, top-quality yarns are imported from Mongolia and cashmere, angora, superfine wool and silk are used in the processing. It is precisely this combination of the finest basic materials, outstanding workmanship and stylish tailoring which results in each garment being naturally comfortable to wear. Inner well-being and outer elegance should complement each other perfectly. Authenticity is the principle behind all windsor. collections. Or, as Frank Wojczewski, Head of Design windsor. women, puts it: "We view fashion not as a product but as a little work of art."

In addition to its clothes collections, windsor. also has a range of perfumes, shoes and accessories, thereby offering an entirely individual lifestyle which is recognisable all over the world. The journey is set to continue.

Holger Rosellen   *Matthias Mey*

COMPANY	UNTERNEHMEN
windsor. / Holy Fashion Group	windsor. / Holy Fashion Group
FOUNDED IN	GEGRÜNDET
1889 (Roos & Kahn), Bielefeld, Germany	1889 (Roos & Kahn), Bielefeld, Deutschland
FOUNDERS	GRÜNDER
Leo Roos, Isidor Kahn	Leo Roos, Isidor Kahn
HEADQUARTERS	HAUPTFIRMENSITZ
Kreuzlingen, Switzerland	Kreuzlingen, Schweiz
CEO	GESCHÄFTSFÜHRUNG
Matthias Mey (Managing Brand Director windsor. men), Holger Rosellen (Managing Brand Director windsor. women)	Matthias Mey (Managing Brand Director windsor. men), Holger Rosellen (Managing Brand Director windsor. women)
EMPLOYEES	MITARBEITER
Around 1,400 employees worldwide and around 2,000 contract workers	Weltweit rund 1.400 Angestellte sowie rund 2.000 Mitarbeiter in Lohnbetrieb
PRODUCTS	PRODUKTE
Classic ready-to-wear clothing, business wear, casual wear, accessories, shoes, bags	Klassische Konfektion, Businesswear, Casualwear, Accessoires, Schuhe, Taschen
EXPORT COUNTRIES	EXPORTLÄNDER
Core markets: Austria, Germany, Switzerland Main export countries: Benelux countries, China, Eastern Europe, France, Middle East, Russia, Slovenia	Kernmärkte: Deutschland, Österreich, Schweiz Export-Schwerpunkte: Benelux, China, Ost-Europa, Frankreich, Mittlerer Osten, Russland, Slowenien

windsor.

RAFFINIERTES UNDERSTATEMENT

Reduktion kann ziemlich aufregend sein. Das beweist die Mode von windsor. Wenn minimalistische, weich fallende Silhouetten durch raffinierte Details betont werden und klare Schnitte mit neuen Proportionen, authentischen Farben und coolen Akzenten aufgemischt werden, dann verwandeln sich Klassiker zu Lieblingsstücken. Viele davon zu kreieren, genau das haben sich die Designer der Kollektionen von windsor. women und windsor. men vorgenommen.

Die beiden Chefdesigner Frank Wojczewski und Tobias Harprecht wissen, nichts ist schwerer als ein Kleidungsstück zu schaffen, das auffällt, indem es nicht auffällt. Jedes Detail ist deshalb von größter Bedeutung: Pikierte Revers, Kragen- und Nahtverarbeitungen auf handwerklich höchstem Niveau gehören ebenso zum unverzichtbaren Repertoire wie hochwertige Einlagen, beste Stoffqualitäten und stilsichere Passformen. „Unsere Kunden schätzen, dass wir hochwertige Mode schneidern, die beim ersten Anprobieren passt", sagt Matthias Mey, Managing Brand Director windsor. men. Das perfekt sitzende Kleidungsstück garantiert ein unverwechselbares und selbstverständliches Tragegefühl. Eine harmonische Einheit zwischen innerem Wohlbefinden und äußerer Eleganz herzustellen, gelingt windsor. wohl deshalb so verlässlich, weil hier Mode nicht als Produkt verstanden wird, sondern immer als ein kleines Meisterwerk.

WINDSOR. IST EINE HALTUNG, DIE VERBINDET

Die Firmenphilosophie von windsor. beruht auf festen Säulen: Stilsicherheit, elegante Leichtigkeit, Verarbeitung bester italienischer Stoffe, klare Schnitte und professionelles Schneiderhandwerk. Diese Grundpfeiler hatten schon die Gründer der Firma – die beiden Kaufleute Leo Roos und Isidor Kahn – im Sinn, als sie 1889 in Bielefeld die Herren-Kleiderfabrik Roos & Kahn gründeten. Damals umfasste die Produktion Bekleidung aus Leinen-, Lüster- und Lodengeweben. Mit den damals revolutionären Erfindungen wie Nähmaschinen und Bügelpressen wurden ab 1902 auch Anzüge und Sakkos gefertigt. 1960 gab der Geschäftsführer Günter Klasing den Anstoß für eine neue Modephilosophie: Herrenanzüge und Mäntel wurden aus leichten Stoffen, in weicher Verarbeitung, mit modischen Akzenten kreiert. Was für windsor. heute selbstverständlich ist, war in der damaligen Zeit ein Experiment. Klasing wählte den Namen des Unternehmens als Hommage an die von ihm hochgeschätzten feinen englischen Tuchwaren. Erst 1977 legte windsor. die erste Damenkollektion vor, mit starken Inspirationen aus der Herrenlinie.

HOCHWERTIG, STILSICHER UND KOSMOPOLITISCH

Seit 2004 wird das Unternehmen von der Schweizer Strellson AG / Holy Fashion Group geführt, und windsor. liefert seitdem einen kosmopolitischen Look, inspiriert durch das pulsierende Leben in den Metropolen der Welt, der sich an

Menschen mit Sinn für Qualität orientiert. Wer windsor. trägt, steht souverän im Leben, schätzt hochwertige Textilien und Stil. Dabei vereint die Premium-Marke den Sinn für Klassisches mit einem Gespür für die Zeit, in der wir leben. Ein Produkt von windsor., ganz gleich ob Anzug oder Kostüm, durchläuft bis zu 225 Arbeitsschritte, bevor es in den Handel kommt. Dabei spielen das Wissen und die Erfahrung der Schneider und Designer eine entscheidende Rolle. Auch wenn All Time Favorites wie Sakkos oder Blazer neu interpretiert werden, verlieren sie nie an Klasse. Maßstab aller Dinge ist Qualität. Die Brustplack wird aus Ross- oder Ziegenhaar gefertigt, die Knöpfe bestehen aus Büffelhorn oder Steinnuss, hochwertige Garne kommen aus der Mongolei. Verarbeitet werden Kaschmir, Angora, superfeine Wolle und Seide. Es ist eben diese Mischung bester Ausgangsmaterialien mit perfekter Verarbeitung und stilsicheren Passformen, die bei jedem Kleidungsstück in ein selbstverständliches Tragegefühl mündet. Inneres Wohlbefinden und äußere Eleganz sollen eine harmonische Einheit darstellen. Authentizität ist die Überschrift über allen windsor. Kollektionen. Oder wie es Frank Wojczewski, Head of Design windsor. women, ausdrückt: „Für uns ist Mode kein Produkt, sondern ein kleines Kunstwerk."
Neben Mode entwirft windsor. Parfums, Schuhe und Accessoires und schafft so einen ganz eigenen Lifestyle, der auf der ganzen Welt wiedererkennbar ist. Ein Ende dieser Reise ist nicht in Sicht.

Inspirations for a windsor.
collection
Inspirationen für eine
windsor.-Kollektion

WOOLRICH
— SINCE 1830

"Woolrich is in people's blood here."
The Employees

THE AMERICAN WAY OF WEAR

In mid-Pennsylvania, where the Susquehanna River meanders through the landscape in wide curves, is the small town of Woolrich, situated at the end of a long tree-lined approach road. Surrounded by timber-framed houses is a wooden building with a weathered façade. This is the old woollen mill, which was established in 1830 and marks the beginning of a success story which would turn the Woolrich label into an iconic brand.

It was here that John Rich, a 25-year-old immigrant from England and son of a Liverpool wool carder, began manufacturing hard-wearing, red-and-black check lumberjack shirts. He travelled around the surrounding forests in a mule cart, selling to the lumberjacks. When work began in the mid-19th century on the construction of vast stretches of railroad through Pennsylvania, he supplied the railroad workers and steam engine builders with warm, weatherproof workwear, such as the railroad vest. All through the First and Second World Wars, the water mill wheels on the Susquehanna River turned ceaselessly to drive the spinning machines so that Woolrich could supply the armies with blankets and other durable items.

To this day, Woolrich remains true to its original concept of producing garments with a purpose. Right from the start, the design and function of the company's outdoor and leisure clothing have been geared to the American way of life and its various occupational groups – focusing on outdoor clothes designed for hunting, skiing and fishing. Occasionally, the firm has faced some rather extreme challenges: in 1939, 1940 and 1941, Woolrich was commissioned by the US government to provide the gear for Admiral Byrd's Antarctic expedition.

Most of the people who work for Woolrich come from the small town of the same name which developed around the old woollen mill. Many of them have worked for over 30 years in the modern production plant where wool is washed, spun and woven into a wide range of products. "Woolrich is in people's blood here", claim Woolrich employees. Everyone knows everyone else – it is like one big family.

Cristina Calori

FROM WORKWEAR CLOTHING TO A LIFESTYLE LABEL

The Woolrich label has been a household name in America since the 1950s. Consequently, even long-standing employees were astonished when, in 1972, the "Arctic Parka phenomenon" ended up becoming such a hit in Europe in the 90s through the Woolrich John Rich & Bros.collection created by WP Lavori in Corso. Originally designed for construction workers building the "Great Alaskan Oil-Pipeline" through the USA's northernmost state during the 1970s, this thickly lined, fur hood parka has also become popular in warmer latitudes – where it has been seen adorning Hollywood stars, such as Penélope Cruz and Sofia Coppola, in their flimsy evening dresses and keeping them warm on the red carpet. The special limited edition of the Arctic Parka released for the 2012 season, which is available in a choice of vibrant colours and made from "Byrd" cloth, a water-repellent, Woolrich-exclusive textile, is the ultimate endorsement of this coat's cult status. Another example of inspired marketing was the prominent product placement of dozens of Woolrich garments in the Hollywood blockbuster "The Horse Whisperer".

Meanwhile, an international design team is developing the label's new look – ranging from parkas to chinos, men's swimwear, as well as lightweight, sportswear for women and a special range of clothes for kids and babies. The past 175 years of designs contained in the Woolrich archives provide a constant source of inspiration for fresh ideas. Another successful marketing strategy was developed by Bologna-based "WP Lavori in Corso", the worldwide licensee of the Woolrich John Rich & Bros. brand. In 1998, Cristina Calori, founder of the company, and creative director, Andrea Canè, launched Woolrich John Rich & Bros. collections, which were specifically targeted at Europe and Japan, and transformed this slightly outdated American brand into a successful lifestyle label, which now also includes a summer collection in addition to the more traditional main collection. To keep abreast of growing competition, WP hired Japanese designer Daiki Suzuki in 2006. He was responsible for creating the higher-priced "Woolrich Woolen Mills" line, a catwalk collection of menswear, designed in New York and produced in the USA. Since 2010, Mark McNairy, Daiki Suzuki's successor, has been responsible for preserving the brand's traditional identity and, under the motto "back to the roots", has

COMPANY	UNTERNEHMEN
WP Lavori in Corso S.r.L.	WP Lavori in Corso S.r.L.
BRAND	MARKE
Woolrich	Woolrich
FOUNDED IN	GEGRÜNDET
1830 (Woolrich),	1830 (Woolrich),
1982 (WP Lavori)	1982 (WP Lavori)
FOUNDERS	GRÜNDER
John Rich (Woolrich),	John Rich (Woolrich),
Cristina Calori	Cristina Calori
(WP Lavori)	(WP Lavori)
HEADQUARTERS	HAUPTFIRMENSITZ
Bologna, Italy	Bologna, Italien
CEO	GESCHÄFTSFÜHRUNG
Cristina Calori	Cristina Calori
EMPLOYEES	MITARBEITER
120	120
PRODUCTS	PRODUKTE
Collections Man,	Herren-, Damen- und
Woman, Kid	Kinderkollektionen
EXPORT COUNTRIES	EXPORTLÄNDER
Europe, Japan,	Europa, Japan,
Russia, USA	Russland, USA

been creating typically American, practical clothing, which is unfussy but modern in style.

Woolrich Inc. in Woolrich, which now boasts the USA's oldest wool spinning mill, is still producing its best-selling products, virtually unchanged since its founding years – for example, the "Buffalo Check Shirt" of 1850 and the lighter, but equally robust "Chamois Shirt" of 1969, made from combed cotton. Even the legendary "Railroad Vest" is still obtainable. At all events, the "American dream", that great concept of freedom which pervades all American history, seems to be woven into every Woolrich creation.

THE AMERICAN WAY OF WEAR

Mitten in Pennsylvania, dort wo der Susquehanna River sich in großen Biegungen windet, liegt am Ende einer langen Allee die kleine Gemeinde Woolrich. Zwischen Fachwerkvillen fällt ein Holzhaus mit wettergegerbter Fassade ins Auge. Es ist die alte Wollmühle, die sich schon seit 1830 auf ihre Holzlatten stützt und mit der die Erfolgsgeschichte der Kultmarke Woolrich begann. Hier nämlich fertigte der damals 25-jährige britische Einwanderer John Rich, Sohn eines Wollkämmers aus Liverpool, robuste, rot-schwarz karierte Lumberjack-Shirts. Vom Maultierkarren aus verkaufte er diese an die in den umliegenden Wäldern siedelnden Holzfäller. Als Mitte des 19. Jahrhunderts endlose Eisenbahntrassen durch Pennsylvania gelegt wurden, belieferte er die Gleis- und Dampfmaschinenbauer mit wärmender, wetterfester „Workwear" wie der „Railroad Vest". Selbst während des Ersten und Zweiten Weltkriegs drehten sich die Schaufeln der Wasserräder am Susquehanna River unablässig, um die Spinnmaschinen anzutreiben: Damals belieferte Woolrich das Militär mit Decken und strapazierfähiger Ausrüstung.

Bis heute bleibt der Familienbetrieb seinem Credo treu, zweckmäßige Produkte herzustellen. Design und Funktion der Outdoor- und Freizeitkleidung greifen seit Anbeginn die Bedürfnisse der US-Amerikaner auf – unter anderem mit Outfits zum Jagen, Skifahren und Fischen. Zuweilen führte diese Maxime zu besonderen Herausforderungen: So stattete Woolrich in den Jahren 1939 bis 1941 im Auftrag der US-Regierung die Antarktis-Expedition von Admiral Byrd aus.

Die meisten Mitarbeiter von Woolrich kommen aus dem gleichnamigen Dorf, das sich um die alte Mühle herum gebildet hat. Viele arbeiten schon seit über 30 Jahren in den modernen Fertigungshallen, wo die Wolle gewaschen, gesponnen und zu umfangreichen Kollektionen verwoben wird. „Woolrich liegt einem hier im Blut", sagen die Mitarbeiter. Jeder kennt jeden – es sei wie in einer großen Familie.

VOM ARBEITER- ZUM LIFESTYLE-LABEL

Die Marke selbst kennt in Amerika seit den 1950er-Jahren jeder. Daher waren selbst langjährige Mitarbeiter erstaunt, als das „Arctic Parka-Phänomen" von 1972 in Europa durch die von WP Lavori in Corso herausgebrachte Kollektion Woolrich John Rich & Bros. in den 1990er-Jahren noch einmal alle Erwartungen der Firma übertraf: Ursprünglich entworfen für die Arbeiter, die Anfang der 1970er-Jahre die „Great Alaskan Oil Pipeline" durch den nördlichsten Staat Amerikas bauten, kommt der dick gefütterte Fellmützenparka auch in wärmeren Breiten zum Einsatz – und schützt Hollywood-Stars in leichten Abendkleidern wie Penélope Cruz und Sofia Coppola vor dem Kälteschock auf dem roten Teppich. Die 2012 lancierte Sonderedition des Arctic Parka, knallfarben und aus der Woolrich-exklusiven, wasserfesten Baumwolltextilie „Byrd", macht die Jacke endgültig zum Kult-Objekt. Eine geniale Marketing-Idee war auch das gezielte Product Placement von Dutzenden Artikeln im Hollywood-Blockbuster „Der Pferdeflüsterer".

Mittlerweile konzipiert ein internationales Designteam den Look des Labels – vom Parka über die Chinos bis hin zur Badeshorts für Herren, eine sportlich-legere Kollektion für Damen sowie eine für Kinder und Babys. Immer wieder sind auch die Entwürfe der vergangenen 175 Jahre aus den Woolrich-Archiven Inspirationsquelle für neue Designs. Die Erfolgsstrategie plante der weltweite Lizenznehmer WP Lavori in Corso mit Sitz in Bologna. Seit Unternehmenschefin Cristina Calori und Kreativchef Andrea Canè 1998 eigene Woolrich John Rich & Bros.-Kollektionen für Europa und Japan lancierten, entwickelte sich das leicht angestaubte amerikanische Unternehmen zu einem erfolgreichen Lifestyle-Label, bei dem auch die für die Marke untypische Sommerkollektion zum Umsatz beiträgt.

Um sich gegen die wachsende Konkurrenz zu wappnen, engagierte WP Lavori 2006 den japanischen Designer Daiki Suzuki. Unter seiner Leitung entstand die hochpreisigere Linie „Woolrich Woolen Mills", eine in New York entworfene und in den USA hergestellte Laufsteg-Kollektion für Herren. Mark McNairy, Nachfolger von Daiki Suzuki, erhält seit 2010 die historische Identität der Marke und kreiert seither unter dem Motto „Back to the roots" typisch amerikanische Funktionskleidung ohne Chichi, aber mit modernen Schnitten.

Woolrich Inc. in Woolrich, mit der mittlerweile ältesten Wollspinnerei der USA, produziert bis heute nahezu unverändert die Bestseller der Gründungsjahre. Etwa das Karo-Wollhemd „Buffalo Check Shirt" von 1850 oder das leichtere, aber ebenso robuste „Chamois-Shirt" von 1969 aus gekämmter Baumwolle. Auch die legendäre „Railroad Vest" ist noch zu haben. Der große Freiheitsgedanke jedenfalls, the American dream, der die Geschichte Amerikas prägt, scheint in allen Woolrich-Kreationen verwoben zu sein.

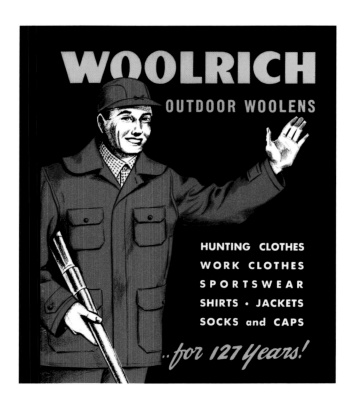

Advertising campaigns,
1957, 1927, 1961
Anzeigenkampagnen
1957, 1927, 1961

Women at work in the beginning of the 20th century
Näherinnen zu Beginn des 20. Jahrhunderts

Men working on a mill
Arbeiter an einer Spinnmaschine

ZIMMERLI
— SINCE 1871

"A promise should be kept. This is particularly true of the world's finest."
Marcel Hossli

UNSURPASSABLE …
THE WORLD'S FINEST

With typical Swiss understatement, Zimmerli, acknowledged minimalist among underwear manufacturers, adheres to a simple creed: simply to be the very best. Elaborate advertising campaigns, extravagant models, excessively large product ranges are not their way of doing things. Let other producers get involved with hip trends! All Zimmerli is concerned with is improving what is already unsurpassable quality by making seams even finer and sourcing even more exclusive raw materials. Cotton is not merely cotton, which is why it is only logical to name a lingerie line after the material from which it is made. The "Sea Island" men's and women's collection is made 100 per cent from this type of cotton, which – as one might expect of Zimmerli – is the rarest and most expensive in the world. It only grows in the ideal climatic conditions of the West Indian Caribbean islands, which is why it constitutes a mere 0.0004 per cent of the world's total cotton production.

EACH GARMENT IS UNIQUE

The high standards necessary in terms of comfort naturally apply to all models. Be it the superfine, fine-rib quality for men's and women's garments made from mercerised and twisted cotton or the super-soft garments made from cellulosic microfibres which absorb and disperse more moisture than any other material: each individual item of underwear is unique and produced exclusively in Zimmerli's own factory in Coldrerio in Ticino, where this outstanding, precision craftsmanship is the responsibility of around 50 highly qualified seamstresses. Marcel Hossli, managing director of Zimmerli, is convinced that the company's greatest responsibility is to uphold the brand's entirely product-orientated philosophy. "A promise should be kept. This is especially true of the world's finest." Thanks to Zimmerli, the "Swiss Quality" label of excellence now also extends to underwear. Interestingly enough, this successful business concept was the brain-child of a woman, Pauline Zimmerli-Bäurlin, who taught herself the necessary skills and, in 1871, began producing stockings and men's socks by machine. In 1874, she invented a new knitting machine, which was able to produce ribbed fabrics and undergarments. Her knitted garments were soon in demand for export and by 1878 they were being offered for sale in the Paris department store of Le Bon Marché. Zimmerli products are now available worldwide in numerous stores in over 50 countries.

Marcel Hossli

THE LABEL WORN BY HOLLYWOOD STARS

Zimmerli enjoys cult status among its fans. The label is particularly popular among Hollywood stars. What better way, after all, to cope with the jetset lifestyle than by wearing Zimmerli underwear which fits like a second skin, providing warmth and a feeling of comfortable well-being? At least his colleagues were sympathetic when Nicholas Cage as the "Bad Lieutenant" in Werner Herzog's film of the same name lamented the loss not of his expensive suit but his "Swiss, 52-dollar cotton underpants" when he was obliged to jump fully dressed into stagnant water to rescue a trapped prisoner from certain death in floods caused by Hurricane Katrina. The emphasis is on simplicity, plain lines and classic styles in both men's and ladies' underwear. The preferred colours are white and black; the women's collection also includes versions in ecru and pink. The traditionally styled men's vests are available as tank tops, muscle shirts, V-necked and round-necked T-shirts. The ultimate in sophistication, these products epitomise the higher standards which would suffer as a result of too many fashion-induced compromises. Zimmerli men's vests are and will remain true men's underwear even if they do also "combine the natural sheen of silk with the softness of cash-mere and the durability of wool". Small wonder, therefore, that Hugh Jackman, who plays the powerful "Wolverine" and likes flexing his muscles in a Zimmerli Richelieu vest, has just been voted the "Sexiest Man Alive".

COMPANY Zimmerli Textil AG & Zimmerli Coldrerio SA	UNTERNEHMEN Zimmerli Textil AG & Zimmerli Coldrerio SA
FOUNDED IN 1871	GEGRÜNDET 1871
FOUNDER Pauline Zimmerli-Bäurlin	GRÜNDER Pauline Zimmerli-Bäurlin
HEADQUARTERS Aarburg, Switzerland	HAUPTFIRMENSITZ Aarburg, Schweiz
CEO Marcel Hossli	GESCHÄFTSFÜHRUNG Marcel Hossli
EMPLOYEES 75 (20 in Aarburg, 55 in Coldrerio)	MITARBEITER 75 (20 in Aarburg, 55 in Coldrerio)
PRODUCTS Daywear undergarments	PRODUKTE Tagwäsche
EXPORT COUNTRIES Worldwide, 50 countries	EXPORTLÄNDER Weltweit, 50 Länder

THE WORLD'S FINEST UNDERWEAR

zimmerli

of Switzerland

UNVERBESSERLICH...
THE WORLD'S FINEST

Die Minimalisten unter den Wäscheherstellern halten sich mit typischem Schweizer Understatement an ein simples Credo: ganz einfach die Besten zu sein. Aufwendige Werbekampagnen, extravagante Modelle, eine maßlos ausgeweitete Produktpalette: Fehlanzeige. Mögen sich andere Anbieter mit hippen Trends beschäftigen, für Zimmerli geht es allein um die Frage, wie Qualität durch noch feinere Nähte, noch ausgesuchtere Rohstoffe unverbesserlich wird. Baumwolle ist nicht gleich Baumwolle, deshalb ist es nur logisch, eine Wäscheserie nach dem Material zu nennen, aus dem sie gefertigt ist. Das Herren- und Damenmodell „Sea Island" besteht zu 100 Prozent aus der gleichnamigen Baumwollsorte, bei der es sich – typisch Zimmerli – um die seltenste und kostbarste der Welt handelt. Sie gedeiht nur unter den optimalen klimatischen Bedingungen der westindischen Karibikinseln, weshalb sie gerade einmal 0,0004 Prozent der weltweiten Baumwollproduktion ausmacht.

JEDES WÄSCHETEIL IST EIN UNIKAT

Die hohen Ansprüche an den Tragekomfort gelten selbstverständlich für alle Modelle, die Damen- wie die Herrenlinie. Ob hauchzarte Feinripp-Qualität aus mercerisierter und gezwirnter Baumwolle oder superanschmiegsame Wäsche aus der Zellulose-Mikrofaser Modal, die mehr Feuchtigkeit aufnimmt und wieder abgibt als alle anderen Materialien: Jedes einzelne Wäscheteil ist ein Unikat und wird exklusiv in der eigenen Produktionsstätte, in Coldrerio im Tessin, konfektioniert. Dort sorgen etwa 50 hochqualifizierte Näherinnen für die hervorragende, handwerklich akkurate Verarbeitung. Managing Director Marcel Hossli, ist davon überzeugt, dass das Festhalten an der extrem produktorientierten Firmenphilosophie des Unternehmens dessen größte Kompetenz ist: „Ein Versprechen soll man halten. Das gilt insbesondere für the world's finest." Dank Zimmerli gilt das Gütesiegel „Schweizer Qualität" auch für Unterwäsche. Interessanterweise verdankt sich diese erfolgreiche Geschäftsidee einer Frau: Pauline Zimmerli-Bäurlin begann 1871 als Autodidaktin mit der maschinellen Fertigung von Strümpfen und Herrensocken. 1874 erfand sie eine neue Strickmaschine, mit der sie gerippte Stoffe und Unterwäsche herstellte. Ihre Strickwaren gelangten schnell in den Export: Schon 1878 finden sie sich im Sortiment des Pariser Warenhauses Le Bon Marché. Heute führen zahlreiche Stores in über 50 Ländern weltweit Zimmerli-Produkte.

DAS LABEL DER HOLLYWOOD-STARS

Bei Zimmerli-Fans genießt der Wäschehersteller Kultstatus. Besonders unter Hollywood-Stars erfreut sich das Label großer Beliebtheit, denn wie ließe es sich am zugigen Set besser aushalten als mit Zimmerli-Unterwäsche, die wie

eine zweite Haut für Wärme und Wohlgefühl sorgt? Zumindest die Kollegen sind also eingeweiht, wenn Nicholas Cage als smarter „Bad Lieutenant" in Werner Herzogs gleichnamigem Film nicht den teuren Anzug, sondern seine „Schweizer 52-Dollar-Baumwollunterhose" bedauert, bevor er in voller Montur ins brackige Wasser springt, um einen eingeschlossenen Häftling aus den Hochwasserfluten des Hurrikans Katrina vor dem sicheren Tod zu erretten.

Ob Herrenunterhose oder Damenslip, die Schnitte geben sich betont schlicht, schnörkellos und modeneutral. Die bevorzugten Wäschefarben sind Weiß oder Schwarz; die Damenkollektion gibt es teilweise auch in Ecru oder Rosé. Die sehr klassisch geschnittenen Herrenunterhemden folgen der Klassifizierung in Tank Top, Muscle-Shirt, T-Shirt mit V-Ausschnitt und T-Shirt mit Rundhals-Ausschnitt. Absolut sophisticated verkörpern die Produkte jene höheren Werte, die durch ein Zuviel an modischen Zugeständnissen nur verlieren würden. Männerunterhemden von Zimmerli sind und bleiben echte Männerunterhemden, auch wenn sich darin „der natürliche Seidenglanz und die Weichheit von Kaschmir mit der Langlebigkeit von Wolle verbinden". Kein Wunder also, dass Hugh Jackman in seiner Rolle als kraftstrotzender „Wolverine", der seine Muskeln vorzugsweise im Richelieu-Unterhemd von Zimmerli spielen lässt, zum „Sexiest Man Alive" gekürt wurde.

Display stand of miniatures representing the available styles. Zimmerli had already won a gold medal for its top-quality knitted products back in 1889 at the Paris World Fair.
Ausstellungsstand mit Miniaturen der verfügbaren Modelle. Zimmerli gewann bereits 1889 auf der Pariser Weltausstellung eine Goldmedaille für die feinsten Strickerzeugnisse.

This style of Richelieu vest has remained a classic since the 1930s.
Modelled in brown: remake of an advertisement from 1963
Das Richelieu-Unterhemd ist in dieser Form schon seit den 1930er-Jahren ein Klassiker. Modell in Braun: Remake einer Werbeanzeige von 1963

The world's finest underwear
zimmerli
of Switzerland
Exclusive Limited Deluxe Retro Edition
1963
Only available in selected Stores!
1963 Richelieu 207 Havanna Edition

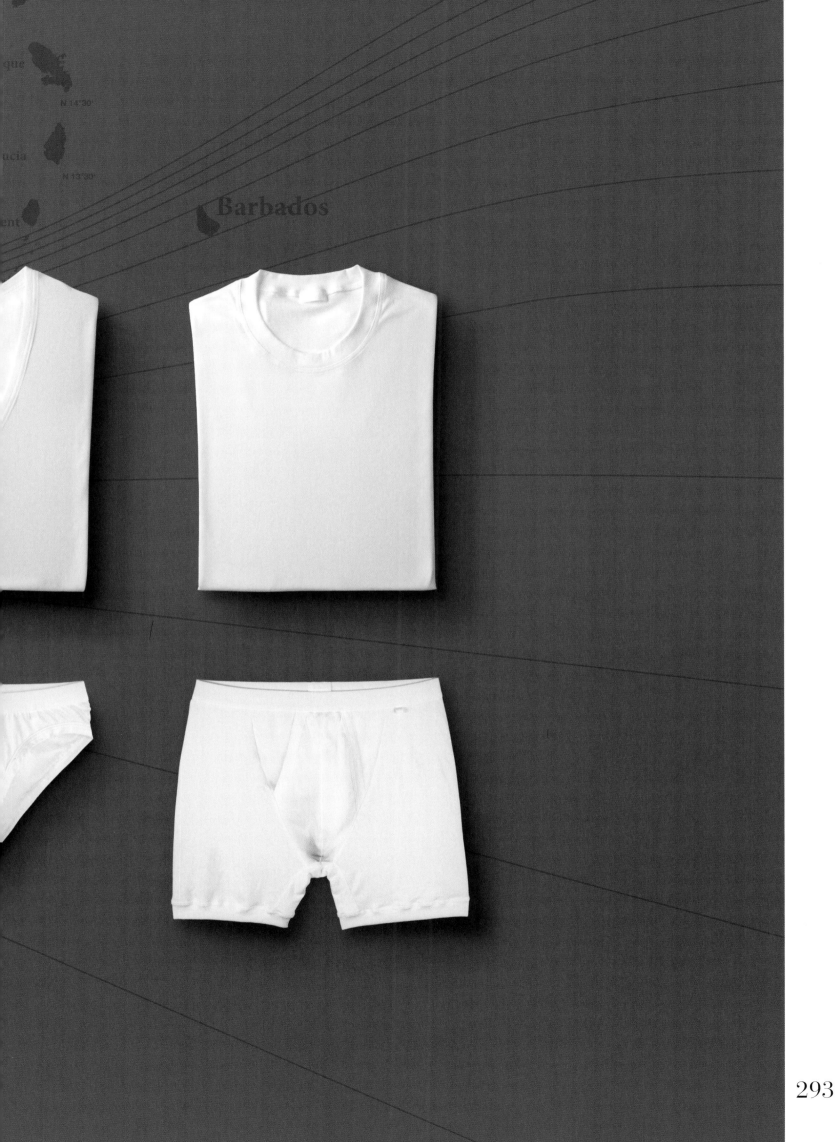

THE AUTHORS

CLAUDIA COSMO

Claudia Cosmo, born 1973 in Cologne, studied Italian and Spanish literature and political sciences from 1992 to 1998 in Cologne and Rome. She works as a freelance writer and has worked for organisations such as WDR and Deutschlandfunk. Since 2001 she is co-organiser of readings of German literature for WDR 1LIVE Klubbing radio, presents readings and cultural events, writes texts for art exhibitions and catalogues and curates her own exhibitions.

For the texts on: Dinkelacker, Eduard Dressler, Franco Bassi, Roeckl, Valstar

MICHAELA KÜHN

Michaela Kühn, born 1972 in Gifhorn, trained at RTL Nord from 1997 to 1999. From 2000 to 2009 she was fashion and culture editor/writer at the RTL Hauptstadtstudio. Since 2009, she has worked as freelance journalist and film maker for various organisations including Holtzbrinck Verlag, René Lezard, Paula Immich, Victorinox, Custo Barcelona, ic! Berlin, Tokyo Bike. She also writes the clothing culture blog for SØR. Michaela Kühn lives in Berlin.

For the texts on: Albini, Barbour, Cerruti, Falke, Gimo's, Gräfin von Lehndorff, SØR, Wigéns

SABINE ELSA MÜLLER

Sabine Elsa Müller was born in Stuttgart. She studied art history, German and ethnology in Stuttgart and Cologne and is the author of numerous articles on the subject of contemporary art. She works as a freelance journalist for magazines such as Kunstforum International, Kunstbulletin, Artist, Kunstzeitung, Art Magazin Online and Artblog Cologne. Sabine Elsa Müller lives in Cologne.

For the texts on: Borsalino, Brioni, Caruso, Eagle, Edsor, Fame, Habsburg, Klemann Shoes, Zimmerli

CAMILLA PÉUS

Camilla Péus, born 1973 in Nairobi, studied art history, sociology and journalism. She trained from 2000 to 2002 with the magazine A&W Architektur & Wohnen. She was then given a permanent position with A&W as editor in Hamburg and as correspondent in Berlin. Since 2009 she has worked as a freelance journalist in Berlin for publications such as AD, ART, Wallpaper, Die Welt, Myself, Brigitte Woman, GG Grund Genug and Food + Travel. She also writes for SØR, compiling texts and supplier portraits for SØR collection catalogues.

For the texts on: Allude, Andrea Fenzi, Ascot, Bogner, Duchamp, Ellen Paulssen, Emanuel Berg, Gant, Hiltl, Hohenberger, Kapraun, Laco, Ludwig Reiter, Regent, Scabal, Seidensticker, van Bommel, van Laack, windsor., Woolrich

DIE AUTORINNEN

CLAUDIA COSMO

Claudia Cosmo, geb. 1973 in Köln, studierte von 1992 bis1998 italienische und spanische Literatur und Politikwissenschaften in Köln und Rom. Sie arbeitet als freie Autorin u. a. für den WDR und
den Deutschlandfunk. Seit 2001 ist sie Mitorganisatorin der WDR 1LIVE Klubbing Radiolesung für
deutschsprachige Literatur, moderiert Lesungen und kulturelle Veranstaltungen, schreibt Texte für
Kunstausstellungen und Kataloge und kuratiert eigene Ausstellungen.

Für die Texte von: Dinkelacker, Eduard Dressler, Franco Bassi, Roeckl, Valstar

MICHAELA KÜHN

Michaela Kühn, geb. 1972 in Gifhorn, volontierte von 1997 bis 1999 bei RTL Nord. Von 2000 bis
2009 war sie Redakteurin / Autorin für den Bereich Mode und Kultur im RTL Hauptstadtstudio. Seit
2009 arbeitet sie als freie Journalistin und Filmemacherin u.a. für den Holtzbrinck Verlag, René
Lezard, Paula Immich, Victorinox, Custo Barcelona, ic! Berlin, Tokyo Bike. Außerdem schreibt sie das
Blog Kleidungskultur für SØR. Michaela Kühn lebt in Berlin.

Für die Texte von: Albini, Barbour, Cerruti, Falke, Gimo's, Gräfin von Lehndorff, SØR, Wigéns

SABINE ELSA MÜLLER

Sabine Elsa Müller, geboren in Stuttgart, studierte Kunstgeschichte, Germanistik und Völkerkunde
in Stuttgart und Köln. Sie ist Autorin zahlreicher Texte mit Schwerpunkt zur zeitgenössischen Kunst.
Als freie Journalistin arbeitet sie u.a. für Kunstforum International, Kunstbulletin, Artist, Kunstzeitung, Art Magazin Online und Artblog Cologne. Sabine Elsa Müller lebt in Köln.

Für die Texte von: Borsalino, Brioni, Caruso, Eagle, Edsor, Fame, Habsburg, Klemann Shoes, Zimmerli

CAMILLA PÉUS

Camilla Péus, geb. 1973 in Nairobi, studierte Kunstgeschichte, Soziologie und Publizistik. Von
2000 bis 2002 war sie Volontärin beim Magazin A&W Architektur & Wohnen. Es folgte eine Fest-
anstellung bei A&W als Redakteurin in Hamburg und als Korrespondentin in Berlin. Seit 2009
arbeitet sie als freie Journalistin in Berlin, u. a. für AD, ART, Wallpaper, Die Welt, Myself, Brigitte
Woman, GG Grund Genug und Food + Travel. Sie verfasst Texte und Lieferantenporträts für die
Kollektionskataloge des Unternehmens SØR.

Für die Texte von: Allude, Andrea Fenzi, Ascot, Bogner, Duchamp, Ellen Paulssen, Emanuel Berg,
Gant, Hiltl, Hohenberger, Kapraun, Laco, Ludwig Reiter, Regent, Scabal, Seidensticker, van Bommel,
van Laack, windsor., Woolrich

THE COMPANIES
DIE UNTERNEHMEN

ALBINI
albinigroup.com

ALLUDE
allude-cashmere.com

ANDREA FENZI
andreafenzi.it

ASCOT
ascot.de

BARBOUR
barbour.com

BOGNER
bogner.com

BORSALINO
borsalino.com

BRIONI
brioni.com

CARUSO
carusomenswear.com

CERRUTI
cerruti.com

DINKELACKER
heinrich-dinkelacker.de

DUCHAMP
duchamplondon.com

EAGLE
eagle-products.de

EDSOR
edsor.de

EDUARD DRESSLER
eduard-dressler.de

ELLEN PAULSSEN
ellenpaulssen.de

EMANUEL BERG
emanuelberg.com

FALKE
falke.com

FAME
fameffcc.com

FRANCO BASSI
francobassi.com

GANT
gant.com

GIMO´S
gimos.com

GRÄFIN VON LEHNDORFF
bsp-leathergroup.de

HABSBURG
habsburg.co.at

HILTL
hiltl.de

HOHENBERGER
weberei-hohenberger.de

KAPRAUN
kapraun-ledermoden.de

KLEMANN SHOES
klemann-shoes.com

LACO
laco-krawatten.de

LUDWIG REITER
ludwig-reiter.com

REGENT
regent-tailor.de

ROECKL
roeckl.com

SCABAL
scabal.com

SEIDENSTICKER
seidensticker.com

SØR
soer.de

STEFFEN SCHRAUT
steffenschraut.com

VALSTAR
valstarino.com

VAN BOMMEL
vanbommel.com

VAN LAACK
vanlaack.de

WIGÉNS
wigens.se

WINDSOR.
windsor.ch

WOOLRICH
woolrich.it

ZIMMERLI
zimmerli.com